COLLUSION

COLLUSION

INTERNATIONAL ESPIONAGE AND THE WAR ON TERROR

CARLO BONINI AND GIUSEPPE D'AVANZO

TRANSLATED BY JAMES MARCUS

 MELVILLEHOUSE PUBLISHING
HOBOKEN, NEW JERSEY

An earlier edition of this book was published in Italy
as *Il mercato della paura. La guerra al terrorismo islamico nel
grande inganno italiano* by Giulio Einaudi Editore.

Melville House Publishing
300 Observer Highway
Third Floor
Hoboken, NJ 07030

www.mhpbooks.com

First Melville House Printing: April 2007

Book Design: Blair & Hayes

A catalog record is available from the Library of Congress.

CONTENTS

COLLUSION

A NOTE

The authors of this book are based in Rome, correspondents for the daily newspaper *La Repubblica*. While they have traveled extensively—to New York, Washington, London, and Tehran—to investigate the episodes revealed here, much of the book is actually set in Italy. It is a key setting, as the book shows, in the American-led War on Terror.

English speaking readers may, however, be unfamiliar with the branches of the Italian government. Of key importance is SISMI, the Italian military intelligence and security service—an Italian equivalent of the CIA. The SISMI headquarters are at Forte Braschi. There is also SISDE, the service for information and democratic security, Italy's domestic intelligence agency—an organization comparable to the FBI. The Chigi Palace, mentioned often in these pages, is the epicenter of the Italian government.

The authors have included a chapter about terrorism-related investigations in Italy. For this, one must know the *carabinieri*, Italian military police. While other specifics of Italian police and judicial proceedings may be unfamiliar, a reader can easily see here the War on Terror's effect on Italy's domestic landscape.

While this book is largely focused on the intricacies of Italian espionage, a thorough reading will show that the implications of what is contained here are far reaching. The point is not only that there have been mistakes in fighting the War on Terror in Italy, or that intelligence agencies routinely work together—which is both obvious and necessary. Rather, this book shows that the character of collaboration between international intelligence agencies has changed dramatically, and corrosively, since September 11, 2001.

CHAPTER ONE

THE YELLOWCAKE FOLLIES

When he discusses the topic today, Hans Blix is still overwhelmed with bitterness and disbelief. The Swedish professor led the United Nations inspectors in Iraq. It was his job to tell the world whether Saddam Hussein did or did not have weapons of mass destruction.

His voice cracks at the memory. To keep his anger under control, he pauses for a moment. He chooses the correct words, the least resentful ones. He says:

> The Italian documents concerning Nigerien yellowcake
> were the most spectacular evidence used to justify the war in
> Iraq. Combined with other information about the aluminum
> tubes, which were to be transformed into centrifuges to
> enrich uranium—another lie—that dossier was the key to the
> Anglo-American military intervention. It was *only* the Italian
> documents that backed up Bush's celebrated sixteen words.

January 28, 2003. The president of the United States delivers his State of the Union address. The occasion is a solemn one.

George W. Bush informs the American people, and the West: "The British government has learned that Saddam Hussein recently sought significant quantities of uranium from Africa." They are sixteen words worth going to war over. It's a short sentence, which effectively splices together a pair of misleading statements.

As Blix recalls, "In January 2003, the American administration already knew that the yellowcake information was false. Fully conscious of the risk they were running by making the information public, they chose to attribute it to the British. It was a way of covering their back, or at least sharing responsibility for what they were saying."

The truth was that from almost the first moment it was clear that there was no proof that the Iraqis were seeking uranium—also called uranium oxide or oxidized uranium—in Niger. The documents that supposedly confirmed Saddam Hussein's shopping expedition were patent forgeries.

The British had not even, in fact, vouched for that dossier. They couldn't: They had only a second-hand acquaintance with it, because it came from a "foreign intelligence agency."

The revelation that Saddam Hussein had been attempting to obtain 500 tons of crude Nigerien uranium (or, as the jargon would have it, yellowcake) emerged, rather, from doctored information assembled by an Italian intelligence snitch. It was SISMI—the Italian military intelligence service, an Italian equivalent of the CIA—that vouched for the information, both in the United States and Great Britain. If the desire for a preemptive war can be traced to Washington, and to the acquiescence of Downing Street, the ace in the hole that George W. Bush was seeking—the evidence he needed to win the hearts and minds of the West—actually came from Rome, courtesy of Silvio Berlusconi's intelligence service.

This is the first tale in this book, and this is the first place the full story has been revealed.

The involvement of the Roman government in these contradictory events, which preceded and legitimized the invasion of Iraq, has a strong whiff of caricature. Indeed, the Italian presence in the affair borders on the grotesque. It's a statement better understood once we meet the key figure in our tale: an Italian named Rocco Martino, the offspring, we've discovered, of "Raffaele and America Ventrici, born in Tropea, Catanzaro, on September 20, 1938." His astonishing role in the whole mess reeks of precinct-house tomfoolery, yet Martino's schemes had far-reaching consequences.

From Rocco Martino to George W. Bush. The leap may, at first, appear impossible, but we'll soon discover that it's neither reckless nor rash. It's merely the result of a coherent (if acrobatic) chain of events, which dishonors the political leadership on both sides of the Atlantic.

ROCCO MARTINO always tries to appear elegant, tidy. No affected style. The right fabrics, in discreet colors—nothing extravagant. In the summer, he wears linen suits, tropical blue or Havana brown; classic herringbone tweeds and gray flannel slacks in the winter; madras and worsted wools in the spring and early autumn. His ties, always of pure silk, are never loud. Blue or white shirts. Italian loafers, quite expensive. Sometimes, he'll wear the more economical French oxfords.

This correctness in his wardrobe must spring from the nature of his work, the manner in which he carries it out, the vicissitudes and catastrophes he has encountered. Above all, Martino wants to appear trustworthy. He believes that his soft white hair, his eye-catching, snow-white, exquisitely maintained mustache, and his plain, non-bureaucratic speech—all badges of the "old-fashioned gentleman"—help him in this ambition. Needless to say, they don't.

Rocco Martino looks like what he is. A lackluster ex-*carabiniere*. A failed spy. Encountering him, you sense the aura of a grifter, even without knowing his history. And once you've had a chance to study his career, the instinct is confirmed.

Rocco Martino was officially employed by was the forerunner

to SISMI—the SID, *Servizio informazione difesa*—for just 18 months, from January 1976 to July 1977. The organization soon showed him the door. According to his record, he was "dismissed for lapses in behavior, having piled up big debts in his dealings with industrialists in Lazio." Best to get rid of such an untrustworthy character, the spymasters seemed to say.

In 1985, Martino was arrested for extortion. As was so often the case, the man was short of money, and he dreamed up the looniest of schemes. First, he asked for a meeting with a branch director at the Banco di Santo Spirito. When that gentleman ushered him into his office, Martino told him that he was a member of Unità, a communist guerrilla group, and that he was there for the money. If the bank didn't pony up, there would be trouble. The director pretended to take the bait. He made a show of being frightened, although he was mainly determined to pay back his visitor in spades. He went off to get the money—and returned with the police. Rocco Martino left the building in handcuffs with his fake beard, donned to disguise himself, hanging askew.

To judge from this episode, Martino doesn't seem to have things together, but it's not mere foolishness (not entirely, anyway) that plagues him. It's that the guy is often overwhelmed by his debts and squeezed by his creditors. So he keeps making desperate moves, which repeatedly land him in hot water or in jail.

Later, in 1987, he was recruited by an official from SISDE— an Italian equivalent of the FBI—to work "on a trial basis" on industrial counterespionage and the Middle East. In 1992, he went into business with an Iraqi of Palestinian origin, now a naturalized Italian, whose brother was an Iraqi arms trafficker. The idea was to start a company that could "keep the products pouring into Iraq, circumventing the embargo."

A year later, Martino was arrested in Germany. In his wallet were some checks that had been stolen during a mugging in Sicily.

Five years after that, he was stopped by the police while he was skulking around the Moroccan Embassy in Rome. When he was searched, officers found documents pertaining to the internal affairs of Syria, Iran, and Libya. He ended up being tried for political and military espionage on behalf of a foreign power. Eventually he was acquitted, but, according to our sources, "SISDE management quashed every official report."

Rocco Martino's checkered resume must have convinced everybody that the approach taken by SID in 1977—that is, firing the little busybody—was the only way to get him out of your hair. Stay away, keep your distance, cut all ties: the only possible option.

But in the shadow world inhabited by spies, that's not what happened. Even a feckless bungler like Rocco Martino was able to find a place in the sun. In 1977, SID turned into SISMI, and Martino continued to work as an "informant" for the intelligence services— until 1999, according to officials in the Italian Ministry of Defense.

1999. It's an interesting year. The end and the beginning of a millennium: a symbolic date. Many expect excitation from the world's numerous crazies. And the paranoiac labors of intelligence services around the world suggest that there is indeed reason to fear the new millennium.

In Italy, Admiral Giuseppe Grignolo runs Department 1 of SISMI. That makes him head of the divisions devoted to arms traffic and trade in illegal technologies. He's also in charge of weapons of mass destruction—WMD—counterproliferation in Africa and the Middle East. He remembers 1999 as the year in which he and other SISMI officials "went around to all the intelligence services, insistently asking for a large-scale collaboration to fight every form of terrorism." It was the era of Y2K, and Osama bin Laden was a hot topic of discussion. Grignolo later recalled that "terrorism was certainly a top-level priority."

Around this time, according to Grignolo, SISMI began "getting a certain number of tips and reports almost every day, especially from our stations in North Africa, Tunisia, Morocco, Turkey, and Libya, about possible attacks. Also, there was talk of the proliferation of weapons of mass destruction in areas like Iran, Libya, and Iraq."

There was also solid intelligence, from a solid source—including a now famous intercepted telex from the Nigerien ambassador in Rome.

The intercepted message was "Telex #003/99/Abnu/Rome." Nigerien Ambassador Adamou Chékou sent the telex to his Ministry of Foreign Affairs in Niamey, the capital of Niger. It read:

> I have the honor of informing you that the Iraqi Embassy to the Holy See [the Vatican] has notified me that His Excellency Wissam al-Zawahie, Iraqi Ambassador to the Holy See, will undertake an official mission to our country on behalf of Saddam Hussein, president of the Iraqi Republic. His Excellency Zawahie will arrive in Niamey on Friday, February 3, 1999, at around 6:25 PM, on Air France Flight 730, originating in Paris. I would be grateful for any arrangements you can make in connection with this visit.

SISMI officials didn't rack their brains over the actual purpose of Zawahie's visit to Niamey. In Niger, the world's poorest country after Sierra Leone, there are only four commercial products: goats, garbanzo beans, onions, and uranium. There was no need for goats, beans, or onions in Mesopotamia. Therefore, Saddam must be trying to get his hands on some Nigerien uranium. That was enough for SISMI officials to start contacting allied intelligence agencies around the world, sounding a "call to arms" against the threat of Arab terrorism. We know for sure that the telex was shared with Britian's MI6.*

In Italy, one person at SISMI who is known to have learned about the telex is Antonio Nucera. At the time a colonel at SISMI, Nucera's knowledge of the telex is important because he is a known friend and comrade of our key player, Rocco Martino. It's been established that in 2000 Martino turned to Antonio Nucera to help put together one of his bungled schemes, the one of crucial importance to our story.

Confirmation of the connection between Nucera and Martino comes from an authoritative source. According to Nicolò Pollari, who spoke to us on the record while director of SISMI, "It's true, in 2000 Rocco Martino was ready to take the gas pipe, ruined, on his last legs. He was in debt, his reputation was shot everywhere. He turned to Nucera because an idea crossed his mind and he needed help." **

Pollari is talkative, generous with details, and often hints at various facts. Usually he's rather reticent and wary, but when we spoke to him on the morning of August 5, 2004, he made an effort to smile as he tosses off a few witty phrases. "I've got plenty to say and your notebook is tiny. Here, take a few sheets of paper, because you've got a lot of writing to do."

---

* A former Italian intelligence operative, who was a pioneer of this sort of information exchange, recalls: "Toward the end of the Eighties, we shared a great deal of information about Saddam's nuclear program with MI6. They were the best, no doubt about it. Back then our interface with London on these issues was a true friend of Italy, Hamilton MacMillan."

**Nicolò Pollari was nominated as director of SISMI on September 17, 2001, and took office on October 15 of the same year. He is a Sicilian, born in Caltanissetta on May 3, 1943. He attended the Guardia di Finanza academy from 1962 to 1966, and rose from second lieutenant in 1964 to major general in 1998 to lieutenant general in 2002. From 1991 to 1993, he directed the Central Unit of the Excise and Revenue Police in Rome, carrying out criminal inquires and investigations to fight terrorism and organized crime in Italy and abroad. He has been awarded university degrees in law, business economics, and political science, and is the author of several publications on legal and economic issues. We spoke to him when he was director of SISMI, but he has since been fired, on November 20, 2006.

On this particular morning, the SISMI chief appears to have barricaded himself behind his desk in the Baracchini Palace. He tips forward on his armchair, his chest jutting out over the desk, his large elbows and hands always in motion amidst the papers organized in folders in front of him.

Pollari is incapable of telling a simple story. He suggests, alludes, skittering from one subject to another without any coherent linkage. At first, it's not clear what he wishes to discuss with such unaccustomed urgency.

In this fog, a folder labeled *Rocco Martino* finally appears in Pollari's hands, and the reason for his anxious efforts becomes evident. Today, the SISMI chief wants to dig a wide moat between himself—meaning the organization he runs—and that scam artist and his colleagues. He keeps insisting that this guy, this Rocco, is bad news, a loose cannon employed by the French secret service. Martino gets a monthly check from Paris, he says, but he's basically a harmless dunce, so ineffectual that he can't be bothered to notice whether a document is authentic or counterfeit. And it's true, he says, that this hapless muddler was able to convince an old comrade-in-arms—such as Colonel Antonio Nucera—to give him a hand. But this was simply a matter of obtaining some *stuff*, which Martino would sell to the French in order to justify his salary. Nothing of real consequence to Italy, he insists. It's obvious that Pollari, with his dubious, mumbling spiel, wants to shove Rocco Martino into the arms of the French—but without harming him, without irritating him, offering him a dignified exit.

On December 5, 1998, Rocco Martino left Italy and took up residence in Luxembourg, at 3 Rue Hoehl, Sandweiler. He hadn't gotten out of the game, says Pollari. Although he was supposedly employed by a security firm as a consultant, he was actually working for French intelligence, with a monthly salary of 4,000 euros. (Martino's stipend may have varied, of course, but this was the sum named by Pollari for the period under discussion.) It's probably more accurate to say he was *also* working for French intelligence at this time, as the thread connecting him to SISMI was still substantial. Indeed, Martino was going great guns. Serving two masters, he sold the French information about the Italians (or information "handled" by the Italians). He sold the Italians whatever he could collect about the French. "This is my profession," he would assert in August 2004. "I sell information." That's the kind of guy he is. He's never too concerned about doing the right thing.

Rocco was short of cash, Pollari says. As he so often did when his pockets were empty, he dreamed up a scheme. The idea seemed brilliant to him: promising, and above all, risk-free. The spark that lit up in his head had to do with some difficulties the French were experiencing in Niger.

A little background. The French control the extraction of uranium in Niger's open-pit mines. The two mining companies, Cominak and Somair, are owned by a giant French enterprise called Cogema (which is owned in turn by the French government). Between 1999 and 2000, an embarrassing fact emerged. The International Atomic Energy Agency, the IAEA, announced that the Libyans possessed 2,600 tons of yellowcake uranium. But although Niger was the major supplier of the mineral to Libya, its official records indicated that less than 1,500 tons had been delivered. Who, then, was smuggling the extra yellowcake out of the country?

It turned out that additional yellowcake was extracted from certain mines in Niger that the French had abandoned because they were no longer productive. For Cogema, this was reason enough to abandon them. Nonetheless, somebody had resumed work in the mines in order to launch a prosperous clandestine operation. Obvious questions followed: To whom were the smugglers selling the uranium? To Libya only? Or to other countries—and if so, which ones? The French were looking for some answers.

At that point, Rocco Martino asked his friend Antonio Nucera for a helping hand.

Can't you give me *something*? he must have said. A piece of information, a good contact, an inside track at Niger's Italian embassy? Anything will do. The French will lap this stuff up. They have a holy fear of being tricked in their own backyard by some operator who will then leave them exposed for the whole world to see. Just think—Martino must have assumed the French were thinking—What if some lunatic in the Middle East puts together an atomic bomb with the uranium smuggled out of Niger? Because the French are desperate to find out who is buying "their" uranium under the table, perhaps they're willing to pay a bundle.

We don't know whether Martino was already aware of the intercepted telex from Ambassador Adamou Chékou. Probably it was something he had heard about via the grapevine. In any case, he would learn about it soon enough, because Martino's friend Nucera knew the whole story. Here was the point of departure that Martino had been looking for. After all, every "fairy tale" worth its salt must begin with a documented fact.

Nucera, then a colonel at SISMI, came to see Martino. He had been transferred, in 1997, from Division 8 to Division 2. Could he be of use to Martino? No problem at all.

Nicolò Pollari says: "Nucera wanted to help his friend. So he invited a SISMI 'source' to lend Martino a hand. This was no big deal, you understand—she was on the payroll, sure, but she wasn't an important or productive source."

The SISMI source worked at Niger's embassy in Rome. She wasn't up to much. She was scraping by, catching crumbs from the table of counterespionage. She had no monthly salary from Italian intelligence: She did piecework, receiving such-and-such a sum for each bit of information. Measly facts, measly pay. And even those amounts, by 2000, were in danger of disappearing. For quite a long time—for a miserably long time—there was nothing for her to spy on, and therefore nothing to sell.

We'll call the source "Signora Laura." *

At the time of her work with Martino, she's sixty years old, more or less. Her face, which must have been lovely, is now faded. She is what we might call the ambassador's factotum: his guardian, assistant, secretary, file clerk, administrator, keeper of the petty cash. She has the look of an old, patient aunt. A French accent. Knowing, complicit eyes. She always speaks in an undertone. Even if she's saying, "Good morning," she exhales the phrase like a tiny, mysterious breath of air, which seems designed to reveal innumerable truths and God knows how many secrets. Signora Laura, too, needs money.

Nucera set up the meeting. It didn't take long for Rocco and Laura to arrange matters. There was this *thing* she could do. Laura felt okay about the situation: Nucera was a bigwig at SISMI, after all. And the colonel was her official "contact." With Nucera's blessing, the two astute swindlers struck a deal. There were already some papers to steal and sell. However, they would need the assistance of a Nigerien insider. Laura picked out the right man. He was the senior counsel to the embassy, Zakaria Yaou Maiga. (According to Pollari, "Maiga spends six times as much as he earns.")

This gang of fumblers, all of them short of cash, was now ready for action. Rocco Martino, Signora Laura, Zakaria Yaou Maiga. As for Nucera, he was just a step behind them, in the shadows.

Maiga set up the plan. He waited for the embassy to close down over the New Year. Then he faked a burglary. The burglars were searching for something, in a confused sort of way. They turned the embassy on Via Baiamonti upside down. Papers everywhere, drawers emptied out, cabinets pried open.

---

* Her real name is Laura Montini; she was first known in Italy as "Signora Laura."

Early on the morning of January 2, 2001, Arfou Mounkaila, the deputy secretary for administrative affairs, reported the crime to the police. He stiffly conceded that these thieves had been real dullards. So much fuss, so much effort, for nothing. Aside from a steel Breil watch and three small bottles of perfume, the intruders had left empty-handed. Mounkaila kept his mouth shut about several other items. Although it was inadvisable to say so, the embassy was actually missing codebooks, stationary, and official seals.

Which happened to be exactly what you needed to cook up a phony dossier.

Rocco and his colleagues rolled up their sleeves. They had the genuine telex of February 1, 1999, from Chékou to the Foreign Ministry in Niamey. Nucera had brought it to them as a kind of dowry. Around this document they assembled a souped-up set of correspondence, buttressed with authentic ciphers and a false "draft agreement." First they added a number of letters, which discussed a putative deal to ship uranium to Iraq via Lomé (in Togo) and Cotonou (in Benin, which happened to be where the 2,900 tons of pure uranium extracted from the Arlit and Akouta mines during the last year were stored).

To these goodies, they added a few diplomatic documents. There was, for example, a letter dated July 30, 1999, from the Minister of Foreign Affairs to the Italian embassy in Rome. There was a letter addressed to Saddam Hussein ("Monsieur le Président"), dated July 27, 2000. And there was a "draft agreement" between the governments of Niger and Iraq, "pertaining to the delivery of uranium, initialed on July 5 and July 6 in Niamey." The protocol had two additional pages attached, entitled *Accord*.

The swindle could have been blown in the distracted blink of an eye, so sloppily had the dossier been assembled. The protocol between Niger and Iraq was initialed by Allele Dihadj Habibou, Minister of Foreign Affairs and Cooperation. His signature also appeared on a letter dated October 10, 2000. But Habibou had stopped leading the nation's diplomatic corps in 1989.

What's more, 500 tons of pure uranium is a sizable enough quantity that it would have aroused the suspicions of anybody with a basic knowledge of Niger and its prize export. Rabiou Hasan Yari, Niger's minister of mining, explains it this way: "Crude uranium is extracted from the subsoil by two companies, Somair and Cominak, both with their headquarters at Arlit, which is almost 750 miles from Niamey. They are owned (56 percent in one case, 34 percent in the other) by France, through a corporation called Cogema—the Compagnie Générale des Matières Nucléaires. Cogema is itself a world leader in the nuclear fuels sector, with the participation of a Japanese company, Overseas Uranium Resources Development (OURD), as well as Germany and Spain. The mineral is not stored in a single place, but sold throughout all of France, Japan, and Spain."

How should we say it? Niger is not free to sell its own uranium, because the production and distribution are controlled by foreign investors.

There's more. The letter of July 30, 1999, makes reference to the agreements negotiated in Niamey—but the agreements themselves are dated a year later, on June 29, 2000. The letter of July 27, 2000, complete with the signature and seal of Niger's president, Mamadou Tandja, alludes to the Constitution of 1965. Yet the nation had ratified four additional constitutions since then, the current one dating from 1999.

The crooks had done shoddy work. That bundle of papers was an omelet made with rotten eggs. What kind of sucker would actually eat it? Rocco Martino, who was now getting down to business, didn't worry about it. He paid off Maiga with a thousand dollars or so. Signora Laura got a slightly smaller sum.

The swindler, says Pollari, was now moving in for the kill. Martino called his contact in the French embassy in Brussels. I have

République Du Niger

Fraternité - Travail - Progrès

Niamey, le 27/07/2000

MONSIEUR LE PRESIDENT,

J'AI L'HONNEUR DE ME REFERER A L'ACCORD N° 381-NI 2000,
CONCERNANT LA FOURNITURE D'URANIUM, SIGNE A NIAMEY LE 06
JUILLET 2000 ENTRE LE GOUVERNEMENT DE LA REPUBLIQUE DU NIGER
ET LE GOUVERNEMENT DE L'IRAQ PAR LEURS RESPECTIFS REPRESEN-
TANTS DELEGUES OFFICIELS.

DITE FOURNITURE EQUIVALENTE A 500 TONNES D'URANIUM PUR
PAR AN, SERA DELIVRE EN 2 PHASES.

AYANT VU ET EXAMINE LEDIT ACCORD, JE L'APPROUVE EN TOUTES
ET CHACUNE DE SES PARTIES EN VERTU DES POUVOIRS QUI ME SONT
CONFERES PAR LA CONSTITUTION DU 12 MAI 1966.

URGENT

EN CONSEQUENCE, JE VOUS PRIE DE BIEN VOULOIR CONSIDERER
LA PRESENTE LETTRE COMME ETANT L'INSTRUMENT FORMEL D'PPRO+
BATION DE CET ACCORD PAR LE GOUVERNEMENT DE LA REPUBLIQUE
DU NIGER QUI SE TROUVE AINSI VALABLEMENT ENGAGE.

VEUILLEZ AGREER, MONSIEUR LE PRESIDENT, L'ASSURANCE
DE MA HAUTE CONSIDERATION.

ANNEXE 1

La direction des affaires juridiques du Ministère des Affaire
Etrangères dans la personne de S.E. Monsieur le Ministre et la
tion du Ministère des Mines dans la personne de M. le Ministre en
Charge, unis en assemblée ont déclaré ce qui suit:

- La Cour d'Etat, appelée à donner son avis conformément à
l'article 20 de l'ordonnance n° 74-13 du 5 juillet 2000, portant
création, composition, attribution et fonctionnement de la Cour
d'Etat, s'est réunie en chambre de Conseil au Palais de ladite
Cour le Mercredi 7 juillet 2000, à neuf Heure;

- Vu la lettre n° 466/MJ/SG du 3 juillet 2000 de M. le Ministre
des Affaires Etrangères et de la Coopération;

demandant de "solliciter l'avis favorable de la Cour d'Etat
sur les point à savoir:

- D'une part si le Protocole d'Accord entre le gouvernement de
la République du Niger et le Gouvernement de l'Iraq, relatif à la
vente d'uranium pur, signé le 6 juillet 2000 à Niamey est conform
au droit interne de la République du Niger, et s'il constitue pour
elle un engagement valable et obligatoire;

- D'autre part, s'il a été dûment signé et approuvé par le
gouvernement d'Iraq conformément à toutes les normes administra-
tives qui lui sont applicables et constituant ainsi pour elle un

engagement valable et obligatoire;

EMET L'AVIS

Que l'Etat du Niger a satisfait à toute les exigences de son droit constitutionnel et de es autres principes de droit pour la prise en charge valable et juridiquement obligatoire de toutes ses obligations resultant du Protocole d'Accord;

Que le représentant de l'Etat du Niger et le représentant de l'Iraq qui ont signé au nom de leur respectif gouvernement, avaient juridiquement pouvoir de représentation.

Où siégeaient Messieurs: Mamadou Malam Aouami, Président de la Cour du Niger; Hadj Nadjir, Conseiller du gouvernement d'Iraq, Mahamane Boukari Conseiller intérimaire du Ministère des Affaires Etrangères du Niger, en présence de M. Bandiaire Ali, Procureur Général de l'Iraq et avec l'assistance de Maître Maiga Ali, Greffier en Chef.

009765280-
01/02 14.57
MINAFET 5208N10
626290 NIGER I

MINAFET 5208NI
626290 NIGER I

TELEX N° 003177/ASMI/RONE   DU 01/02/99

OBJET: S.E.M. LE MINISTRE DES AFFAIRES ETRANGERES
----   ET DE L'INTEGRATION AFRICAINE.
                     NIAMEY

J'AI L'HONNEUR DE PORTER A VOTRE CONNAISSANCE QUE L'AMBASSADE
D'IRAQ AUPRES DU SAINT SIEGE VIENT DE M'INFORMER QUE S.E.
M. WISSAM AL ZAHAWIE, AMBASSADEUR D'IRAQ AUPRES DU SAINT SIEGE,
EFFECTUERA UNE MISSION OFFICIELLE DANS NOTRE PAYS EN QUALITE DE
REPRESENTANT DE S.E. M. SADDAM HUSSEIN, PRESIDENT DE LA REPUBLIQUE
D'IRAQ.
S.E.M. ZAHAWIE ARRIVERA A NIAMEY LE VENDREDI 05 FEVRIER 1999 VERS
19 H 25 PAR VOL AIR FRANCE N° 730 EN PROVENANCE DE PARIS.

JE VOUS SAURAIS GRE DES DISPOSITIONS QUE VOUS VOUDRIEZ BIEN FAIRE
PRENDRE A CET EFFET.

   TRES HAUTE CONSIDERATION

SIGNE: S.E. ADAMOU CHEKOU
-----   AMBASSADEUR NIGER ROME.

626290 NIGER IN

MMINMAFEHT IITWMPPILMMMMM

0029

REPUBLIQUE DU NIGER

CONSEIL DE RECONCILIATION· NATIONALE

MINISTERE DES AFFAIRES ETRANGERES
ET DE L'INTEGRATION AFRICAINE

DIRECTION DES AFFAIRES JURIDIQUES
ET CONSULAIRES

Niamey, le ___ 30 JUIL 1999

N° ⊇--05055 ___ /MAE/IA/DAJC/DIR

URGENT

HONNEUR VOUS DEMANDER BIEN VOULOIR CONTACTER S.E.
L'AMBASSADEUR D'IRAQ M. WISSAM AL ZAHAWIE POUR CON-
NAITRE REPONSE DE SON PAYS CONCERNANT FOURNITURE
D'URANIUM SELON DERNIERS ACCORDS ETABLIS A NIAMEY
LE 29 JUIN 2000.

PRIERE SUIVRE CE DOSSIER TRES CONFIDENTIEL AVEC
TOUTE DISCRETION ET DILIGENCE.

NASSIROU

TA/KA

REPUBLIQUE DU NIGER

CONSEIL MILITAIRE SUPREME

MINISTERE DES AFFAIRES ETRANGERES
ET DE LA COOPERATION

DIRECTION
DES AFFAIRES JURIDIQUES
ET CONSULAIRES

N°_____ MAE/C/DAJC/

№ 0 7 2 5 4

Niamey, le 10 OCT. 2000

LE MINISTERE DES AFFAIRES ETRANGERES
ET DE LA COOPERATION

à

Monsieur l'Ambassadeur du Niger/
à

ROME

OBJET: Protocole d'accord entre le Gouvernement
=====================================
du Niger et le Gouvernement d'Iraq
=================================
relatif à la fourniture d'uranium
=================================
signé les 5 et 6 Juillet 2000 à Niamey.
=======================================

     J'ai l'honneur de vous faire tenir ci-joint, pour informa-
tion, copie du Protocole d'Accord signé à Niamey entre la Republique du Niger et le Gouvernement d'Iraq concernant la fouhiture
d'uranium que l'Etat nigerien à émis au sujet du Protocole cité en
objet./.

P.J. : 1

RÉPUBLIQUE DU NIGER

ACCORD

something for you, he said. When he showed up for the appointment in Luxembourg, we can imagine that he may have felt a fresh pang of conscience, then told himself that it wasn't his job to say whether the stuff was authentic or not. He could always swear on a stack of Bibles that he believed the papers were real. His only duty was to lay his hands on something, then pass it along to the man at the embassy, as they had agreed. As for the rest, they would see. All he did was sell information. It's up to the buyer to evaluate the merchandise, isn't it? Rocco Martino collected his money and left for the Côte d'Azur.

The wild and crazy spy simply adored Nice. Or so says Pollari.

NOW IT WAS the spring of 2001. Osama bin Laden was in his encampment in the peaks of Tora Bora, or God knows where. Mullah Omar was ruling (and terrorizing) Kabul. Mohammed Atta and his fellow "martyrs for Allah" were attending flight school in Florida. George W. Bush had occupied the White House for just a few months; terrorism and Al Qaeda were not high priorities on his agenda. After the inauguration, White House anti-terror adviser Richard Clarke had made a vain attempt to draw the president's attention to the terror network, and to stress that it must be destroyed. Nothing happened.

So it went in Kabul, in Florida, in the White House, while the dossier of junk thrown together by Rocco Martino made its way to Paris in the spring of 2001. It's not known what the French initially thought of that bundle of useless, nonsensical papers. It's reasonable to assume that the whole package would have ended up in the trash can after an initial reading—if, that is, September 11 had never taken place. It was the attack on the United States that put the fraudulent dossier back in business.

Onward, then. It's the spring of 2001. Nobody yet foresees the inferno that will explode on September 11.

According to Pollari's version of events, Rocco Martino was working for the Direction Générale de la Sécurité Extérieure (DGSE). (DGSE operates under the authority of the French Ministry of Defense. It is in charge of military intelligence, strategic information, technological intelligence, and foreign counterespionage.) He had worked for SISMI as well, and could still count on a good friend at the agency, Colonel Antonio Nucera. The French needed information about smuggled African uranium, and Rocco, in dire straits himself, sensed an opportunity. He turned to Nucera, who hooked him up with a SISMI informant, Signora Laura. She in turn corrupted Zakaria Yaou Maiga, senior counsel to Niger's embassy in Rome.

The two, Laura and Zakaria, stole some documents, smeared some additional ones with false information, then turned the whole dossier over to Rocco.

Rocco, who "didn't even know where Niger was," had no way of determining whether the documents were authentic or forgeries, nor did he really care. He sold them to those "pricks at DGSE," and that was that.

"There's the whole story of the phony dossier," finishes Pollari.

Pollari's reconstruction of events surrounding the phony dossier had already been proposed in the Italian Press when we spoke with him—by an investigative piece in *Libero* and in a *Panorama* column— where it was amply "documented" by anonymous SISMI sources. In this version of events, SISMI knew nothing. Even though, smack in the middle of this intrigue, we find a SISMI colonel, a SISMI informant, and a SISMI collaborator ("until 1999"), all of them hovering like bees around a flower—the Nigerien embassy in Rome—that SISMI had been observing for years. Is it possible, despite all this, that SISMI knew nothing, noticed nothing, saw nothing, heard nothing?

They can't, of course, have it both ways.

It's clear that either SISMI was paying these half-assed dilettantes, or Pollari's reconstruction is false, evasive, misleading.

One detail seems decisive. Why would Nicolò Pollari, who took control of SISMI on October 15, 2001 (which is to say, *after* the embassy break-in), feel obliged to defend the gang of thieves in question—and with them, the crude dithering of a bureaucracy he had been charged with reforming? Wasn't this mess a perfect opportunity for the new director to rid himself of some deadwood, line up fresh sources, and develop a more modern espionage organization, as he had promised?

Basic caution dictates that the head of SISMI knows more than he's saying—and certainly more than he wishes to share with the public. One might reasonably speculate that Pollari had a hand in this fraudulent business (*after* he took office, *after* September 11). Perhaps, we think, he ran it and guided it. This would be another story entirely, which we'll be tackling soon.

A judicial inquiry by the Procura di Roma—that is, the Italian public prosecutor's office—begins to help confirm these speculations.* The prosecuting attorney, Franco Ionta, investigated several "falsehoods" and "unknown persons." The obvious key witnesses—Rocco Martino, Signora Laura, and Antonio Nucera—however, were considered merely "persons in possession of information." Witnesses. Not suspects.

Only witnesses? It's worth recalling that in 1998, Rocco Martino was investigated for political and military espionage, in connection with a similar case: He was—to repeat—nabbed near the Moroccan embassy in Rome in possession of documents pertaining to the internal affairs of Syria, Iran, and Libya. Ionta tries to explain it this way:

---

* The Public Prosecutor in Rome opened an investigation of the Nigerien dossier in July 2003, just a few days after the publication of documents in *La Repubblica* that demonstrated the dossier's falsity. The probe was shelved two years later, then reopened in early December of 2005.

> I had to ascertain whether the three were aware that
> the documents were not trustworthy. My course of
> action was clear. I had to hear them out, as persons in
> possession of information. Their statements, which were
> consistent, indicated that the senior counselor to the
> embassy had created the dossier. Unfortunately, Zakaria
> Yaou Maiga is a diplomat, with full immunity. So I
> was forced to close the case and dismiss all charges.

If we place the prosecutor's statement alongside Pollari's, a worrying trend emerges. Both attempt to put distance between the burglary and the Italian government. They say Rocco Martino was employed by Paris, that Zakaria Yaou Maiga was employed by Niamey.

What did this have to do with SISMI? What did this have to do with the Italian government? Once again, we stumble across some rather irregular details. When Rocco Martino's house was searched, the police seized two suitcases of documents and CD-ROMs. Nobody—neither the prosecuting attorney nor the police investigators—took the trouble to examine their contents, limiting themselves to a quick glance. A strange procedure, given that Martino was Italian and could have been prosecuted. It's impossible even to figure out who had custody of these papers before they were returned to Martino. According to the prosecuting attorney, the police investigators had them. According to the police investigators, the prosecuting attorney had them. Antonio Nucera, as it turned out, was not even interrogated by the magistrate. Instead, he made his statement to the Reggio Calabria branch of DIGOS at Vibo Valentia, which we assume had very little knowledge of the case.

The facts seem to indicate that there was pressure to short-circuit the inquiry in a hurry. That seems clear. The preliminary investigation was practically predetermined to conclude with a dismissal of all charges. No further discussion would be necessary—

the politicians, the Parliament, the media, and the security services could simply forget about it.

ALAIN CHOUET lives in southwest France, north of Nîmes, and he enjoys a rustic retirement. With a smile, he calls the locale "a land that's always been a refuge for undesirables. In the eighteenth century, it was the Protestants fleeing from Calvinist persecution. These days, it's former Communist mine workers."

He's a man with a gentle manner. White beard, snow-white hair that's thinning at the temples. Brown eyes, an exceedingly lively gaze. He seems calm, reflective, and yet always detached. He's wearing a soft Breton sweater of cobalt wool with a high collar, moleskin pants, and a knee-length black leather jacket. There are traces of mud and dirt on his shoes. He's a quiet man, at peace with himself. With, perhaps, a hint of remorse—he appears to have no regrets. "I had thirty-four unforgettable years," he recalls. "Now I've reached the age where I can devote myself entirely to my passions."

Until 2002, Alain Chouet was the number-two man at DGSE.[*] He was, he tells us, the man who oversaw the "yellowcake case" on behalf of the French foreign espionage agency.

Says Chouet:

> I know what happened. When and how it happened.
> In this story, I was in charge of French intelligence. I
> made the decisions. I communicated with the Americans
> and exchanged information with them regarding this

---

[*] A third-generation Parisian, Alain Chouet was born in 1946. He studied Arabic and was awarded degrees in law and political science. He worked for DGSE for more than three decades, winning numerous awards and citations and serving in Beirut (1974-76), Damascus (1976-79), Paris (1980-85), and Rabat (1985-88). He also worked for the Ministry of Defense and the French mission to the United Nations before assuming leadership of the SRS in 2002.

affair. During the period under discussion, I ran the
Service de Renseignement de Sécurité, which is in
charge of antiterrorism, foreign counterespionage,
and WMD counterproliferation. I can tell you exactly
how things went, and I will. With one understanding:
I will attest only to the facts that I personally know.

As Alain Chouet tells the story, the dates and the protagonists start
sliding around. Among the first surprises: Rocco Martino's resume
changes before our eyes. It's true that the Italian swindler does
occasionally work for the French. But not in counterespionage—he
works for the Ministry of Foreign Affairs. And they're not his only
client, we should add, because he's always short of cash, so he sells
the same information to the West and to the East. To the French
and to the Egyptians. To the English and to the press, assuming that
they're willing to fork over a few thousand euros.

Martino's carousel spins especially fast during the Balkan crisis
of the nineties. Italian intelligence has good sources in that region—
and Rocco, of course, has excellent contacts in Italian intelligence.
Martino (to give just one example) feeds information to the French
during the secret negotiations in Rome, letting them know when the
Belgrade delegation arrives, who's taking part, who's meeting with
who, and so forth.

None of this, however, has anything to do with counterespionage.
Says Chouet:

> Rocco Martino knocked on our door for the first time in
> June 2002. He showed up at our embassy in Luxembourg
> and asked to speak with one of our people. He said
> he had important documents on the uranium traffic
> between Niger and Iraq, and was asking $100,000 for the
> material. Now, I've spent too much time in the Arab souk
> to swallow that kind of bait. I told my men: First we look

at the material. Then, if it interests us, we talk about the
price. I asked Jacques Nadal, our station chief in Brussels,
to meet this Italian in Luxembourg. Nadal saw him at
the end of June 2002. Martino showed us the papers.
Nadal bundled them up and sent them to Paris. In Paris
we compared them with papers that we already had.

Surprise number two: The French counterespionage agency was
already in possession of the fraudulent Nigerien documents before
Martino's 2002 meeting with Jacques Nadal. Where did they
come from? Who passed them along? Who was their (so to speak)
progenitor?

At a restaurant, Chouet orders a glass of red wine, a Perrier, and
a veal kidney. While he waits, he applies a brown Gauloise to the
flame of a Zippo with a faint floral engraving. He continues:

At the beginning of the summer of 2001, the CIA circulated
some information that was as generic as it was alarming.
"Iraq," they told us, "is trying to acquire uranium from an
African nation." The Americans traced their suspicions back
to a trip the Iraqi ambassador to the Holy See had taken
at least two years before, when he visited several Central
African nations. As usual, the Americans didn't reveal the
source of this information. Washington didn't say anything
about Niger—they were talking generically about Africa.
The United States knows that not a leaf falls in our former
Francophone colonies without us knowing about it. Above
all, when we're talking about counterproliferation. And
besides, no matter how generic the information was, it meant
more to us than to other countries. In the wake of the Gulf
War [1991], France couldn't allow anyone to accuse us of
underestimating Saddam Hussein's rearmament program.

It doesn't take much to determine that the information—the first report of an Iraq-Niger meeting—had been provided to the Americans by the Italian intelligence services. It was the SISMI division staffed by Giuseppe Grignolo, a close contact with the CIA after all, that had intercepted the telex from the ambassador in Rome. We know, too, that the news had been "shared" with the English via MI6. Had it also been entrusted to the CIA, in view of SISMI's excellent rapport with the Firm? It's quite probable.

There is also room for a second hypothesis: It was the British who passed along the news to Langley. That wouldn't change much. The idea would be that the documents had "slipped away" from Italy. Whatever the details, we know—according to Chouet—that the Americans knew rumor of the Iraq-Niger deal in 2001 and, by 2002, had possession of Martino's bogus dossier.

Chouet continues:

> When the Americans came calling in the summer of
> 2001, I immediately rolled up my sleeves. I told my men
> in Africa to get down to work. In Niger, obviously, but
> also in Mauritania (you'll soon see why). The results
> were totally negative. At the end of August 2001, we
> cancelled the alert. And after the attack on the Towers,
> between September 2001 and the spring of the following
> year, that information on the uranium trade turned into
> background noise again. Then something happened.

What happened was this: On September 21, 2001, Admiral Gianfranco Battelli (Nicolò Pollari's predecessor at SISMI) sent a cable to Langley with news of a trip "undertaken by Iraqi personnel to Niger in '99, during which they had made inquiries about the production of crude uranium in that nation's two mines, and asked how that material might be exported."

Says Chouet:

I don't know what happened between Rome and Washington.
I know that the CIA was still knocking on our door with
the uranium story in the late spring of 2002. The end of
April, I would say, and early May. This time, there was
an undeniable urgency to their questions. In comparison
to the previous summer, the Americans were now more
precise. They pointed to a specific country: Niger. They
offered a wealth of details. In fact, they entrusted to us all
the information that we *later* discovered was contained in
Rocco Martino's dossier (which had completely disappeared
from the radar). As usual, Langley said nothing about the
source. They mentioned neither Martino nor SISMI. All
they asked was that we verify the material. The pressure
from Langley was considerable. The CIA asked for an
immediate response on the validity of the information. In
the wake of 9/11, the relationship between DGSE and the
CIA was excellent, and therefore I organized a mission under
deep cover. During late May and June of 2002, my boys
were busy in Niamey. The mission, in accordance with our
operative guidelines, was concealed from both our Foreign
Ministry and diplomatic corps. I assigned twenty percent of
our best agents to the squad—men with a deep knowledge
of Niger and all the issues connected to yellowcake. They
remained in Africa for a couple of weeks, and when they
returned, their findings were simple, even blunt: "The
American information on the uranium is complete bullshit."

When I read the report, their findings seemed completely
consistent with what I knew about Niger and Saddam.
I knew that if Saddam wanted to acquire yellowcake in

Niger—but why would he buy more, since he already had enormous quantities?—he would never assign an ambassador to negotiate the deal. The dictator trusted nobody in his Foreign Ministry. Just imagine him sending those ambassadors all over the world! No, he would have sent one of his sons for a deal like that.

There's another reason that I believed the report my boys delivered: We already knew the reason for Wissam al-Zahawie's trip to Niger. At all costs he needed to find an African country willing to accept the Iraqi regime's stockpile of toxic waste in exchange for cash. Mauritania, which Iraq had been using as garbage dump up until that time, had notified Baghdad that it no longer intended to stink up its own land. I sent along our findings to the CIA. The Americans seemed extremely disappointed by what they heard. I understood their frustration—but I understood it even better when the CIA, unhappy with the outcome, sent us part of their dossier in late June of 2002, almost as if they wanted to demonstrate how reasonable their urgency had been. They sent a sheaf of papers to Paris via the usual intelligence channels. I recall that there were no more than ten or so pages. It included a brief introduction in which the CIA sketched out the significance of the dossier—and then, no more than three complete documents. All it took was a quick glance at those papers to conclude that they were junk. Crude fakes.

The document that caught my eye made reference to the Iraqi ambassador to the Holy See. Gazing at the page, I recalled the strange, generic bulletin from the CIA during the previous summer. At that point I told

myself: "Get a load of these Americans. They've had
this stuff for a year and they're telling us about it only
now, after we've already sent two missions to Niger."

They still didn't tell us where they had obtained that
stuff—not then, not later. But we figured it out on our
own. We might be French, but we're not total idiots! In
the first place, those documents (insofar as you could read
them) originated in the Nigerien embassy in Rome, and
we knew precisely where *that* was. What's more, during
the very same period that the CIA was sending us the
documents, Rocco Martino appeared on the scene. I already
mentioned that Nadal met with him in Luxembourg.
When Jacques sent Martino's papers to Paris, we compared
them to the dossier the Americans had transmitted to us
just a few weeks before (which we had already decided
was fake). The documents were identical. We concluded
that Rocco was the source of the "bullshit" palmed off
on the Americans. The same nonsense that had made the
rounds in the summer of 2001. We also concluded that
Rocco was trying to palm off those same documents on
the Germans at the Bundesnachrichtendienst [BND].* The
Germans asked our advice and we told them it was trash.

Here, a third surprise. Late June 2002.
     The CIA, which already had the 1999 telex, sent some of the
Niger documents to Paris. These were the materials assembled by
Rocco Martino, Signora Laura, and Antonio Nucera. How did they

---

* The Bundesnachrichtendienst, or BND, has been the foreign counterespionage
arm of the German Federal Republic for forty years. Its general headquarters is in
Pullach, near Munich. Reformed by August Hanning, who was its chief for seven
years (1998-2005), it is now directed by Ernst Uhrlau.

end up in the hands of the CIA? And what did SISMI know about the comings and going of those documents?

Alain Chouet, busy with his veal kidney, shrugs his shoulders:

> Don't ask me! I'm telling you that I received a "taste" of those documents from Langley in the summer of 2002, and that they were the same ones the Italian was trying to palm off on us. We met with Rocco Martino a second time. It was toward the end of July 2002. We told him that his papers were junk, fakes. Meanwhile, we checked out who he was, and discovered that he was a former Italian intelligence agent.[*]

---

[*] SISMI now accuses French intelligence not only of manipulating Rocco Martino, but of deliberately misleading the Americans about the fraudulent nature of the Nigerien dossier. (Relevant articles have appeared in numerous Italian dailies, including *Il Foglio, Il Riformista, L'Unità,* and *Il Giornale.*) SISMI points the finger to a meeting between the French head of counterproliferation and a U.S. State Department official on November 22, 2002. On that occasion, says SISMI, the French alluded to a report that the Iraqis had tried to procure uranium in Niger—and vouched for the reliability of this intelligence. According to this version of events (which is partially based on the U.S. Senate's report on prewar intelligence), the French withheld any knowledge of the fraud until March 4, 2003, at which point they informed Washington that they already possessed the identical "documentation" of the supposed transaction. When the authors shared this scenario with Chouet, he replied: "Let me repeat for the millionth time. First: Our Foreign Ministry has no idea what DGSE is doing at any given time. That's the rule. It's a common practice, for other intelligence agencies as well as ours. Second: We [at DGSE] tipped off the CIA in the spring of 2002. Third: Pay attention to the specific wording of the U.S. Senate report. It doesn't say that the French *informed* the Americans on March 4, 2003. What it does say is: 'On March 4, 2003, the American government *learned* that the French had based their initial analysis of the uranium sale on the same documents that Washington now possessed.' That is, until that date, *somebody* was sitting on that information. Maybe somebody in Washington. Certainly not somebody in Paris.... I should add one more thing. In my two years as head of DGSE, I had occasion to meet with George Tenet, who was then director of the CIA. I participated in various talks between Paris and Washington. Now, if I said that a certain thing was 'possible,' that word turned into 'probable' in Tenet's mouth."

Alain Chouet's tale contradicts (and corrects) three essential points in the reconstruction of the affair offered up by the chatty Nicolò Pollari.

Rocco Martino, the swindler who disseminated the false documents, didn't work for DGSE. In fact, DGSE encountered him for the first time in the summer of 2002.

That summer, the CIA was already in possession of at least part of Rocco Martino's phony documents.

And contrary to what Pollari told the parliamentary commission (and the reporters he summoned to his office at the Baracchini Palace), it was not the French who transmitted the phony documents to Washington, but the Americans who transmitted them to the French, asking them to help verify the dossier. The French examined the papers and, toward the end of July 2002, denounced them as fakes.

Chouet's tale reveals the crude cosmetics of reality. Of course, his reconstruction puts his own nation in an advantageous light. Yet it is solidly, credibly confirmed by the Americans and the Germans, by the CIA and the BND.

Wolbert Smidt worked for the BND for 35 years, attaining the rank of senior director before leaving in 2003. Having served as station chief in Paris, he knows France well, and on the eve of the Iraqi war, he led the agency's Intelligence Collection Department. He recalls:

> In 2002, the BND concluded that Iraq was in no shape
> to build nuclear weapons. We learned very quickly about
> the existence of false documents tied to Nigerien uranium.
> Those papers were circulated among European intelligence
> agencies. Obviously, we were all asking the same question:
> Were the documents authentic or not? And in each case—this

fact must be stressed—the European agencies came to the
same conclusion: The documents were false. It was so easy
to figure this out that I'm sure the CIA must have come to
the same conclusion, and communicated it to the White
House and to the other American intelligence agencies.

In Washington, a U.S. official (who prefers not to reveal his name
and the agency for which he works) confirms Chouet's version of
events. Paris, he says, informed the CIA that the documents were
false after "exhaustive research on the ground." He says: "At the
time, I recall, Alain Chouet's report completely contradicted our
understanding of that situation." And meanwhile, Chouet's account
is also amply confirmed by a former high CIA official and a French
government official.

The former CIA official remembers it this way: "It's true, we
contacted the French for the first time in the summer of 2001, before
September 11, and then once again in 2002. Now, I can't tell you the
details of the final report that Paris sent in 2002, but I can definitely
recall the conclusions it drew. They were the same ones that Chouet
mentioned."

That is, the documents were forgeries. A French government
official adds: "In January 2003, we heard Bush refer to the
yellowcake in his State of the Union address, and to the related
British intelligence. Our first thought was that we were dealing with
a fit of lunacy. We knew that the rumor had absolutely no basis.
Nonetheless, we checked it out one more time, leaving no stone
unturned in our effort to figure out what was going on."

In the face of such evidence, which collectively supports the
French version of events, the Italians have precious little to offer. As
an accountant might say: all debit, no credit. The Italians produced
a judicial inquiry without a shred of objectivity. A string of

communiqués from the Chigi Palace—the epicenter of the Italian government—essentially confirms Pollari's story as a matter of faith. Indeed, the first note issued by the Chigi Palace on October 24, 2005, was followed by three more (October 26, October 29, December 5), all of which essentially toed the same line. None of the messages delved much into the development of the "yellowcake affair." They simply affirmed that neither the Italian government nor SISMI had known a thing about it, despite all evidence to the contrary. Above all, there is a thick, intervening cloud of dust, which keeps the facts at an unmistakable distance.*

There are, however, various circumstances that force us to tell this story by rearranging certain pieces on the chess board.

Let's begin with the arrival of Nicolò Pollari at the Baracchini Palace. He was appointed head of Italian intelligence two weeks after September 11, and officially took the reins the following month, on October 15, 2001. He immediately said: "I need between 50 and 100 field agents right away—at the latest, over the next few months."

---

*Anonymous sources at SISMI released color photos to the press (*Il Riformista,* October 29, 2005 and *Il Giornale,* December 3, 2005) that documented Rocco Martino's meetings with individuals whom Italian military intelligence called "his French contacts." Two of the photos depicted Martino seated in a bar, conversing with a man identified as Jacques Nadal, the DGSE agent in Brussels. The other two images were shot out in the open, and show the Italian swindler standing next to a tall man with short hair. (These photos were taken from behind.) The parties responsible for leaking the pictures clearly wished to demonstrate the relationship between Martino and French counterespionage, thereby suggesting that the SISMI informer was a French agent. In reality, they were sowing confusion. According to the same anonymous SISMI sources cited by one of the newspapers (*Il Giornale*), the photos in question were actually taken in the spring of 2004—that is, a year after the disclosure of the falsified documents and a good three years after SISMI first passed on its summary of the bogus information to Washington. It's obvious, then, that the photos prove nothing about DGSE's role in the dissemination of the dossier. They merely prove that, in 2004, Martino was being trailed and photographed by SISMI.

The new chief wanted to get right down to business. He understood that the state of things was advantageous to him, that it offered opportunities previously unknown to anybody in his position. He had ample room to maneuver. The threat of Islamic terrorism was taking root everywhere, anywhere. It might incubate the most deadly sort of delirium. The very fate of the nation, you might say, now depended upon the preventive efforts of its spies, who, almost overnight, found themselves at the center of the political, military, social, industrial, financial, and media scenes. They were virtually everywhere, because the defense of the nation's security was an all-embracing task.

Never had the spies been paid so many courtesies. Never had they been so pampered. Pollari realized that the government and the undersecretary in charge of the secret services, Gianni Letta, had granted him a great deal of autonomy, along with an abundance of human and financial resources and the freedom to operate inside and outside Italy's borders. In return, much was expected of SISMI. Silvio Berlusconi in particular was eager to draw a winning hand, which would earn him a coveted spot with the United States, now that the Americans had been attacked and wounded by Islamic fundamentalism. He insisted upon it. For him it was a political priority, right up there with cutting a pesky business tax, reforming the telecommunications and judicial systems, and modifying the Constitution. The Italian premier didn't even consider the idea of being an extra on the international stage. If he couldn't be the featured player, he was determined to be a guest star at the very least.

Nicolò Pollari was no slacker. He set up shop 24 hours a day in a small office at the Baracchini Palace. Just a few dozen square meters. A window through which the sun never shines. Throw in some dark wooden paneling and you've got a suffocating scene, dominated by papers. Papers everywhere.

Pollari trusted nobody. He kept all the most important dossiers in his own office. To the left of his desk, there was another, horseshoe-

shaped table, covered with a breaking wave of files. Pollari divided
the agency into watertight compartments. The left hand knew not
what the right hand did. Those at the lower level had no idea what
their superiors were up to. Often they were working on the same
dossier, with the same objectives. One department against another.
One senior official against another. The newest hires—often drawn
from the ranks of the national police, especially from the Guardia
di Finanza—locked horns with the old fogies from the navy and the
"young lions" from the carabinieri. The competition was insane.
The rivals tripped each other up, stabbed each other in the back, all
fighting for the same slice of pie.

This hellish climate was exactly what Pollari wanted. He thought
that such ruthless competition could bring a stodgy, stumbling,
bureaucratic institution back to life. He asked his men to dive
headlong into the dark well of modern radical Islam. Who were the
terrorists, and where could they be found? What were they doing,
and what were they planning? Did they have tools and supplies? Did
they have money? Where had they come from? Were there any who
perhaps might be willing to collaborate, to pass on the occasional tip
in exchange for cash or a long-term visa?

Pollari demanded information, news, warnings, reports. He
seemed less concerned about how they were gathered, or to what
degree they could be verified. He told his staff: Bring me the goods
on the rogue states, on Iraq, Iran, Libya, Syria. Find out what sort of
overseas programs are being developed by Hezbollah and Hamas,
by the Kurds and Salafis and Wahhabis, by the Islamic Jihad.

THE AMERICANS were obsessed with the need to evaluate how dangerous
Iraq was. This was a top priority. It was a source of terrible anxiety.
Did Saddam Hussein have weapons of mass destruction? If not,
was he any shape to build them? How long would it take? What
did he still need to complete the weapons? Was Baghdad connected

to the attacks on the Twin Towers? Was Mohammad Atta—the lead 9/11 hijacker—an Iraqi agent? Had there been, since 1993, a state sponsor behind bin Laden, as Deputy Secretary of Defense Paul Wolfowitz insisted? That link could be proven—no, it *had* to be proven. It was a matter of national security. And equally, it was a matter of political utility. It was necessary to buttress the instincts of President Bush, who had prowled the White House on the evening of September 12, ordering deputies to "see if Saddam was involved."

As it turned out, it was the neoconservative camp within the Bush administration that took over—attempting to compile intelligence about Iraq and terrorism. The neoconservatives had two fundamental philosophical principles. First: We live in a dangerous and terrifying world. In this world, America must have the maximum freedom of action to defend itself from attacks, to project its power without being bogged down by allies, rules, international institutions. Second: An America ultimately liberated from the snares of coalition politics and international law must use its power to tip the global equilibrium in its favor, even intervening to modify the internal nature of those regimes that may represent a danger. This was the principle that could (and must) legitimize a military intervention in Iraq, if only to find evidence of that nation's weapons of mass destruction.

"Fuck Saddam," Bush told his subordinates at the White House. "We're taking him out." The members of the neoconservative team were delighted that the president's War on Terror had, in the words of David Frum and Richard Perle—two key administration hawks—jolted the "national security bureaucracy out of its comfortable routines."

The CIA, the neoconservatives believed, was an oasis of moderation in Colin Powell's State Department and incapable of proving that Saddam had WMDs for an elementary reason: "[T]hey weren't up to the job." They believed the CIA had gradually become an agency "with very strong, mostly liberal policy views, and these views have again and again distorted its analysis and presentation of its own information."

The agency would have to be outflanked, then. Stuck in a corner. Rendered harmless. It was impossible to combat terrorism with the same men, the same bureaucracy, the same methods that had left U.S. territory undefended on September 11. How could *those* people now defeat Osama bin Laden and tear out the roots of Islamic terrorism, which were taking hold in the fertile terrain of rogue states such as Iraq?

Dick Cheney decided to do something. To do it alone. He bypassed the institutional structures of the intelligence services. He put together a vest-pocket agency with his own associates. It was an operation that closely resembled Team B—an alternative intelligence arm of the 1970s, which had employed Paul Wolfowitz to report on the effective danger of the Soviet nuclear arsenal.

The whole business was less intricate than you might think. To get things moving in the right direction, you merely needed to exaggerate the enemy's capabilities. You selected one-sided data and intelligence sources. You tossed away the information that contradicted your scenario, and emphasized any clues that supported it. "In a trade where information is always malleable, and where the person organizing and evaluating the information is given notable leeway, it's always easy to bend a case to one's own ends," argues journalist Federico Rampini.

It's an old trick. It resurfaced during the war in Vietnam, when the problem solvers at the Pentagon—as convinced as the neoconservatives that they could resolve any crisis—remained blind and deaf to reports by the intelligence services that the strategy in Vietnam was a catastrophe.

This informal team of Cheney's men was run out of the Pentagon's Office of Special Plans (OSP) and headed by Undersecretary of Defense for Policy Douglas Feith. The OSP itself was a mini-agency that did not collect intelligence so much as create it. How they accomplished this has been precisely described by Robert Baer, an outspoken former CIA field officer in Iraq.[*]

In a conversation with us, he explains:

> The method is called competitive intelligence—that's the term used by insiders. The team (or should we call them a gang?) works in the following manner. A piece of intelligence, normally provided by a source who tells you exactly what you want to hear, is passed along to an allied intelligence agency or to another source, who will pass the "news" in turn to a friendly agency. At the same time, that information, which has just been put into circulation, is generically dropped into an official white paper and marked to the attention of the Secretary of Defense and Vice President Cheney and (through them) the president, who is thereby put under pressure. The news now becomes *classified*. At this point, the president requests more information on the subject, and asks each of our intelligence agencies to search for proof of what he has just read in the white paper. The CIA puts its men on the job, as does the Department of Defense, the NSA, the DIA, and so forth. While our intelligence agencies are searching for proof, allied agencies keep popping up with the same news—and since they like to make Big Brother happy, they assert that things are exactly as the White House supposes them to be. In this way, the news is repeatedly confirmed. It also becomes superfluous

---

[*] Baer currently lives in a cabin in Silverton, Colorado, high in the Rocky Mountains. He left Washington with relief: "It was the smartest decision of my entire life. All I brought with me was a deck of cards and my two Labradors, Hersh and Risen… that's right, I named them after the two best investigative reporters in America."

to check the reliability of these sources, since they're "allied
agencies" that are telling us what we want to hear.
Our intelligence agencies take this evidence back to the
president. Obviously, such a great distance has now been
created between the original source of the news and
its ultimate application that it's impossible to figure out
who supplied the information in the first place—or to
evaluate its credibility. What matters is that a false piece of
information has now become a true one. It's also become
classified, and capable of impacting political decisions.

Competitive intelligence only appears to multiply the number of
sources. In reality, it's a vicious circle, a disinformation technique.
Once they've been manipulated, hypotheticals turn into facts, and
theories turn into *indisputable* facts. To put it another way: Doug
Feith's OSP approached the War on Terror in the same way that a
Madison Avenue ad agency would approach the launch of a new
product. In the fall of 2001, the product the OSP needed to sell to
the world was the invasion of Iraq.

For the White House, Saddam was a constant torment, a
psychotic nightmare. Washington (and its CIA station in Rome)
wanted nothing from the Italian government—from its intelligence
agencies, from its judiciary—so dearly as they wanted information
about Iraq and its weapons and its link to Al Qaeda.

At Forte Braschi, SISMI's headquarters, an idea began to
take shape. There's something we *know*, muttered the second-tier
bureaucrats. Let's bring it to the attention of the director.

Pollari, in his cluttered office, was also asking his subordinates
what the agency *had*. He was told about the "Niger dossier." The
related note that his predecessor, Gianfranco Battelli, had sent to
Langley on September 21, 2001, was added to the pile of papers
beside his desk.

As far we can tell, nobody pointed out that the information was fraudulent. They wanted to make a good impression on the new boss. Nobody found the time to explain to Pollari that they were dealing with a dirty trick. Nobody. Certainly not Colonel Alberto Manenti, named as head of the WMD unit to keep Rocco Martino's old friend Antonio Nucera from occupying that post. "Manenti is a competent officer," says one source at Forte Braschi, "but he's absolutely incapable of saying No to his boss. He won't clash with their beliefs or hunches."

Let's assume this is the correct version. Pollari, who still didn't know the extent of his own agency's risky business, gave the green light to Operation Niger. Or rather, a few days later, he felt a powerful itch to be at the center of the Great Game with his American friends. He understood how helpful it could be to heap Washington's plate with treats; to satisfy, as rapidly as possible, the cravings of the important ally. It could put him at the crossroads of various strategic initiatives. It could give him a truly international role and, even more important, access to information that would improve his performance on the home front.

THE DAYS OF SHOCK and anguish for the West were days of excitement for Rocco Martino. In the air he smelled the fresh scent of money. All he had to do was *mention* a dossier, a tip, for his new clients—and, in the wake of what happened in New York and Washington, he got offers from everywhere, the West, Africa, the Middle East. There was plenty of work to do, and Signora Laura might be useful once again. Martino believed that his career had been resurrected: an unexpected gift. According to an "insider" at Forte Braschi, however, it wasn't merely that Rocco believed in this resurrection—he was *encouraged* to believe in it.

At the former SISMI headquarters on Viale Pasteur, Antonio Nucera was well aware of the fervor now reigning at the Baracchini

Palace. For the colonel, it must have been almost routine to learn that the telex intercepted in 1999 and Battelli's note to the CIA had been transferred from the archives to the director's desk. Was it Nucera who blabbed to Rocco that SISMI planned to share the telex with its American ally?

The "insider" has no intention of naming names: "Let's just say that an emissary from SISMI met with Rocco."

Whoever he was, the emissary, we're told, deliberately spilled the beans to the debt-ridden Martino: At the highest levels of the SISMI, there was a focus on Niger and uranium. The emissary exerted no pressure. He moved cautiously, with calculated wariness. Almost distractedly. All he needed to do was raise his comrade's expectations: He had already foreseen the reaction. Martino must believe that he could sell whatever documents Signora Laura might remove from the embassy on Via Baiamonti.

One can imagine the two colleagues having a good laugh together, each for his own reasons. There would soon be a brisk market for stolen papers—why not take advantage of it by trying to sell their dossier?

"How?" asked Martino, but he already had a few ideas. The emissary weighed in with his own. They listed some possible clients. At the top of the list, they put down MI6, the British intelligence agency. (MI6 carries out foreign intelligence activities on behalf of the prime minister, but reports directly to the foreign secretary.) After thinking it over for a few days, they added the Egyptians. They even met with an agent of the Mukhabarat, according to Pollari. Soon, however, they let that idea drop: Everything always got too complicated with the Arabs. If things got messy, they might shoot. Plus you never knew quite what you were getting into with those guys.

The English, led by MI6 Director Sir Richard Dearlove, were more generous—and, as everybody in this world knew, they were easy to satisfy. Out of choice, and out of long habit. Since the autumn of 1997, their I/Ops unit had been gathering and disseminating "trash" about Iraq's weapons of mass destruction. The English were no less intent than their friends at the CIA upon proving that Saddam was trying to build a nuclear weapon. So they would be the clients for whatever documents Signora Laura could manage to steal.

When Rocco Martino sensed new business at hand, he got fired up. He dropped his impression of an old-fashioned gentleman and raised his voice. He became fidgety, impulsive, and brusque with everybody. He cursed and sometimes insulted whomever got in his way. This happened with Signora Laura, who was causing him some major trouble. Good God, he lamented, that woman couldn't seem to steal a thing. In reality, SISMI was roasting him over a low flame. As the Signora reveals: "Nucera brought me some papers, which I was supposed to slip in among the documents I was passing along to Rocco."

This is the story put together by a reliable source, who was able to hear firsthand the Signora's reconstruction of the relationships between a certain functionary at the Nigerien embassy, Rocco Martino, and Colonel Antonio Nucera of SISMI.

If we credit Signora Laura's version, it was SISMI who dreamed up the false yellowcake dossier. Assuming that she's telling the truth, it was the crew at Forte Braschi that patiently cooked up the fraudulent papers, which Martino would then disseminate throughout Europe. And after *that*, SISMI agents would show them to a CIA field officer in Rome.

But let's return for a moment to Rocco's activities. Before trying his luck with the French and the Germans, he began in London. He stopped by "Legoland," the MI6 headquarters on the Albert Embankment. He introduced himself as a double-dealing SISMI courier. Nobody in Rome lifted a finger to stop him, even though his every step was monitored, tracked, and photographed by Italian intelligence.* SISMI, therefore, lulled the swindler into thinking he had a golden opportunity on his hands. They accompanied him on his peregrinations as a door-to-door salesman of stolen secrets. They did so to protect him, rather than to stop him. May we fairly conclude that the Italian intelligence service used this curious "channel" to share fraudulent information with the English without dirtying its own hands?

Exactly, insists Rocco Martino. In 2003, having just returned to Italy from Nice, he made his way to Rome: elegant, bronzed, cheerful, he insisted on being called "Signor Morini." At that point he tidied up and sharpened his story. He also minimized his own contribution, taking a few discreet steps toward the sidelines. He placed his own mission in a very institutional framework. He also declared that he had reconstructed the entire affair, including the chapters of which he had no direct knowledge, with "a friend at Forte Braschi."

As Martino put it: "At the end of 2001, SISMI transmitted the yellowcake dossier to the British at MI6. They 'passed it along' without evaluating it. They only noted that it had been received from a 'credible source.' It's a routine procedure. Part of the normal exchange of information among allied nations."

Martino didn't admit to being the postman. He didn't say that he had received that "parcel" from his old employer. All he insisted was that SISMI had sent the documents to London.

Fine. The English got the delivery. Then what? According to

---

* According *Il Giornale*, October 29, 2005: "According to intelligence sources [at SISMI], from 1999 through the spring of 2004, Martino would have about thirty meetings with his secret contact, who was working out of 65 Rue Ducale, Brussels— an establishment with the French tricolor fluttering outside. He would pass along information in exchange for a regular stipend of several thousand euros. SISMI tailed him, photographed him, eavesdropped on him…. Everything that passed through his hands was copied, microfilmed, analyzed."

Martino: "After that first communication, an intense exchange of information began with MI6. There were various meetings, here and in London, between English and Italian officials. During the same period, the British transmitted the material to the Americans. As usual, they saw no reason to ask the Italians for permission to use the information."

Who took care of this matter in Italy? Who was told about the operation and updated as it progressed? According to Martino, "At SISMI, it was run by the Division 3. There were analysts working on it, who oversaw our links with foreign intelligence and wrote daily reports for the director of the agency. And as usual, they would compile a short summary note—a single page—for the staff of the foreign minister and for CESIS, who would in turn brief Letta and Berlusconi." (CESIS is the Comitato esecutivo dei servizi di informazione e sicurezza, which allows the Italian president to ensure that both SISMI and SISDE pursue the same political ends. The committee has no day-to-day tasks, but CESIS does deliver a report on the activities of both agencies to Parliament every six months.)

ANOTHER YEAR PASSES. It's July 2004.

By now the swindler wishes to be called "Signor Giacomo." He meets a journalist from the *Sunday Times* in the Eurostar lounge in Brussels. This time around he's even more blunt. So much for institutional discretion. He no longer adopts the tone of a lofty State functionary, whose only sin was being more talkative than he should have been and more greedy than he deserved to be. He's in trouble. MI6 has released his name to the *Financial Times*. The investigative teams from the networks and the American journalists are hunting him down with more determination than the Roman judiciary. Rocco must lever himself out of the corner. He wants to spill the beans, perhaps in exchange for several thousand euros. In his possession he has 24 hours of tape recordings, notes with names and telephone numbers, documents, and a CD-ROM, all of which will confirm his story. He has a great desire to show his evidence, and to document that "the drama of the false dossier was engineered by the Italian government."

His key recollection is as follows:

> I got a call from a former colleague at SISMI. I was told
> that a woman at the Nigerien embassy in Rome had a
> "gift" for me. I met her, and she gave me the documents.
> SISMI wanted me to circulate those documents without
> any further involvement from the agency. I did so. It's true,
> I had a hand in the dissemination of those documents, but I
> was duped. Both the Americans and the Italians are behind
> this story. We're dealing with a disinformation operation.

If you examine them closely, there's not much difference between the story as reconstructed by Rocco Martino and Signora Laura, and the one recounted by Nicolò Pollari. In both scenarios, the protagonists are the same, as is the tissue connecting them.

There's the disgraced spy (Martino); his friend, also a spy (Nucera); the shabby source at the embassy (Signora Laura); the false dossier assembled with the help of a Nigerien spendthrift; the discreet input from Forte Braschi; the trip to London; the sale of the documents, which everybody in Italy knows are false, to British intelligence, which then passes them on to the CIA, which has them authenticated in turn by SISMI. At this point the basic plot is no longer in doubt, just as the role of SISMI is no longer debatable— clearly the agency steered the entire business.

When the unreliability of the documents was made public in July 2003, the crew at the Chigi Palace soon realized that they were in serious trouble. The staff of Silvio Berlusconi and Undersecretary of the Government Gianni Letta, a Berlusconi associate, instinctively fired off a quick note:

The reports that Italy has transmitted to foreign
intelligence agencies documents obtained from
Niger or Iraq are totally groundless.

It's understandable that the government needed to muddy the trail, to produce its own version of events. But cutting the cord so cleanly, by denying any involvement whatsoever, seemed more dangerous and compromising than an admission of "indirect" involvement, so the gang at Chigi Palace decided that it better correct their flat denial in a hurry. Too many people knew the score, and the government didn't want to leave itself in a vulnerable position. Twenty-four hours later, toward the end of the evening, with the editorial offices distracted and the newspapers already gone to press, Gianni Letta sent Filippo Berselli, the Italian undersecretary of defense, over to parliament. There Berselli was charged with reading out a convoluted note written by Nicolò Pollari.

Naturally Berselli confirmed that "no documentation was ever handed over by any part of SISMI." And he repeated that "in regard to the hypothetical transmission of documentation to the intelligence agencies of Great Britain and the U.S., no document obtained from Niger or Iraq in connection with the delivery of crude uranium was ever handed over by any part of the agency."

What happened, then? The moment came for some hedging, some admissions. Berselli finally tried to clarify certain matters. Again, a key admission:

Following the usual procedures, we did share the contents
of certain findings with the intelligence agencies of
allied nations, with the goal of obtaining eventual
verification and an examination of the problems that
are facing us in a wide-ranging international context.

Only "in April of 2002" it was claimed, "was the information offered to the intelligence agency of another allied nation."

Pollari hid the facts behind a fake, hair-splitting brand of eloquence. In the note he read, Berselli could have said: Our information was too generic and therefore we worked with the CIA and only in the spring of 2002 did we involve the English at MI6. It would have been more clear—but that wasn't an option for the director. And therefore he didn't reveal that he kept asking the allies to confirm information that he himself had put into circulation via Rocco Martino—fully aware, of course, that it was trash.

Nicolò Pollari wasn't acting alone: The game was too lively, the stakes too high. On July 16, 2003, Undersecretary Gianni Letta testified before the Parliamentary Commission on the Oversight of Security Services. At that moment, Letta must have possessed a good deal of information that would have helped to clear up the whole imbroglio. Yet he uttered no names, no dates, no details. He produced no documents. Instead he fudged, he whittled away at the facts, and when there was no other choice, he explained that the information requested by Parliament could not be furnished, since that might endanger "the secrecy of certain sources and operations in progress."

IN THE UNITED STATES, it's easy to gather evidence proving the involvement of the Italian government. We can track down proof that SISMI and the various functionaries are simply not credible when they deny informing the CIA about Saddam's bogus shopping expedition in Niger. Nor are they credible when they insist that they heard of Rocco Martino's dossier only *after* February 2003.

In Washington we can establish that as early as October 2001— only 34 days after the attacks on the Twin Towers—Italian agents allowed the CIA field officer in Rome to examine the (obviously false) "draft agreement" between Niger and Iraq. This overture parallels another move that Italian intelligence was making. SISMI was sharing the information in the dossier with London, too. They didn't analyze the data. They didn't say: It's good, it's bad, it's dubious. They simply said that the source who had procured it was "credible." London then contacted Washington. The British didn't say that the information came from an Italian source. All they said was: We have evidence that Saddam Hussein is buying uranium in Niger.

American intelligence, under pressure to give the hawks what they wanted, suddenly found itself in possession of one report (Saddam is buying uranium in Africa) and two "allied" confirmations (the Italians and the British). In reality, of course, the original report and its subsequent confirmations came from a single hand. And that hand belonged to the swindler Rocco Martino, manipulated and controlled by SISMI. It's Robert Baer's "competitive intelligence" at its very best.

In Italy, we all know how Berlusconi is. He likes to amuse people, to entertain them. He hogs the spotlight, he explains, he declaims. He's always performing, even when he's forced to improvise like a ham actor around a script he doesn't know, has never read, and can hardly imagine. Often he hits the wrong note. His riff on the "superiority of Western civilization over Islam," which he unleashed in front of the television cameras just a few days after September 11, was a conspicuous gaffe. (The comment was made to the press during the Berlin summit conference, on September 26, 2001.) For George W. Bush, who was just then seeking the support of moderate Arab nations in the War on Terror, it was a most unwelcome comment. Berlusconi's visit to the United States was subsequently announced and then delayed, announced again and cancelled again. Finally, on October 15, 2001, he was welcomed to the White House. There he sat in the drawing room overlooking the Colonnade, and examined the garden with so much interest and attention that Bush decided to give him a guided tour of the rose bushes and magnolias.

Berlusconi wore his big smile, reserved for special occasions. He was in Washington to say: "I'm there for you." And in the spectacle that was now shaping up in Afghanistan, he had no wish to be a mere extra. To his ally, who was preparing to wage war against the Taliban and Al Qaeda, he offered bases and logistical support for military operations. If necessary, pilots and seamen. And ground troops, "if they are requested."

He was asked: "Did the United States make any specific requests?"

Berlusconi responded: "No, we didn't go into details. That will be up to our military experts, who are already working together."

He nodded, a pensive look on his face, while the American president observed that "this will be a war on many fronts: the financial front, the intelligence front.... The Al Qaeda network must be eliminated throughout the entire world."

Berlusconi "didn't go into details" with George W. Bush. But Gianni Castellaneta, a diplomatic adviser to Chigi Palace, made it clear that the new director of SISMI—who took office that very same day—was working with allied nations on some "extremely interesting intelligence."

On the same day that Berlusconi dined in the West Wing, Pollari's SISMI shared two interesting pieces of news with the CIA. First: The negotiations regarding Niger's sale of crude uranium to Iraq had been going on since 1999. And second: The sale of the mineral had been authorized by the State Court of Niger in 2000.

These were not easy days for George Tenet. The CIA director was under siege. Couldn't he have stopped the massacres of September 11? As it turned out, all the necessary information, or almost all of it, had been right under the nose of his analysts. All they had needed to do was pick out the correct details from that imposing flow of information. Nobody did so. They had overlooked the clues, cried the neoconservative think tanks, because they had been blindsided by "ideological prejudice or institutional bias."

For the neoconservatives, of course, ideological prejudice was the infectious virus that had sickened the CIA and now might possibly kill it. Regarding terrorism, the agency got it wrong, more or less in the same way (and for the same reasons) that it had gotten the Soviet Union wrong during the Cold War. Or so said the clergy of the American Enterprise Institute, a neoconservative think tank.

Such convictions, such ideological prejudices, caused the analysts to recoil "from reporting facts that would have demanded a forceful U.S. response to the Soviets."

We can't blow it again, was the mantra out at Langley. The director knew that he would be cut no further slack. Every trail, every clue, every rumor, must be tracked down, checked, confirmed or disproved. Otherwise the agency would be destroyed or irreparably "reformed."

Faced with this new intelligence from the Italians, the CIA hesitated. And Nicolò Pollari made it his business to convince them that the dossier wasn't pure garbage. On October 18, 2001, the new director took pen and paper in hand and wrote a reassuring, one-and-a-half page note to the agency. The news about the uranium was solid, he declared, and it had been taken seriously because the source, "a woman in the Nigerien embassy in Rome," was "credible." Pollari didn't mention her name, but he noted that "in the past, she has furnished SISMI with cryptographic ciphers and copies of embassy paperwork."

Now the CIA put aside any reluctance. On that same day, October 18, its analysts drew up a complete report, which was distributed throughout the American intelligence community. It read:

> According to reports by a foreign intelligence agency,
> Niger, at the beginning of this year, planned to ship
> several tons of uranium to Iraq in accordance with an
> agreement concluded last year. Iraq and Niger have been
> negotiating this business since 1999, but according to the

foreign agency, the State Court of Niger gave its approval
only this year.... Once it has been enriched, the quantity
of uranium is sufficient to produce an atomic bomb.

Now the crew at Langley got to work. First of all, the "boys" in
Niamey were put on the job. The response from Niger arrived by
return mail in a diplomatic pouch, on November 20, 2001. In a
cable sent from the American embassy in Niger, we read: "The
French-led mining consortium excludes any possibility that Niger
would be able to divert to Iraq some three thousand tons of uranium
produced in its two mines."

Meanwhile, the Italian dossier also crossed the desk of the U.S.
State Department's Bureau of Intelligence and Research (INR).
There it was examined by the Strategic, Proliferation and Military
Affairs Office. This division was led by Greg Thielmann, an "analyst
on intelligence questions pertaining to national security" with more
than 25 years of experience.*

Thielmann's division was not a large one. During that period,
it employed sixteen analysts. These were people with an excellent
reputation in Washington. They were appreciated for their
extraordinary abilities and notable tenacity. Like most of the State
Department's intelligence offices—and in contrast to what the

---

* Educated at Princeton, Greg Thielmann worked at the State Department as an
analyst on questions pertaining to national security and counterproliferation.
On the eve of the Iraq war, he was the Director of the INR Office of Strategic
Proliferation in Military Affairs. In that capacity he worked under John Bolton, who
was then Undersecretary of State for Arms Control and International Security.
Bolton was annoyed, then infuriated by Thielmann's skeptical attitude toward
reports of Saddam's WMD arsenal. Eventually he punished his subordinate by
excluding him from daily staff meetings. (According to a piece in *The New Yorker*
of October 27, 2003, Thielmann was told: "The undersecretary doesn't need
you to attend this meeting anymore. The undersecretary wants to keep this in the
family.") Thielmann left the State Department in 2003.

neocons were always insisting—it was dedicated to the truth of facts, whatever they happened to be, with the awareness that a fact, if true, can do no harm. And because it helps the political leadership to make fully informed decisions.

Thielmann recalls:

> I received the report. It was a summary that Langley had
> gotten from one of its field officers stationed in Rome. The
> agent stated that thanks to the cooperation of the Italian
> military intelligence service, he had seen some papers that
> documented Iraq's efforts to acquire more than 500 tons
> of pure uranium from Niger in the beginning of 2001.
> (He hadn't, however, been able to make copies of the
> papers.) As they always do in these cases, the CIA had
> shared the report with every other intelligence agency,
> including ours, because they wanted us to evaluate it. The
> moment I read it, that piece of paper headed straight
> for the wastebasket. No matter how you looked at it, the
> story didn't hold up. For at least two good reasons.

Two reasons.

> The first reason. We knew that Iraq already possessed five
> hundred metric tons of enriched uranium in its warehouses
> at Tuwaitha, routinely authorized by the AIEA. A quantity
> sufficient to produce at least two nuclear devices. So it
> made no sense for Saddam to buy a rather hefty amount
> of pure uranium in a country like Niger, where the mines
> are controlled by the French Congema consortium, which
> also includes the Spanish, the Germans, and the Japanese.
> How was it possible that none of these countries, all of
> them our allies, was aware of what had been going on?

The second reason.

> Purely empirical. You go with your gut, your instincts. That's
> often the best way to get your bearings. One of my most gifted
> analysts regularly shared his findings with the CIA, and in
> circumstances like this, I would turn him loose on the agency,
> because he might come up with some additional clues about
> the source of the information. In fact, we routinely indexed in
> our database all sources of information pertaining to weapons
> of mass destruction, and this allowed us to create a sort of
> archival record of their credibility.... So the CIA couldn't
> answer our questions. For weeks, they kept telling us that they
> were trying to obtain certain additional data. Starting with the
> actual documents upon which the report was based. However,
> they kept repeating that Italian intelligence was certain that
> Iraq had at least attempted to buy uranium from Niger—as
> if that were an independent confirmation of the report.

There were no documents to examine. The documents remained in
the hands of the Italians, and SISMI was "certain." In Washington,
nobody knew about Rocco Martino's dreams of glory, about Signora
Laura, about the spendthrift Zakaria Yaou Maiga. They had never
heard of Colonel Antonio Nucera. Nobody in Rome felt obliged to
stop that train, which had begun to gain a great deal of velocity in
Washington—too much velocity, perhaps, even for those who had
put it on the tracks.

Worse: In Rome, the dossier had been scrubbed clean of the
blatant errors that might cause the Americans to smell a forgery. As
a result, the decisively bogus dossier now looked genuine. It was an
elementary job; the swindle took place in plain sight.

The evidence of this can be found by comparing the original
forged dossier—which is now on the public record—with a

description of the "scrubbed" dossier given by U.S. officials familiar with the documents.

The changes are confirmed by the U.S. Senate's *Report on the U.S. Intelligence Community's Prewar Intelligence Assessments on Iraq*, which notes, on page 36:

> Reporting on a possible uranium yellowcake sales agreement between Niger and Iraq first came to the attention of the U.S. Intelligence Community (IC) on October 15, 2001. The Central Intelligence Agency's (CIA) Directorate of Operations (DO) issued an intelligence report from a foreign government service indicating that Niger planned to ship several tons of uranium to Iraq. The intelligence report said the uranium sales agreement had been in negotiation between the two countries since at least early 1999, and was approved by the State Court of Niger in late 2000. According to the cable, Nigerien President Mamadou Tandja gave his stamp of approval for the agreement and communicated his decision to Iraqi President Saddam Hussein. The report also indicated that in October 2000 Nigerien Minister of Foreign Affairs Nassirou Sabo informed one of his ambassadors in Europe that Niger had concluded an accord to provide several tons of uranium to Iraq.

By now we're familiar with the documents "prepared" by SISMI's Antonio Nucera, then consigned by Signora Laura (a SISMI source) to Rocco Martino (a SISMI collaborator).

Among the documents, there was one authentic item. This was the telex of February 1, 1999, sent by Ambassador Adamou Chékou to the Minister of Foreign Affairs in Niamey: "I have the honor of informing you that the Iraqi Embassy to the Holy See has notified me that His Excellency Wissam al-Zawahie, Iraqi Ambassador to the Holy See, will undertake an official mission to our country on behalf of Saddam Hussein, president of the Iraqi Republic."

Around the authentic telex, our friends had assembled the fraudulent correspondence. There was the letter dated July 30, 1999, from the Ministry of Foreign Affairs to the ambassador in Rome, signed Nasirou Sabo. There was also the letter addressed to Saddam Hussein ("Monsieur le Président") from the president of the Republic of Niger, dated July 27, 2000, in which he authorized the agreement to sell Iraq 500 tons of uranium each year. And there was a second letter addressed to the ambassador in Rome, dated October 10, 2000, from the minister of foreign affairs, Allele Dihadj Habibou—this one devoted to the "draft agreement" for the uranium sale. To this last item the swindlers had attached a two-page "agreement," which noted the approval of the State Court "in accordance with Article 20 of Ordinance 74-13 passed on July 5, 2000."

As we have seen, the swindle could have been unmasked at once. The letter of July 30, 1999, was signed by Nasirou Sabo, who was no longer Minister of Foreign Affairs by that date. Additionally, it made reference to the agreement concluded in Niamey on June 29, 2000—that is, *a year later*.

The letter of July 27, 2000, from Mamadou Tandja, the President of Niger, mentioned the Constitution of 1966. Yet the Constitution then in force had been issued in 1999.

And finally, the letter of October 10, 2000 (regarding the "draft agreement") was signed by Allele Dihadj Habibou, who hadn't been the minister of foreign affairs and cooperation since 1989.

When the senior SISMI officials got to work on this shabby dossier, however, they chucked out the letter of July 30, 1999. The reference to an agreement made a full year later was simply too incongruous. As for the letter to Saddam Hussein from Mamadou Tandja, they passed the document on in spite of its flaws.

The 1999 telex was no problem. It was authentic. That was more than you could say for the letter from Allele Dihadj Habibou. He hadn't been in the appropriate ministry for more than a decade. But a little bit of retouching could fix that. By looking at both sets of documents, it is evident that—before the document was shared with the CIA—someone had transferred Nasirou Sabo's signature from the July 30 letter to the October 10 letter—which made perfect sense, since Sabo *had* been the Foreign Minister between 2000 and 2001. Now the dossier was ready. Still, it needed to be handled with discretion. Passing it directly to the CIA was still too risky.

What if they discovered the manipulation of the signatures? They allowed the CIA agent just a quick glance.

As Greg Thielmann has already recalled, the CIA agent in Rome "had seen some papers that documented Iraq's efforts to acquire more than 500 tons of pure uranium from Niger in the beginning of 2001." He hadn't, however, been able to make copies of the papers. Instead the field agent hurriedly jotted down the information he was able to glean from the dossier.

What did Pollari know about the bunglers who had concocted this fakery? True, he had vouched for Signora Laura. But he had been at SISMI just a few days: It's hard to tell whether he was praising her in earnest or had been fed bad information by a colleague. As was his habit ("I don't trust anybody in this place"), we assume he would have personally verified any story this important—especially once the CIA asked for additional help from the Italians. But in the wake of his original cable, as SISMI sent a second report to the CIA, and then a third, Pollari's tone never changed.

Let's return to the Senate report for a moment:

> Reporting on the uranium transaction did not surface again
> until February 5, 2002 when the CIA's DO [directorate
> of operations] issued a second intelligence report which

again cited the source as a "[foreign] government service."
Although not identified in the report, this source was also
from the same foreign service. The second report provided
more details about the previously reported Iraq-Niger
uranium agreement and provided what was said to be
"verbatim text" of the accord. Subsequently, the governments
of Niger and Iraq signed an agreement regarding the
sale of uranium during meetings held July 5-6, 2000.

On February 12, 2002, the Pentagon's Defense Intelligence Agency
(DIA) drew up a report entitled *Niamey Signed an Agreement to Sell 500
Tons of Uranium a Year to Baghdad*. During the morning briefing, Dick
Cheney read it. He asked the CIA officer for more information.
In response, the CIA director in charge of WINPAC (Weapons
Intelligence, Nonproliferation and Arms Control) produced a note
"for limited distribution" that stated: "The information on the
alleged uranium contract between Iraq and Niger comes exclusively
from a foreign government service report that lacks crucial details,
and we are working to clarify the information and to determine
whether it can be corroborated."

That put the ball back in SISMI's court. Could they verify those
documents? Was there additional evidence?

Pollari never shifted. Perhaps he was under pressure from the
government, which wanted to help its greatest ally topple Saddam.
To return to the Senate report one last time:

> On March 25, 2002, the DO issued a third and final
> intelligence report from the same "[foreign] government
> service." The report said that the 2000 agreement by
> Niger to provide uranium to Iraq specified that 500
> tons of uranium per year would be delivered in [phrase
> deleted from report]. As in the two previous reports,

the foreign government service was not identified. The foreign government service did not provide the DO with information about its source and the DO, to date, remains uncertain as to how the foreign government service collected the information in the three intelligence reports.

At this point, who was going to confess that in order to make the information "digestible," the Italians had doctored the papers by transferring Nasirou Sabo's signature from one letter to another?

In most cases, Thielmann's unit pays no further attention to reports that are deemed unreliable. They simply indicate that the file "has been archived"—and they do so verbally. Otherwise the 16 analysts would spend every minute writing memoranda, merely to contradict the tons of rubbish tangled in the nets of America's intelligence agencies. This time, however, somebody must have put the squeeze on Thielmann and his group. In the face of White House pressure, they realized that a verbal communication was insufficient. So instead of closing the file, they decided to draw up a report. They would put it down in black and white. According to Thielmann, this was largely at the behest of the CIA, which understood precisely what the administration hawks had in mind.

Theilmann recalls: "With my approval, the African desk of the INR drafted a memorandum that was passed along to Powell. We noted that the information gathered by the CIA was inconsistent. That the story of the uranium sale was false. That a whole bunch of things that had been sent to us were bogus."

The memorandum was signed by Greg Thielmann on March 1, 2002. This was a week before the CIA completed its own independent report, which put down in writing the findings of a former ambassador, Joseph C. Wilson, who had just returned from a mission to Niger. As it happened, Langley had been unwilling simply to dump the Roman rubbish in the lap of the State

Department. They wanted to scope out the situation with their own eyes. Without informing the State Department, then, they sent Joe Wilson to Africa.

IT WAS A COLD FEBRUARY morning in 2002. Joe Wilson crossed the Potomac in his car and headed for Langley.

It wasn't unusual for the CIA to request a meeting with Wilson.* During the 22 years of his diplomatic career, he was often called upon to share his knowledge of the countries in which he had served. This time, the CIA wanted to discuss the uranium industry in Niger. Wilson recalls:

> The participants in the meeting were drawn from the
> intelligence community's experts on Africa and uranium, and
> included staff from both the CIA and State Department...
> I did not know any of them personally.... They were
> interested and interesting professionals but as anonymous as
> you would expect in a bureaucracy that places a premium
> on secrecy.... My host opened the meeting with a brief
> explanation of why I had been invited to meet with them.
> A report purporting to be a memorandum of sale of
> uranium from Niger to Iraq had aroused the interest of

---

* Born in 1949, Joseph C. Wilson IV served the United States as a diplomat from 1976 to 1998. In 1988 he was named deputy chief of mission (DCM) at the U.S. Embassy in Baghdad, a post he still occupied during Iraq's invasion of Kuwait in 1990. Between then and the beginning of Operation Desert Storm, he was the only American diplomat to remain in Iraq—and also the last one to personally encounter Saddam Hussein. During the 1990s he was ambassador to Gabon and São Tomé and Príncipe and advisor to the National Security Council on African politics. In 1998 he married Valerie Plame, who worked as a covert CIA agent until her cover was blown in 2003. In 2004 Wilson published *The Politics of Truth* (New York: Carroll & Graf Publishers, 2004), an account of his diplomatic career and of his entanglement in the so-called Nigergate scandal.

Vice President Dick Cheney. His office, I was told, had
tasked the CIA to determine if there was any truth to the
rumor....The report, as it was described to me, was not very
detailed. For example, it was not clear whether the reporting
officer—not present at this meeting—had actually laid
eyes on the document or was simply relaying information
provided by a third party. The amount of the uranium
product... involved was estimated to have been up to five
hundred tons but could also have been fifty, suggesting that
the account had been written from memory (and an imperfect
one at that) rather than with the document at hand....

I was skeptical, as prudent consumers of intelligence
always are about raw information. Thousands of pieces
of data come over the government's transom on any given
day, but a lot belongs in the category of "rumint," rumors
passing as fact.... Rumint is a necessary if unfortunate
reality in a world where many people will sell you what
they think you want to hear, as opposed to simple facts.

At the end of the briefing—after I'd answered questions on
topics ranging from security arrangement to transportation
routes for the yellowcake—I was asked if I would be
willing to travel to Niger to check out the report in
question, which, if credible, would be very troubling.

Joe Wilson arrived at Niamey's Hamami-Diori International
Airport on February 26, 2002. It was a Tuesday, and, according to
Jeune Africa/L'intelligent, he had a *large sourire*—a broad smile—as he
disembarked. He knew the city and the country well. He had worked
there on behalf of the United States Agency for International
Development (USAID) from 1976 to 1978, and returned during the
1990s when he was employed by the NSC.

A limousine from the embassy awaited him at the airport.

First stop: the Hotel Gaweye in the city center. With "his perfect French and his Golden Boy manner, he installed himself in Suite 424/425, which offers an unspoiled view of the river and of the Kennedy Bridge."

First meeting: Ambassador Barbara Owens Kirkpatrick.

After civilities had been exchanged, Wilson discovered that they hadn't told him the whole story at Langley. There had already been two follow-up reports on that "draft agreement" for the sale of uranium, and both had been unable to verify the deal.

Joe Wilson recalls:

> Kirkpatrick told me that not only had she discussed the issue with President Tandja, but that before I showed up, she had accompanied General Carleton Fulford [deputy commander of the U.S. European Command] to a meeting with the president and other members of the government. Kirkpatrick added that Fulford believed the story of the uranium sale to be false. Both her report and Fulford's had been passed along to our intelligence community and widely circulated. Kirkpatrick had been sure that they had settled the question once and for all.

That's understandable.

Thielmann was right. That dossier deserved to go straight into the trash—and he came to this conclusion without even knowing that two other investigators had already labeled it as unreliable.

Knowing that there had already been two negative reports, Wilson asked himself why yet a third report was requested. What the hell was going on? This question Wilson put on hold for the moment. He was in Niamey to do a job, and he intended to do it, even if Kirkpatrick and Fulford had already dealt with the same question. Three days were sufficient for him to get the job done, although flight schedules extended his stay in Niger to a full week.

Wilson spared himself an avalanche of official meetings. They would only be a waste of time. So there was no meeting with President Mamadou Tandja. No meeting with Allele Dihadj Habibou, the administrative head of Cominak (one of the two companies that mined Niger's uranium). The ambassador preferred to interview other government officials and a couple of key men in the mining industry. Nothing he heard contradicted the conclusions drawn by Kirkpatrick and Fulford—but there was one intriguing detail. A trifle, really. In retrospect, though, it further convinced Wilson that the uranium sale had never happened, and would never happen—and that the "draft agreement" shown to the CIA field officer by the Italians was false.

In his book, Wilson recalls a conversation with one of his sources:

> He mentioned to me that on the margins of a ministerial meeting of the Organization of African Unity (OAU) in 1999, a Nigerien businessman had asked him to meet with an Iraqi official to discuss trade. My contact said that alarm bells had immediately gone off in his mind. Well aware of United Nations sanctions on Iraq, he met with the Iraqi only briefly and avoided substantive issues. As he told me this, he hesitated and looked up to the sky as if plumbing the depths of his memory, then offered that perhaps the Iraqi *might* have wanted to talk about uranium. But since there had been no discussion of uranium—my contact was idly speculating when he mentioned it—there was no story. I spoke with this Nigerien friend again in January 2004, and he recollected our conversation in 2002. He told me that while he was watching coverage of press conferences in Baghdad prior to the Second Gulf War, he recognized the Iraqi information

minister Mohammed Saeed al-Sahaf, known to Americans as "Baghdad Bob," as the person whom he had met in Algiers.

This is the stuff of comedy. Al-Sahaf was the so-called minister who stood on the terrace of the Palestine Hotel while the Bradley Fighting Vehicles were speeding into the streets of Baghdad, assuring the TV networks in all seriousness that "the Iraqis are winning the war."

Wilson's work was done. He bade his Nigerien friends farewell with a Pantagruelian banquet of *mechouis*, or roast goat. Back to Washington. It was March 4, 2002.

Again, we can look to Wilson's book, where he recalls:

> Within an hour of my return to Washington in March 2002, a CIA reports officer, at my request, arrived at my home. Over Chinese takeout, I gave him the same details of my trip and conclusions that I had provided to Owens-Kirkpatrick in Niamey before my departure. These included the account of the meeting between my Nigerien contact and the Iraqi official on the margins of the OAU meeting, as well as my observations about where our government might inquire further if it was not persuaded by my report or those of the ambassador and the general whose inquiries had preceded mine. He left, and I went back to my life as a business consultant, with no further official contact with the CIA for the next year and a half.

Although years have passed, Thielmann is still infuriated when he thinks about the whole business. As he says: "That's right, nobody in the CIA told us that Wilson had been sent to Niger to verify the information. Nobody told us that the ambassador had been given the same kind of sketchy information compiled by the field officer in Italy—I found out only later, when I was chatting with Wilson.

And there's more. When Wilson returned to Washington in March, and was debriefed by the agency, the information he passed on was deliberately minimized by Langley. Even the source remained anonymous! By now, of course, we had already written up our own conclusions at Strategic Affairs. Then we got a note from the CIA discussing 'information gathered by an American citizen in Niger, which is impossible to verify at this time.'"

To summarize the whole affair: The CIA refused to credit the information from the diplomats in Niamey. The CIA sent Wilson to Niger. The CIA turned a deaf ear to many of Wilson's findings, and—perhaps more important—to the information they had meanwhile gathered from Alain Chouet's DGSE. The CIA also cut the State Department out of the loop, even though they were working on the same file.

Indeed, the CIA wanted to muffle even the slightest rumor of fraudulence. They kept silent about having "a portion of the documents" in their possession by "the late spring of 2002,"—according to Chouet's version of events—and continued to request "proof" and verification of already discredited information. The summer was almost over by now. Things hadn't turned out very well for the CIA. The State Department hadn't backed down. The INR hadn't backed down.

The agency's "sources" at the Iraqi National Congress, always eager to make themselves useful, knew nothing about the whole fairy tale.

It was September, and the White House needed to close ranks. Time was running out, as was any semblance of patience at the White House.

Dick Cheney continued to push the intelligence agencies. He wanted hard evidence of Saddam's arsenal. This pressure had a tormenting subtext: If there was no definitive proof of the link between Osama bin Laden and Saddam Hussein, and no definitive proof of the presence of weapons of mass destruction in Iraq, that was only because the intelligence agencies *had failed to find them*. Even the agencies had to admit that such evidence *could* exist—perhaps in the very places they hadn't yet searched. Keep looking.

Donald Rumsfeld put it in a nutshell: "The absence of evidence is not necessarily the evidence of absence." For the spies, however, this argument sounded like an order, a threat, and a piece of career advice: Keep looking, and behave as if the evidence will inevitably surface, and if anybody doesn't like this solution to the problem, you can find another job.

Thielmann put it this way: "George Tenet, the director of the CIA, kept waffling and showing signs of weakness. He knew that he couldn't reasonably insist on the credibility of the uranium deal. But at the same time, to avoid disappointing the president and Cheney and Rumsfeld, he concealed everything that disproved the story. Even worse: He waited for SISMI to pass the information to the British, so that somebody could tell the White House (in September 2002) that the story now had two confirmations. One from the Italians, one from the British. In reality, it was always the same lies bouncing from one agency to another."

The fraudulent dossier—which lacked any concrete evidence showing either the acquisition of uranium or even an attempt to acquire it—had begun to spin in circles like a top. The evidence of its inauthenticity was simply swept under the carpet.

The "Wilson report" (which did not add "any new information to clarify the issue," according to the Senate intelligence report) was not "brought to the attention of the Administration," but rather "distributed through routine channels." The Senate Select Committee on Intelligence also noted that "the CIA's briefer did not brief the Vice President on the report, despite the Vice President's previous questions about the issue."

This didn't make Thielmann feel any better. Indeed, he was disturbed when he read draft portions of the National Intelligence

Estimate—the most authoritative national security document, which is periodically revised by the director of the CIA, based on information gathered by all U.S. intelligence agencies, and submitted to the upper ranks of the current administration—pertaining to "Iraqi programs for weapons of mass destruction." They were parroting the story of the uranium sale as if it were credible! Theilmann couldn't sit still for that. His unit asked that the following note be appended to the relevant section: "The suggestion that Iraq sought to acquire uranium in Africa is, in the judgment of the INR, highly dubious." In the final text of the National Intelligence Estimate submitted by the CIA to Congress on October 1, 2002, this dissenting footnote "inadvertently" drifted to a spot sixty pages after the relevant text. ("Nobody has ever been able to explain that error," Thielmann notes.)

After a frenetic September, packed with meetings, briefings, and communications between Washington, London, and Rome, the fraud attained even greater heights. Over the course of two weeks, the Niger claims were broadcast around the world.

September 24, 2002. A fifty-page dossier released by the British government affirmed that Iraq was attempting to acquire uranium in Africa. Tony Blair insisted that Baghdad had "sought significant quantities of uranium from Africa, despite having no active civil nuclear power programme that could require it." In Washington, White House Press Secretary Ari Fleischer backed this. British contention.

September 26, 2002. Colin Powell told the Senate that Iraq's attempt to obtain uranium was proof of that nation's "nuclear ambitions."

At Forte Braschi, meanwhile, insiders were calling these "magnificent" days for Nicolò Pollari. "The director seems to be on cloud nine." He had plenty of reason to feel that way. Although news of the uranium sale was arguably the offspring of one swindler and one reckless SISMI agent, it was Pollari who had raised it to maturity.

Finally, September 9, 2002, a Monday.

Pollari's self-esteem was at its very pinnacle. Less than a year after taking office, he was a real player in the Great Game. Accompanied by a delegation that included several SISMI division heads (among them Alberto Manenti), Pollari was received at the White House by National Security Advisor Condoleezza Rice and her second-in-command, Stephen Hadley.

It is an important moment, but not really, as it would turn out, the end of this story.

CHAPTER TWO

A FINE ITALIAN TUBE

When you say the word *uranium*, the layman immediately thinks of an atomic bomb. In fact, it's not as simple as that. As Hans Blix points out in his book, there are a great many intermediate steps between the raw mineral and its lethal application: "Uranium, extracted from the subsoil and concentrated in yellowcake, has to pass through many elaborate industrial and chemical processes before becoming an explosive which is compatible with atomic bombs."

Centrifuges are among the main tools necessary for this industrial process. They allow technicians to separate the fissile elements of uranium from the nonfissile ones. It's obvious, then, that if Baghdad starts procuring aluminium or steel tubes like those used in centrifuges, this may confirm the speculation that Saddam is trying produce nuclear weapons. Especially if he seems to be stocking yellowcake at the same time.

A now familiar story: In early 2001, American intelligence agencies got wind of an Iraqi plan to buy 60,000 high-potency aluminium tubes in Hong Kong. In June of that year, the CIA intercepted the tubes in Jordan, before they could be shipped to Iraq. What they found were 7075-T6 tubes: the preferred sheathing material for a low-cost missile system, at $17.50 a pop. Still, the tubes were made of an extremely hard alloy, which might allow them to be used as rotors in a uranium centrifuge. The CIA insisted that the tubes had been procured for this latter purpose.

First, a word of explanation. Iraqi scientists had two options for enriching uranium. The first process, involving the construction of enormous calutrons, was so primitive that it had been abandoned in the United States more than five decades before.* It was highly unlikely that anyone would use such an inefficient technology at this point, and in any case the remaining Iraqi calutrons had been destroyed at the end of the first Gulf War.

The second method uses a "cascade" of centrifuges to separate out the constituents of uranium. The process calls for sixteen thousand separate centrifuges, which must remain synchronized as they rotate at high speeds: a challenge even for the most sophisticated plants. It turned out the Iraqis had already tried their hand at such a cascade, with disastrous results. As the IAEA inspectors discovered, Baghdad had brought in German technicians and purchased special steel from Swiss firms. Yet the Iraqis failed to mold the centrifuges correctly, which ruined the whole show.

Why, then, would Saddam's technicians persist in producing fissile material with centrifuge technology? Wouldn't it have been easier to buy enriched uranium on the black market? And if Saddam had decided to take another shot at building a workable cascade, how long would it take him to complete the job? The answer, according to many scientists, was six to ten years.

What's more, there were still doubts about whether the tubes seized in Jordan were really intended for that purpose. The U.S. Department of Energy was aware that for years, the Iraqis had used

---

* The word *calutron* is derived from the California University Cyclotron. It refers to a device for separating isotopes 235 and 238 from uranium; the device fuctions by means of mass spectrography.

aluminium tubes to make combustion chambers for small, platform-based missiles. As the *New York Times* later put it: "Back in 1996 the inspectors of the International Atomic Energy Agency examined some of these tubes, also made of 7570-T6 steel, in a military complex, the Nasser metallurgical plant in Baghdad, where the Iraqis were known to be building missiles. According to the IAEA, about sixty thousand of the tubes for missiles were 900 millimeters long, with a diameter of 81 millimeters and a surface thickness of 3.3 millimeters. The tubes being sought now by Iraq had exactly the same dimensions; a perfect match."

Were the tubes for missiles, then, or for the rotors in a uranium centrifuge? In this case, too, the question landed on the desk of the INR's Office for Strategic Affairs. Langley requested an assessment. The CIA explained that "the allied intelligence services of eleven nations—including Italy—have intercepted on the black market, and on the open market, evidence of substantial Iraqi activity directed at acquiring these aluminium tubes for the building of centrifuges."

The Strategic Affairs group had already heard such rumors, as had Australian intelligence and any number of other interested parties. Yet Greg Thielmann was sceptical in the extreme. As he recalls: "It immediately struck me as an unlikely story and I decided to stake my reputation on it. I personally expressed my doubts as to whether those tubes confiscated in Jordan could be used for the building of centrifuges. I went on to argue that they were intended for artillery projectiles. On this point Colin Powell wouldn't budge. He had been a general, after all. He tossed his experience as a soldier into the ring. He stressed his conviction that tubes of that kind were too thick to be made into artillery projectiles: not even the American army made projectiles that big, let alone the Iraqis."

Colin Powell defended his theory in front of the UN Security Council on February 5, 2003. His words:

I am no expert on centrifuge tubes, but just as an old Army
trooper, I can tell you a couple of things: First, it strikes
me as quite odd that these tubes are manufactured to a
tolerance that far exceeds U.S. requirements for comparable
rockets. Maybe Iraqis just manufacture their conventional
weapons to a higher standard than we do, but I don't think
so. Second, we actually have examined tubes from several
different batches that were seized clandestinely before
they reached Baghdad. What we notice in these different
batches is a progression to higher and higher levels of
specification, including, in the latest batch, an anodized
coating on extremely smooth inner and outer surfaces.
Why would they continue refining the specifications, go
to all that trouble for something that, if it was a rocket,
would soon be blown into shrapnel when it went off? *

In Washington, the INR decided to entrust the analysis of these
objects to the Oak Ridge National Laboratory, whose scientists
produce uranium for the American nuclear arsenal. In early 2002,
the Oak Ridge staff delivered a very precise verdict. The tubes
were too narrow, too heavy, too long, and too brittle to be used in
centrifuges. Instead they were intended for the construction of a
particular type of artillery projectile, a model that the Iraqis had
decided to copy from an Italian artillery projectile. Italian?

Thielmann shakes his head slowly. He turns a stern gaze upon his
interlocutor. He repeats: "Italian! An Italian artillery projectile."

The projectile in question was the Medusa 81, an air-to-ground

---

* In reality, the IAEA inspectors verified that the tubes, intercepted in Jordan, had
been anodized because the Iraqis wanted to protect them from the elements:
Saddam's deputies stored them out in the open, and the inspectors later discovered
thousands of old, rusted, useless tubes.

missile deployed by Italian army and navy helicopters. It was hardly a surprise that the Iraqis possessed plenty of Italian weaponry, or that they would seek to duplicate it during the straitened era of the international embargo.* During the early 1980s, the cream of the Iraqi air force had been trained in electronic warfare by Selenia, an arm of the IRI Finmeccanica group, a private Italian industrial group. They also did their basic flight training at Italian bases, including Latina, Amendola (Foggia), and Galatina (Lecce). But that only raises another question. The Italians, like the Americans, had confiscated a supply of the aluminium tubes. They had them at their disposal, tested and examined them. Surely they recognized them as *their* tubes—the very kind used to manufacture the Medusa 8. There was, however, no communication of this fact to Washington.

Italian intelligence held back what it knew until November 2003, eight months after the invasion of Iraq. This foot-dragging was carefully documented by the so-called Silberman-Robb Commission:

> Although some elements of the American intelligence
> community were aware that the Iraqi 81-millimeter
> Nasser projectile model was probably an adaptation of
> the Italian Medusa air-to-ground system, neither the DIA

---

* Ever since the oil crises of 1973 and 1979, the Italians had promoted major economic, commercial, and technological exchanges with Iraq in order to keep the petroleum flowing (in 1974, the Italian import-export ratio with Iraq was an unfavorable 100/40). Eventually the government in Rome furnished Baghdad with nuclear-related technology. In 1979 they built their trade partners a laboratory for the production of radioisotopes, as well as facilities for chemical engineering and fuel testing (the latter run by SNIA-Technint). In 1980 the government signed a contract to provide five research labs for the nuclear reactor at Osirak. For these facilities, plus a mini-armada of naval vessels—including four *Lupo*-class frigates, six corvettes, and a logistics vessel—the Iraqs would pay 1,500 billion lire: Italy's most impressive weapons sale since the end of World War II.

> nor the CIA—the two main proponents of the theory
> that tubes had a nuclear purpose—obtained the technical
> specifications of the Medusa until Operation Iraqi Freedom
> was well under way.... Only in a classified intelligence
> report of November 2003 did the CIA finally obtain from
> the Italians the technical specifications of Medusa.

Having already precipitated the scandal of the Nigerien uranium sale, the Italians had apparently returned for a second round of mischief. Let us put it more succinctly. There is adequate evidence to show that SISMI also played a major role in the cobbling together of intelligence about the famed aluminium tubes. Here, of course, we begin a new story.

Pollari, it must be said, played his hand very carefully. He understood that the Bush Administration's rush toward war—and his own government's desire to join the adventure, using every public and private means at its disposal—offered him considerable opportunities. The real battle was being fought in the corridors of Washington; all Italian intelligence needed to do was stay in formation. Bring up the rear and provide support. Confirm information that was useful to the hawks—confirm it prudently, that is, right before London and Washington decided to go public with the news. Pollari could maintain a high profile when it was advantageous, then hide when the going got slippery. Played in this way, it was an easy game. Safe, like betting on a race that was already over.

ONE CAN'T really talk about Iraq's uranium enrichment program without talking about Judith Miller. It was this prominent journalist and Pulitzer Prize winner at the *New York Times* who picked up the story of the aluminium tubes and made a dramatic and crucial scoop. There is, however, another reason to discuss her career here. Judith Miller's operating procedures—and the network of individuals, organizations, lobbies, and ideologies that support them—can shed

some important light on the political processes at work in Italy and
the United States.

On September 8, 2002, Judith Miller and Michael Gordon
published a long, front-page article in the *New York Times*. In it, they
discussed the aluminium tubes that might enable Saddam to build
an atomic bomb:

> In the last 14 months, Iraq has sought to buy thousands
> of specially designed aluminum tubes, which American
> officials believe were intended as components of centrifuges
> to enrich uranium…. The diameter, thickness and other
> technical specifications of the aluminum tubes had
> persuaded American intelligence experts that they were
> meant for Iraq's nuclear program, officials said, and that
> the latest attempt to ship the material had taken place in
> recent months…. Iraqi defectors who once worked for the
> nuclear weapons establishment have told American officials
> that acquiring nuclear arms is again a top Iraqi priority.

Miller and Gordon concluded:

> Hard-liners are alarmed that American intelligence
> underestimated the pace and scale of Iraq's nuclear program
> before Baghdad's defeat in the gulf war. Conscious of
> this lapse in the past, they argue that Washington dare
> not wait until analysts have found hard evidence that Mr.
> Hussein has acquired a nuclear weapon. The first sign of
> a "smoking gun," they argue, may be a mushroom cloud.

"I'm not exaggerating," insists Roberto Reale, in the best Italian
investigation of the media during the war. "It is absolutely reasonable
to state that it was this article in the *Times* that gave the green light
for an acceleration of the war." This judgement has since been

seconded by U.S. Congressman Henry Waxman, and by much of
the U.S. Democratic Party leadership, which has urged a complete
re-examination of America's prewar intelligence.*

Waxman says: "People were talking about Iraqi weapons of
mass destruction for a decade, and for a decade nobody invaded
Iraq. Nobody can deny in good faith that on the eve of the invasion,
our main concern was always the threat of chemical and biological
warfare. The simple truth is that what made the war possible was the
transformation of those weapons into the spectre of an atomic bomb.
This was stated quite clearly by none other than Paul Wolfowitz. He
noted that the 'evidence' of Saddam's nuclear rearmament was (and
I quote) 'the decisive argument in gaining the consent of American
public opinion to military intervention in Iraq.'"

The September 8, 2002, article in the *Times* suggested that
Saddam was busily rearming, and that he had the technological savvy
to wage an aggressive war against the United States and its allies.
Didn't the imminent arrival of those tubes prove how dangerously
close the dictator was to adding nuclear weapons to his arsenal?

Here was the proof the hawks in the Bush Administration had
been waiting for. They had been pining for an unimpeachable source
to shore up the theory of the "smoking gun," which the Iraqi tyrant
would sooner or later aim at America. The fact that Miller worked
for the *New York Times*, that notorious hotbed of liberal opinion, was
an added bonus in this case.

To Roberto Reale, the Italian media expert, the events that
followed Judith Miller's scoop seemed like a carefully prepared show.
As soon as the *Times* hit the newsstands, it sparked off a round-robin
of strategic television appearances—what Reale calls "a propaganda

---

* In November 2005, the Democrats called for a closed session of the Senate—a
dramatic and desperate bit of procedural arm-twisting—and under the leadership
of Jay Rockefeller and Carl Levin, the minority party forced the Republican majority
to commit itself to "Phase Two" of the Intelligence Committee's investigation.

offensive of perfect efficiency, worthy of a military operation." Dick Cheney, Colin Powell, Donald Rumsfeld, and Condoleezza Rice rushed over to the TV studios to comment on the breaking news, waving the "centrifuges" in the public's face as proof of clear and imminent danger. It was as if they had found Saddam's fingerprints on an actual nuclear device.

In the frightened and furious memory of many Americans, it was the "mushroom cloud" evoked by Condoleezza Rice on CNN's *Late Edition* that made the strongest impact. Her comments were so effective that President Bush repeated them almost word for word on October 7, as Congress prepared to vote on the resolution for war in Iraq: "America must not ignore the threat gathering against us. Facing clear evidence of peril, we cannot wait for the final proof—the smoking gun—that could come in the form of a mushroom cloud."

But the most explicit endorsement of Miller's article came from Dick Cheney on *Meet the Press*. The picture he painted of Saddam's nuclear ambitions was menacing, intimidating—and completely unfounded, as the Italian government and its intelligence agencies already knew. The vice president noted: "We do know, with absolute certainty, that he is using his procurement system to acquire the equipment he needs in order to enrich uranium to build a nuclear weapon."

Nearly two years later, in May 2004, the *New York Times* would apologize for that article, as well as for eleven others, all but one of which had been written or co-written by Miller. The coverage "was not as rigorous as it should have been," acknowledged the editors. "Information that was controversial then, and seems questionable now, was insufficiently qualified or allowed to stand unchallenged."

In the paper's admission of responsibility—which is what interests us here—there is also a revelation of the working methods that lay behind Judith Miller's war chronicles and the plague of disinformation they produced: "We depended on information from exiles, in particular the group of Ahmad Chalabi, and the accounts of these exiles were often eagerly confirmed by United States officials convinced of the need to intervene in Iraq."

The *Times* sketched out a triangle, whose vertices were occupied by Ahmed Chalabi, the Bush Administration, and the paper itself. Questionable information had a way of bouncing from one side to the other. The process worked something like this. First, Chalabi would pass along some dubious facts to Judith Miller. The Pentagon (or the NSC, the CIA, the OSP, or perhaps the vice president's staff) would anonymously confirm these facts for Miller. The *Times* would publish the facts in one of Miller's articles. And once they were printed, the administration would cite them chapter and verse.

Again, this is what the spies call *competitive intelligence*. Yet the Miller System is only one segment of the whole enterprise.

AHMED CHALABI was the darling of the Washington hawks.

Born in Iraq in 1944, Chalabi was educated in the United States. He earned a mathematics degree from MIT in 1965 and a doctorate from the University of Chicago four years later. It was at the latter institution where he studied with Albert Wohlstetter, a specialist in nuclear weapons. A foreign-policy hawk and director of the RAND Corporation, Albert Wohlstetter seems to have inspired the character of Dr. Strangelove, who appeared first in Peter George's satirical novel *Red Alert, Two Hours to Doom*, then in Stanley Kubrick's eponymous film of 1964. Wohlstetter introduced his prize pupil to his circle of friends, which included such once-and-future hawks as Richard Perle, Dick Cheney, Donald Rumsfeld, Paul Wolfowitz, and former director of the CIA James Woolsey.

Over the next couple of decades, Chalabi devoted much of his energies to founding and running the Petra Bank in Jordan. In 1989 some fiscal irregularities forced him to scuttle over the Syrian border concealed in the trunk of a car. In the wake of the first Gulf War, however, Chalabi reinvented himself as an advocate of regime change in Iraq—with considerable assistance from the CIA.*

After the Gulf War, the CIA appointed a public relations agency, the Rendon Group, "to help to organize, advise and run the Iraqi opposition." In turn, the Rendon Group created the Iraqi National Congress (INC). The flacks at Rendon chose the group's name, coordinated its strategies, and connected it to the Washington power network via James Baker and Brent Scowcroft. They transformed a hollow shell into a political entity sponsored by the United States and capable of serving American interests. "Had it not been for the Rendon Group," said one State Department official, "Chalabi's group wouldn't even be on the map."

The INC was cooked up in 1992. In no time at all, Chalabi had a thriving operation on his hands. The key members of his staff—led by an all-American boy, fundamentalist Christian, and

---

* Until the military coup that unseated Faisal II in 1958, the Chalabis were probably the wealthiest family in Iraq. The founder of the family fortune—Ahmed's great-grandfather—was a tax collector in Kadimiah, a city near Baghdad. His son prospered by ingratiating himself with the British. And *his* son multiplied his riches by redeeming the debts of an influential member of the royal family. After the 1958 revolution, however, the Chalabi family fled to Lebanon and put down roots there. Ahmed was educated in the United States, then returned to Lebanon to teach at the American University in Beirut. In 1977 he moved to Jordan, where he founded the Petra Bank. Within ten years, Petra was the second-largest bank in the region. In 1989, however, all the Jordanian banks were required to deposit 30 percent of their foreign currency reserves in the central bank—and Petra seemed to be missing the necessary cash. Ahmed slipped across the Syrian border, hidden in the trunk of a friend's car. Jordanian investigators were to discover a $215 million deficit at Petra, and when detectives from the Kroll agency tried to figure out where the money had gone, they calculated that the total losses run up by Chalabi enterprises around the world amounted to nearly $1.5 billion. Ahmed Chalabi was tried in absentia, along with forty-seven associates. He was found guilty on thirty-one charges, and sentenced to twenty-two years in prison. But since his trial took place before a military tribunal (thanks to Jordanian martial law), Chalabi cannot be extradited under international law.

former director of the Rendon Group named Francis Brooke—
reported directly to the undersecretary of defence for policy, Paul
Wolfowitz.

In a conversation with the authors, Brooke characterizes it this
way: "The first Gulf War had just ended. I was a boy, and the job I
had been offered was incredible. Nineteen thousand dollars a month
for three months' work in London. Not bad. Even though I had to
pay my own living expenses, it was a lot of money. And the job
sounded pretty banal. They said I had to organize and coordinate
a campaign against Saddam's regime. Soon, though, I realized that
things were a bit different than they seemed."

"First of all, I found out that the funds for my salary were
provided by the CIA," he continued. "Also, I discovered that it wasn't
just a question of campaigning against Saddam in Europe—we were
helping to build an opposition in exile. So it was that, in autumn 1991,
I met Dr. Chalabi. And it was a meeting that changed my life."

In 1995, Chalabi attempted to overthrow Saddam by force of
arms. Setting up shop in northern Iraq, which was controlled by
the Kurds, he assembled a small staff and an armed militia. To get
the revolt rolling, he planned to bribe the tribal chiefs in the area
around Mosul. This strategy failed miserably: The chiefs pocketed
his money and did nothing. And although Chalabi's Iranian friends
had promised to help, they too held back. The military attack by his
tiny personal militia, supported by a few Kurdish allies, petered out
within a couple of days.

The CIA knew nothing of this venture (or so the agency claimed).
At once, they disowned the INC. Yet Chalabi was not the type to be
easily discouraged. His defenders within the neo-conservative camp
were quick to leap to his defence—and the money kept flowing in.
Brooke, who served as Chalabi's treasurer as well as his aide-de-
camp, recalls the influx of American dollars: "The first money from
American taxpayers reached us in 1992. Chalabi, at that time, was
in northern Iraq, and the CIA was paying the INC three hundred

thousand dollars a month. The contributions went on until 1997, in exactly the same amounts. Between 1997 and 2000, the CIA faucets were turned off. We began to negotiate with the Clinton Administration and obtained the [Iraq Liberation Act of 1998], which again authorized payments to support the INC. In the spring of 2000, the State Department started to supply funds again. This time, three hundred and forty thousand dollars a month. With the Bush Administration the payments continued, but the paymaster changed. Beginning in the summer of 2002, INC funds came from the Pentagon instead of the State Department. The money was paid to a firm registered in Virginia of which I am still chairman, Boxwood Inc. The payments stopped in May-June 2004, when Chalabi came under investigation for spying."

During the long prelude to the Iraqi invasion, Brooke was a frequent visitor to the Pentagon. Meanwhile, CIA and Defense Intelligence Agency (DIA) officials put in regular appearances at his brownstone home in Georgetown: "Sure, we had (and we continue to have) relations with the CIA and the DIA. During the actual invasion of Iraq, CIA operatives ate and slept with our own intelligence staff. And as far as the Pentagon is concerned, yes, I know and have had relations with the Office for Special Plans. With whom? I can say that Harold Rhodes is a friend and a good person, though it is not strictly correct to say that he works for the OSP—his job is at the Office for Net Assessment, where they do pure analysis. I would describe it as the Pentagon's think tank."

Greg Thielmann characterizes the relationship a bit differently: "The Office for Special Plans threw Chalabi scraps of intelligence, which the INC reworked, enriched, exchanged independently with the intelligence services of allied countries, and then brought back to Washington. And when anyone tried to check the evidence for this information, they found themselves facing an apparent series of interlinked confirmations. In reality, a single hand had once again dealt all the cards. And with false information."

IN OCTOBER 2001, just weeks after the attack on the Twin Towers, the London office of the Iraqi National Congress seemed like the best place in Europe to collect information about the supposed link between Iraq and Mohammed Atta. At the time, the authors of this book travelled there. Despite the swanky headquarters at 169 Knightsbridge, the facilities themselves were fairly underwhelming. You would never have known that James Woolsey had just flown to London and delivered a $4 million check from the State Department.

Check or no check, the place looked shabby. There was no security. On the ground floor a fat bored man sat behind a crooked desk with a gray telephone, picking his nose. Upstairs was Nabil Musawi. Tall, athletic, and sure of himself, this former manager of a Leeds pizzeria had become Chalabi's "colonel," and the boss gave him plenty of latitude: "Anything Nabil says has the same force as if I'd said it myself."

When we spoke to him, Musawi did not say much, but the little he did say allowed us to glimpse the early card game devised by Chalabi and the Office of Special Plans. The first question of the day was: What did the INC tell James Woolsey that was worth four million dollars? Musawi, who at the time asked to be described merely as a "member of the INC," told us: "We supplied Mr. Woolsey, and therefore the Pentagon, which appointed him, with evidence gathered during conversations with at least three Iraqi deserters. These men provided information proving the links between Iraq and the attacks of September 11, between Saddam and infection with anthrax. Naturally this is a work in progress, because the deserters have to be constantly moved from their refuges in the Middle East, and are waiting for visas for Britain or the United States. But one of them—an official of the Iraqi secret services—was interrogated by the CIA in Ankara last week."

This official, Musawi went on to explain, had told the CIA that in September 2000, he had seen "some Al Qaeda members being trained to hijack a Boeing 707 in the Salman Pak camp, on the outskirts of Baghdad." No doubt there would be more such interrogations, Musawi told us.

The game plan—when we first visited in October 2001—was already crystal clear. The INC would collect and control the Iraqi refugees. Whether they were genuine was almost beside the point. Chalabi's men would indoctrinate deserters according to their own needs, altering the equation, suggesting how the dots should be connected. Osama with Saddam Hussein. Mohammed Atta connected to Baghdad and anthrax and flying lessons and God knows what else. After wrestling with some initial doubts, the deserters got ready to face the CIA interrogators. Once the operation got rolling, the machine could supply Washington with whatever it needed.

Only two weeks later, the machine had kicked into much higher gear. The blackened sign from a real estate agent remained on the white door at 169 Knightsbridge. Inside, however, the scene was very different. The fat man was gone. In his place, huddled around a new desk and a telephone exchange with twenty-odd black buttons and little red lights, sat three men armed with handguns.

Upstairs, Nabil Musawi was wearing a black leather jacket with padded shoulders and a black round-necked cashmere pullover, over beige corduroy trousers. He seemed even more self-confident. His profession, he now explained with some earnest gestures, obliged him to ask questions. Iraqi deserters claiming to have information might be bluffing, sometimes not. He would listen to the answers, compare them with what he already knew or what others had told him, assess their reliability, vagueness, or falsity. And then, with great patience, he would start all over again.

For more than 24 hours, Musawi told us, he had been interrogating a new Iraqi deserter in London: his fourth such assignment. This guy was a 34-year-old officer in the special security forces in Baghdad, and one of Saddam Hussein's personal interpreters. On October 31, 2001, he had been brought to London from a small village in the heart of Europe, where he was in hiding, to report on the Iraqi training camps used by Osama's Arab-Afghanis. He also claimed to have information on Saddam's bacteriological and chemical weapons, and on the connection between Iraq and the attacks of September 11. This, argued Musawi, was still the key question.

When we spoke, Musawi stated it simply:

> The United States accuses Osama. Now, Mohammed
> Atta's links with Iraq can be documented by seven episodes.
> Osama's links with Iraq can be documented with nine pieces
> of evidence. But who and what can confirm Atta's links
> with Osama? Where is the proof? There isn't any, because
> Atta has never worked for Osama. Atta has always been an
> agent of the Iraqi secret services…. Atta planned the details
> and the objective of the operation. He did so not with bin
> Laden, nor with the other 18 suicide bombers, but with
> Faruq al-Hijazi and Ahmad Khalil Ibrahim Samir al-Ani,
> two officers of the Mukhabarat, the Iraqi secret service…
> The Twin Towers were an obsession for Saddam. By striking
> them, he wanted to paralyze America as America had
> paralyzed Iraq during and after the Gulf War. He tried in
> 1993 with an Iraqi agent, the Palestine-born Ramzi Yousef.

In 2001, we were sceptical of the credibility of the INC's account. It was clear that the Iraqi opposition had every reason to drag Saddam Hussein into the War on Terror. Even so, we thought, the facts gathered at 169 Knightsbridge would certainly be checked and verified by the intelligence agencies of the United States and its allies, that is, dubious information would be identified and discarded.

IT TURNED OUT that Chalabi had been playing a long game. It dated back to 1998, when the White House was still occupied by Bill Clinton.

At that time Chalabi was already connected to the key players in the campaign for regime change in Iraq. There was the "brain trust" of the American Enterprise Institute. The spin doctors and boosters of the Republican Party. The former director of the CIA, James Woolsey. And there was Charles Duelfer, the technician whom the White House and the CIA had put in charge of the search for the weapons of mass destruction in Iraq. The procedure was exactly as it would be five years later.

The Iraqi National Congress produced intelligence required by the current policy makers. Then this intelligence, whose source remained a secret, would be delivered to the press in order to nudge public opinion in the right direction.

Chalabi's earlier efforts at disinformation were witnessed firsthand by Scott Ritter, who worked in Iraq as a UN inspector from 1991 to 1998. What role did Ritter play in the whole mess?

Ritter served in the first Gulf War as a Marine officer and has the curt manner of a military man, along with an unbounded faith in the empiricism of "bare facts." Everybody in Washington knows him. These days, many avoid him, because he never concealed his defiant opposition to the war in Iraq. And because of a journey he made to Baghdad in October 2002, hoping that he could persuade Saddam Hussein to readmit the UN inspectors to the country.

Ritter and Chalabi met for the first time on January 24, 1998, in those same Knightsbridge offices. As Ritter recalls: "The London meeting was requested and authorized by Richard Butler, then mission chief of the United Nations. Chalabi was eager to link up with UNSCOM. After a handshake, he asked if we had liked the intelligence about the Iraqi palace of Gabal Makhul, which was supplied by one of the deserters whom he had interrogated in Germany in November 1997. His question shocked me. Until that moment I had always thought that the deserter was an asset—an American 'resource' under German protection. Chalabi smilingly corrected me. 'I'm the one who controls him,' he said. 'The deserter is one of my spies. I have an important spy network all over Iraq, even within the regime. I can give you any information you need. Just tell me what you want.' At that moment all the alarm bells should have started ringing in my head."

In 1998, then, Chalabi already controlled a network of "informers" in Iraq, who were ready to accredit "any information" necessary to Washington or the United Nations. Whether the information was true or false didn't matter. And the source of the information could always be concealed, or presented as an American intelligence "resource."

Ritter wasn't happy with this situation. However, the deputy head of the UNSOM mission, Charles Duelfer, kept him under pressure. As Ritter tells us, "I collected Chalabi's findings. He gave me a series of 'speculative reports' on the use of Iraqi mobile laboratories to manufacture chemical weapons. Over the next few days, he continued to send us information, part of which was already known to us. But that wasn't what struck me. What struck me was the fact that all the 'new' information was contradicted by what we had learned for ourselves on the ground in Iraq. Even the descriptions of the places were not accurate. Obviously, for those who had no experience of Iraq, Chalabi's intelligence was quite spectacular."

Within a few months, Chalabi had lost any credibility in the eyes of the UN inspectors, with one important exception: the deputy head of the inspection team. "Duelfer continued to press me to use the INC's material," recalls Ritter.* And Chalabi himself was eager to bring Ritter into his circle, as Ritter would discover: "In early June 1998 I arrived in Washington, where I was to meet some CIA officials. I contacted Randy Scheunmann, the national security adviser to Trent Lott, who was then leader of the Republican majority in the Senate. Randy said to me: 'Why don't you meet

Chalabi? He's in Washington. He's expecting you for dinner at his house in Georgetown.'"

Ritter was surprised by the invitation. After their first meeting in London at the INC office, he thought he had seen the last of Chalabi. What he didn't know was that the Man from Petra had won the heart of the Republican Party—and made enormous progress in constructing the right "story" for Iraq.

Ritter says:

> When I knocked on the door of his house in Georgetown, Chalabi hadn't arrived home yet, and the door was opened by Francis Brooke. I had hardly sat down when we were joined by Max Singer, a well-known consultant for the

---

* Charles Duelfer is an important figure in the construction of the "case" against Iraq. On the eve of the war, Duelfer left the United Nations and worked as an analyst for the Center for Strategic and International Studies, a noted Washington think tank. In his office there, which was buried in papers, he spoke to the authors in February 2003. At that point he considered the resurrection of Iraq's nuclear program a virtual certainty, which only the imprudent could ignore. "The Baghdad regime has lied about its weapons of mass destruction," he said, "and it's still lying. These weapons exist, and Saddam will make use of them. From 1993 to 2000, in Iraq, I realized the extent of their fakery. I saw proof in Baghdad that disarmament had never even begun…. Listening to the doubts and the subtle distinctions in the Blix report, I was assailed by a sense of compassion. I thought once more of a certain morning in September 1995. Again I saw the face of Tariq Aziz." To maintain that Baghdad was lying, and that the Blix report was essentially wastepaper, Duelfer clung to the testimony of Iraqi defectors. He was aware that such testimony had a tainted source (Chalabi) and little credibility with the public. In a shrewd but deceptive move, he attributed at least some of that information to Tariq Aziz, a former Foreign Minister he had encountered in Baghdad during his first ONU inspection mission. Many of Aziz's claims—the hidden arsenal, the missing stocks of chemical and biological agents, the mobile laboratories—had in fact been disproved by that very ONU mission. Yet now the fibs were filing back in through the front door. Peddled as intelligence findings by the CIA, they were presented to the United Nations by Colin Powell as proof of Saddam's lies.

Hudson Institute and for BESA, a strategic institute at the
University of Bar-Ilan in Israel. In Washington, Singer
was considered a leading authority on political warfare. He
had been commissioned by Trent Lott's office to write a
paper entitled "The Chalabi Factor," which emphasized the
importance of Chalabi and his INC as the most effective
opposition to Saddam's regime. I was given a copy. I was
asked to read it. It outlined a political scenario in which
Chalabi and the INC, exploiting the weakness of the regime
in the north and south of the country, would establish itself
in the Bassora area, with control of the oil wells. That would
guarantee the "political viability" of the plan to overthrow
the regime. According to the paper, Chalabi was the right
man for the operation. I felt very uneasy. What was a guy
like me, a United Nations inspector, doing at Chalabi's
dinner table discussing the overthrow of Saddam Hussein?

With this paper, the Republicans planned to attack Bill Clinton's
indecisive attitude toward Saddam. The INC struck them as a
perfect tool: a kind of mallet that might open some strategic cracks
at the White House. With this goal in mind, it's interesting to note
which guests showed up at Ahmed Chalabi's house in Georgetown.

Ritter says: "Within the hour Chalabi arrived, accompanied by
a tall man in a grey suit, Stephen Rademaker, and his wife Danielle
Pletka." In early June 1998, Rademaker was the legal counsel to the
House Committee on International Relations. His wife, a well-known
right-wing Republican, was on the staff of the Senate Committee
on Foreign Relations. After September 11, both would be appointed
to very different posts. Rademaker, who had worked on drafting
the legislation that created the Department of Homeland Security,
would be sworn in on August 12, 2002, as Assistant Secretary of
State for Arms Control. His wife would become vice-president of
the American Enterprise Institute.

Of the dinner, Ritter recalls: "They started discussing the paper Singer had brought, while Chalabi made a great show of preparing the aperitifs. Then, to my great surprise, Rademaker and Brooke started talking about the plans to overthrow Saddam. About before and after. They told me that the first step would be a 'purge' of all Baathists. They added that agreement with the Sunni leaders had already been reached. Then Chalabi whispered some words in Brooke's ear, and his assistant vanished and returned to the sitting room with three pages, entitled *Military Plans*."*

With the benefit of hindsight, we can see that Ritter was getting a preview of the plan for regime change. Of course, Chalabi would need to burnish his image a little after his failed operation in Kurdistan. He would need to transform himself back into the quintessential Iraqi patriot. But nobody doubted he was the right man for the job: least of all the last guest to arrive, James Woolsey, who would later attempt to pin the September 11 attacks on Baghdad.

Why did this company of cowboys want Ritter on hand? After a long evening in Georgetown, he finally figured it out. At that very moment, in June 1998, the UN inspector had an explosive report in his possession. His UNSCOM unit had obtained fragments of the ballistic missiles that the Iraqis had destroyed in compliance with a United Nations mandate. According to the Iraqis, the destroyed missiles had been armed with chemical weapons, including sarin, anthrax, and botulin. But when UNCSOM technicians carried out their initial examination at the military laboratories in Aberdeen, Maryland, they found something else. The fragments seemed to contain degraded traces of the chemical agent VX, one of the most

---

* The "military plans" were drawn up by General Wayne Downing, whose unit was in charge of intercepting and destroying Iraq's SCUD missiles during the first Gulf War. Downing would be hauled out of semiretirement after September 11 to serve as Deputy National Security Adviser for Combating Terrorism (a job he left only eight months later, in April 2002).

deadly nerve gases known to man. According to the Iraqis, they had worked on producing VX in their own labs, but never with any success.

For the campaign that the Republicans were preparing to launch—and for the "resurrection" of Chalabi—that report was pure gold. It didn't matter whether the lab results were definitive or not. All they had to do was blur the source of the information, deliver it to the front page of a great newspaper, and wait for the political ripple effects.

Ritter did in fact tell his dinner companions about the report. Then, after a nearly sleepless night, he went to discuss it with Trent Lott in the senator's offices on Capitol Hill.

The cat, however, had already been let out of the bag. On June 23, 1998, two days before the mission chief of UNSCOM, Richard Butler, spoke to the Security Council, the *Washington Post* ran a banner headline: "Tests Show Nerve Gas in Iraqi Weapons." In the accompanying article, the Iraqi National Congress was given credit for the information.

"Today I keep thinking about those 48 hours in Washington," Ritter says. "I think about my error in telling Chalabi and the Republicans about those laboratory results, which were later disproved by French and Swiss laboratories, proving that the Iraqis had not lied. I think I was a witness to the birth of the 'Chalabi scheme,' which would drag us into the senseless war we are in today."

IT'S A LONG WAY from Georgetown to 169 Knightsbridge. But both Ritter's dinner companions and Nabil Musawi were operating under the same assumption: that Saddam Hussein was the controller of all terrorism aimed at the United States. This assumption is the backbone of a whole theoretical system, which has long been the brainchild of Laurie Mylroie, a neoconservative writer.

In Europe, few people have ever heard of Mylroie. In America, this Pentagon consultant and American Enterprise Institute stalwart attained at least some temporary visibility on the eve of the first Gulf War, when she wrote a quickie book with Judith Miller called *Saddam Hussein and the Crisis in the Gulf*. But Mylroie had bigger fish to fry. She has made a career out of demonstrating the precise link between Iraq and anti-American terrorist acts. Mylroie has published this theory of hers in another book, *The War Against America: Saddam Hussein and the World Trade Center Attacks*.

Mylroie's theory struck many observers as paranoid and obsessive: It was the Butcher of Baghdad, she argued, who advises, finances, arms, and trains all anti-American assassins. If the United States wishes to regain its security, it must annihilate Saddam. Musawi repeated this scenario—as did Paul Wolfowitz and Richard Perle—without the slightest addition or variation. But Musawi's special task was to insert the names of the Iraqi deserters into Mylroie's tableau to provide links between Saddam and the archipelago of terror. Bin Laden, meanwhile, is demoted to a marginal figure, a puppet, an almost folkloristic icon.

Chalabi, of course, expected something in return. He dearly wanted to be the next president of Iraq. On the cold, foggy day in January 2002 when we spoke with him, he had every reason to expect a bright future. He adjusted the lapels of his magnificent pinstripe suit, which he wore over an eccentric pair of black leather boots. And with a tremor of excitement in his voice, he told us: "I'm just waiting for the moment to move. You'll see, that day will arrive very soon. See you in late summer! In Baghdad, of course...."

The combination of intelligence, disinformation, and psychological warfare is very old. After September 11, that ancient strategy was revived with a few surprising and significant innovations. Originally a technique for deceiving the enemy beyond one's borders, it was now used to confuse friends, and to reduce internal opponents to silence. Meanwhile, modern technology has given the technique a whole new life. A piece of news surfaces in Kirkuk. The confirmation pops up in Prague, while yet another witness says he is ready to corroborate it in Singapore. A third source surfaces in Khartoum. Who will be able to keep up with this pingpong ball as it bounces from one corner of the earth to another?

IN ORDER TO understand how the scenario played out in Italy, we had better keep an eye on SISMI. We've already seen the agency defending Rocco Martino, the very swindler whom Forte Braschi had sent around Europe with his bogus dossier. We've observed the shame of the aluminium tubes, which SISMI curiously failed to recognize as Italian missile shells. But before returning to Nicolò Pollari and his colleagues, let's take a look at the Italian press, which was being manipulated as shamelessly as its opposite number in America.

During the very same hours when Judith Miller was reviewing the investigation of September 11, the Italian newsweekly *Panorama* was preparing a scoop for the issue of September 12-19, 2002. It described the "latest coup of Iraqi agents on the international market for uranium trafficking."

Pino Buongiorno, deputy editor of the magazine, informed his readers that the Iraqis were up to no good:

> At stake was a consignment of half a ton of uranium.
> Officials of the Mukhabarat, the Iraqi secret service, bought
> it for cash through a Jordanian import-export firm, in far-
> off Nigeria, where some arms dealers had smuggled it after
> stealing it from a nuclear depot in a republic of the former
> USSR. The five hundred kilos of uranium were shipped to
> Amman. From there, travelling overland, they reached their
> destination after a seven-hour journey: a factory twenty
> kilometers north of Baghdad, called Al Rashidiyah, known
> for the production and processing of fissile material.

Later in the article, Buongiorno noted:

> [George Tenet] alerted allied secret services to the possibility
> that other operations, similar to the one in Nigeria, might
> be carried out over the coming weeks. Much of his concern
> was focused on Germany. In recent years, Iraq has tried to
> acquire both technical finesse and industrial components
> (easily converted to military use) from Leycochem. They
> have also tried to buy the much sought-after aluminium
> tubes for gas centrifuges from German sources. But
> Tenet's warning is also aimed at Italy, where Saddam
> Hussein may try to acquire some futuristic agricultural
> machinery that his scientists can transform into weapons
> of mass destruction. There is no doubt that, especially in
> the last four years, the Baghdad dictator has accelerated
> his military plans…. This has been revealed to German,
> British, and American intelligence by the most recent
> Iraqi deserters, such as the nuclear scientist Adnan Said
> al-Haideri, who fled to the U.S. in 2001 via Bangkok.

A good many of the details are confused (Nigeria versus Niger, five
hundred kilos versus five hundred tons). And of course the article
features some pure invention, including the tortured journey of the
smuggled uranium from the former USSR to Africa, Jordan, and
Baghdad. What we should note, though, is that the recipe in *Panorama*
does include all the right ingredients. Uranium, aluminium tubes,
Iraqi deserters, weapons of mass destruction.

For most readers, Pino Buongiorno's article was an absolute
revelation. True, the Americans media had alluded to "an operation
which prevented the acquisition of stainless steel tubes for uranium
enrichment." But nobody else had described the successful acquisition
of uranium, nor revealed the hard numbers pertaining to Saddam's
shopping expeditions in Africa. (The fact that Buongiorno had

mixed up kilos and tons was only a slight offense in this context.) Even Tony Blair, who would be the first head of state to mention the deal, kept his mouth shut until September 24, 2002. And on that occasion, he limited himself to mentioning "significant quantities of uranium."

Buongiorno was a seasoned journalist. Naturally he had checked the information with his contacts in Italian military intelligence. How worried should Italy be? Which Italian firms had been approached by Iraqi intermediaries, and where were they located? What did Forte Braschi know about those aluminium tubes? Was it true that SISMI, too, had intercepted a consignment of them? And what about that uranium story?

At Forte Braschi, officials decided that the fruit was ripe. It was time to pick it, while it was still on the tree: time to reap the rewards for all the undercover work they had done over the past year. This was exactly how Pollari liked to play the game. His American ally was now ready to go public with the intelligence it had gathered. Why not share his own findings with the Italian government, even the Italian public? With prudence and ambiguity, perhaps. But where was the risk?

Thus did senior SISMI officials confirm the stories of the African uranium and the aluminium tubes to *Panorama*. It's possible they got carried away and added a little extra detail. In any case, Pino Buongiorno's scoop became Nicolò Pollari's opening gambit in Italy. It was a move with highly significant timing.

Let's recall that on September 9, 2002, three days before the *Panorama* article came out and the day after Judith Miller's scoop, Nicolò Pollari was in Washington. At the White House, he visited the offices of National Security Adviser Condoleezza Rice and her deputy Stephen Hadley. With him was a delegation of Italian intelligence officers, including Colonel Alberto Manenti, head of the WMD nonproliferation unit.

The timing of the meeting is interesting: The French had already shot down the uranium story. So had Joe Wilson. So had the State Department office led by Greg Thielmann. In the early days of 2002, the only allies the hawks could rely on were the United Kingdom and Italy: MI6 and SISMI. According to NSC spokesman Frederick Jones, the visit was no more than a courtesy call: "Fifteen minutes, no more."

Stephen Hadley, now National Security Adviser himself, "has no memory" of the what they talked about. Did the issue of the Nigerien uranium even come up? He "has no memory" of that either.

One can only take his word for it. Yet the gaps in Hadley's memory do not alter the fact that, in that first month of September 2002, the SISMI director had detailed knowledge of the two key arguments with which the American administration was selling the atomic nightmare to the world.

Pollari knew all about Rocco Martino's bogus story, having already accredited it on three different occasions and shared it with MI6. He also knew perfectly well that the "mysterious" aluminium tubes were a knock-off of the Italian Medusa 81 missile, rather than parts for an immense cascade of centrifuges.

During those September meetings, then, Pollari was in the best position to make a responsible choice. He could have told his American interlocutors—technicians and politicians alike—that the story of Saddam's nuclear rearmament was nonsense, that he knew the tale of the Nigerien uranium, like that of the centrifuges, was rubbish. His other option was to buttress or indulge his ally's convictions, perhaps by just maintaining a discreet silence.

Pollari, in the most benevolent hypothesis, chose silence. Over the next 13 months, he did not send the CIA the technical specifications for the Medusa 81 system. Stephen Hadley, encouraged by the silence—or confirmation—from the Italians, contacted the CIA on

September 11. Might the president finally unveil the uranium story in early October, when he was slated to give a speech in Cincinnati, Ohio? Yes, he was told.

OCTOBER 2002. With a large bundle of papers at his elbow, Nicolò Pollari was sitting at the oval table of the Parliamentary Commission for Oversight of the Secret Services. The table was too large for that long, narrow room. The discussion was fairly routine. Even boring. Until the SISMI director took out a single sheet from his heap of papers and addressed the group: "We know for certain that a Central African republic is negotiating with Iraq to supply it with natural uranium." He looked up, and after a theatrical pause, he added: "Unfortunately, we do not yet have any documentary evidence, but we do not despair of obtaining it."

Pollari had made his move, and it was a very cunning one. He slid the "product" right under the eyes of his political and institutional overseers, but declined to furnish definite, documentary proof. He would allude to "documentary evidence" only a month later, in November. Yet he never produced a single document.

This calculation would have been impeccable, were it not for an additional factor: the money-grubbing Rocco Martino. After an insider told him that Pollari had confirmed the Niger-Iraq negotiations, the swindler saw a chance to make some easy cash.

Rocco called a journalist he had met several years before. She now worked for *Panorama*. Her name was Elisabetta Burba. In a subsequent issue of the magazine, she recalled the whole scenario:

> In October 2002, I was in the Balkans doing an investigation on the UCK [the Kosovo Liberation Army]. The office called me on my mobile phone: "Elisabetta, someone left a message for you." I called back. On the other end, I heard an echo of the past. "Do you remember me?" Of course I did: thanks to this man, I had made two international scoops. "I've got

something for you," he said. In short, conspiratorial sentences, he presented his merchandise: proof that "our moustachioed friend" had bought uranium in an African country. He said he had plenty of evidence: contracts, letters, agreements.... All smuggled out of that country's embassy in Rome.

Rocco Martino asked *Panorama* for a hundred thousand euros: a sum the magazine was not prepared to pay. Burba writes:

> When I got back to the office, I found other documents that had arrived by fax. There was the coded original and the version decrypted by my source. One said that the uranium was to be transported to Iraq via Turkey, the other that the goods were to be put on a Gabonese ship and that the transfer would take place in international waters.

The swindler was inspiring some great excitement at the newsweekly. The editor-in-chief, Carlo Rossella, told his staff: "If this stuff is genuine, we've found the smoking gun." He came up with the idea of "going to the Americans"—surely they would be able to tell if the papers were authentic. At once Rossella called Ambassador Mel Sembler, who was a friend of his. Burba met three CIA men in Rome. She explained that she had been authorized to give them photocopies of several of the documents. Then she took her leave.

Elisabetta Burba had gotten the hardest assignment: a trip to Niger. She would pretend she was there to investigate dinosaur fossils, from *Ouranosaurus nigeriensis* to the *Afrovenator abakensis*. In the meantime, she was to contact some reliable sources about the uranium deal.

Burba did her job with rigor and determination. She soon learned, according to her article, that in Niger "there are only two factories that turn uranium into yellow powder. They put it into four-hundred-liter drums, half-filled, two hundred kilos per drum. Then the drums are sent to Cotonou, where they are put onboard ship. Organizing a trade of this kind involves huge problems of transport and security: the roads are all infested with bandits. It would take an enormous deployment of men and equipment to protect two thousand five hundred drums so that they could be moved halfway across Africa and shipped to Iraq via Turkey."

Burba returned to Italy and delivered the bad news: "There's little or no evidence to confirm the story." Nor did any confirmation arrive from Via Veneto. "We can't tell you that the documents are false, nor that they are authentic," said an official. Burba told her editor that the story didn't hold up. Better to drop it.*

Thus, Rocco Martino's attempt to wring a few last euros out of his dossier had no consequences in Italy. (He would also attempt to sell his stash to the newspaper *Il Giornale*.) The public wouldn't even learn of it until July of the following year. In the United States, however, it was a different matter. Alarm bells went off all over Washington when it was learned that those documents were in circulation.

Out at Langley, the question was: "What the hell is going on?" It was clear to the CIA that those papers needed to be avoided like radioactive material. Better to know nothing about them. You never

---

* In the same issue of July 31, 2003, Carlo Rosella wrote a brief editorial about the whole affair. Addressing the magazine's readers, he explained: "If we hadn't done all that laborious investigation, we would have stumbled into an enormous scandal (or into an enormous trap). We would have printed falsehoods. It would have put the magazine's credibility at risk. For this reason we chose such unimpeachable sources as the American Embassy." Excluding Elizabetta Burba, who behaved like an absolute professional, the staff at *Panorama* seemed to have been blindsided by the whole business. Or perhaps they realized that the reconstruction of events offered by the top brass was deliberately inconsistent and evasive. In any case, it's impossible to believe that Rosella, Buongiorno, and Giorgio Mulè had forgotten their own cover story of a few weeks before, which revealed Saddam's cash purchase of five hundred kilograms of uranium in Africa (in Nigeria rather than Niger, they claimed incorrectly, of course).

saw them, never read them, never even touched them. By the time the parcel of "Rome papers" reached Washington on October 16, the backpedaling was already in full swing.

During a regular meeting, the INR distributed the loot to the various agencies. Four CIA officials were present. None of them, in the coming months, would be able to remember if they had obtained the documents during the meeting. Out at Langley, the distancing mechanism was even less subtle. The papers simply disappeared. Only after an internal investigation by the agency's general inspector did a copy turn up in the safe of the Nonproliferation Unit.

Meanwhile, the staff at the Center for Weapons Intelligence, Nonproliferation and Arms Control (WINPAC), who check all such documents as a matter of course, was unable to obtain a copy until January 16, 2003. At that point they had to request it directly from the State Department.

The truth is that those papers, the fruit of competitive intelligence, were effective only if they were absent. They needed to seep into the metabolism of the allied secret services like a bacterium, bounce about clandestinely among the spies and policy makers, and never come to light. Once they actually materialized, things began to change.

By the time Colin Powell addressed the UN Security Council on February 5, for example, he omitted all reference to uranium in his speech. Why the sudden caution? Powell had persistently asked the CIA to get more details about the Iraq-Niger deal from that notorious "allied intelligence agency." In a cable to Langley, his staff pressed them once again: "The question of Niger uranium may be an integral part of the Secretary of State's speech to the United Nations. Are you able to provide us with the contract for the deal signed in 1999 and [assure us] that your information does not come from the secret service of another government?"

The CIA contacted SISMI, which replied that it did "not possess

a copy of the contract," although "the information did originate in
our country."

Langley now wanted to dig a deep, water-filled, fenced-in
moat between itself and SISMI. Everybody at the CIA knew the
documents were fake. They couldn't (and wouldn't) say so, but it was
too much to expect them to hang themselves on such rickety and
improvised gallows. Least of all George Tenet. Testifying before the
Senate Intelligence Committee in July 2003, the director asserted
that "until February 2003, Langley had never seen the fake Niger
documents, whose existence we learned about from the Italian secret
services in late 2001."

In this new season of its existence—"the season of rebirth," they
call it at Forte Braschi—SISMI wanted to achieve some independence
from the United States without sacrificing opportunities or protection.
The two agencies did an awkward dance. SISMI would yield and
withdraw; the CIA would make overtures, then warily pull back.

CHAPTER THREE

ROMAN BLUNDERS

The War on Terror offered Italian intelligence agencies certain possibilities, certain powers. And the zigzagging paths they took to attain these prizes also cleared the way for some unscrupulous moves on the part of the Italian judiciary. This terrain, which had already been cultivated by the spies and spooks, now became a happy hunting ground for some of Italy's more ambitious judges and prosecutors. In this context, too, public opinion was carefully nudged in a desired direction—which is to say, a general sense that there was a "concrete and imminent" danger of terrorist attacks. *Here. Now.* Those frightening shadows created a brand of fear so diffuse, intense, and stratified that it tended to flatten every critical or dissenting observation.

This was the ideal environment for those in Italy who wished to fashion a parallel legal structure—a special branch of criminal law, devoid of constitutional principle and largely administered by the police. As Italian legal theorist Luigi Ferrajoli has explained, these enterprises have involved a wide range of corner-cutting devices. There is, for example, preventive detention. Then there are security measures, preventive measures, precautionary police procedures, and some creative methods for maintaining public order. As is often the case in Italy, the lack of legal safeguards only multiplies the temptations of power. Those seeking to grasp power lose interest in proven crimes. How much more productive it seems to tackle potential crimes, *future* crimes. In some judicial districts, the abuses were glaring. What prevailed was, according to Ferrajoli, "the shallow and authoritarian argument that justice must guard against the criminal rather than the crime; that justice must determine whether a suspect is dangerous (rather than guilty), that it must devote more attention to the enemy's identity than to the evidence of his crimes."

It would be another story if the culprits here were motivated by conformity, a mad desire for power, or ideological ardor. What matters, though, is their habit of launching inquiries and legal proceedings without any rhyme or reason. All that's required is a backdrop of hysteria and some wafer-thin evidence. Nobody is too concerned about it. The only thing the media bothers to report is the sentences handed down by the criminal courts.

Two stories from Italy will illustrate exactly what we're talking about.

THE PLACE: THE CITY OF ANZIO, on the seacoast, just thirty miles south of Rome. It all happened on Via Furio Anziate, a tiny street with only two buildings leading to the lighthouse and to the Grotte di Nerone, those gaping caves where the waves break and sizzle. At 2:00 AM on October 4, 2002, an agitated spectacle suddenly unfolded at the entrance to Number 4. This was the house owned by Signora Benita Pergola, the one "where the Arabs live." In the flickering blue light from the carabinieri vehicles, two men emerged, their wrists cuffed behind their backs.

A few miles away, on a glassy stretch of black water, the spectacle was soon repeated. A helicopter pointed its searchlight down at the *Titanic*, an old fishing vessel. A patrol boat pulled up alongside the older boat. The officers were searching for a 42-year-old Egyptian,

Mohammed Khaled Mohammed al-Zahed, who had worked onboard as a cabin boy for the past five years. When they raided the house on Via Furio Anziate, they had found his two comrades, also Egyptians.

Who were they? Fattah Abd el-Salah Ali e-Gamal, 41 years of age. And Ahmed Mohammed Magdj Shalabej, 40 years of age.

At dawn on October 4, Lieutenant Alessandro Perrino announced the capture of these three Egyptians to the nation (and to the American ally). Evidently the prisoners had been planning to turn Memorial Day into a bloodbath: They would attack the military cemetery at Nettuno on the very day set aside to commemorate the American landing at Anzio on January 22, 1944. They were also going to attempt a slaughter of the innocents at a McDonald's restaurants in Rome, and possibly at Leonardo Da Vinci International Airport.

The evidence gathered during the arrests fired the imagination of every newspaper columnist. The house on Via Furio Anziate appeared to be a goldmine of clues, a virtual advertisement for violent aggression. That was certainly the impression given by the search-and-seizure report. In the bathroom, in the space between the ceiling and water heater, the carabinieri found a 9-millimeter Beretta pistol, "oiled and ready for use." According to the confiscation report, the pistol had a legible serial number. A cartridge with seven shots was inserted in the weapon, which was additionally wrapped in a cotton rag. In the same recess, they also found seven bricks of TNT. In the bedroom, they seized any number of damning items: "a small map of the McDonald's franchises in Rome, and another of Leonardo Da Vinci Airport"; some telephone calling cards; souvenir postcards; telephone books; books in Arabic; a plastic bag containing battery holders "with electrical wires attached to the two terminals"; two laminated ID cards; a handwritten notebook including the hours for prayer; and two hands from a clock (color: black). They also seized a photocopy of a local street map, including the area around the Anzio-Nettuno military cemetery. On the map, the suspects had marked two spots with a *x*: an entrance to the cemetery, and the location of a structure commemorating the Allied landing.

And that wasn't all.

On the afternoon of October 4, Benita Pergola made her way to the carabinieri barracks in Anzio. The news that her three tenants had been arrested cheered her immensely. A year before, she had rented the apartment to el-Gamal, who paid his rent under the table. She despised the man, but not the money he handed her each month. In any case, she planned to get rid of him at the end of July 2002, when she would be able to rent the house to some wealthier tenant who wanted a seaside retreat for his family. Alas, things didn't turn out that way. El-Gamal had nowhere else to go, and he refused to leave Via Furio Anziate.

On September 22, two weeks before the raid, she and her tenant had a final, furious quarrel. They almost came to blows, and the landlady told her tenant he was "in serious trouble." She was true to her word: On September 25, the carabinieri dropped by for a visit. On that occasion they found only al-Zahed at home. They asked to see the lease and receipts for the rent, and found everything in order. Apparently the dispute was over.

The arrest of the Egyptians on October 4, then, was a gift for Signora Pergola: a de facto eviction. Five days later, she returned to the house and then immediately called the barracks, with a story and a gift of her own.

She explained that she had gone back to Via Furio Anziate with her husband. First they discovered that "the Arabs had changed the locks." Having gained entrance, they found the house a complete shambles, and began to "put things in order," jamming the "Egyptian junk" into "twenty black garbage bags." In the course of these activities, Signora Pergola had opened a cupboard and noticed a white plastic bag inside. Opening the bag itself, she came upon a "belt" wrapped in a blanket.

At once the Public Prosecutor in Rome ordered a new search. And on October 12, in the cupboard indicated by the landlady, the carabinieri found an item they hadn't noticed eight days before: "a leather belt with internal pockets designed to house objects or other materials." Which is to say, a "kamikaze belt."

Now the prosecution had its ducks in a row. The weapons (the pistol), the explosives (a kilo and a half of TNT), the belt to be worn by the martyrs, the targets (the military cemetery, McDonald's, Leonardo Da Vinci Airport). And best of all, they had a perfect culprit: Fattah el-Gamal.

Like his companions, el-Gamal worked as a fisherman. (One of the three, Shalabej, also made some extra change by peddling toys and knickknacks in the street.) Those who wondered what Al Qaeda could possibly have to do with this poor character were greeted with sarcastic condescension: Didn't they realize that the world had been turned upside down in the wake of 9/11? Didn't they realize that terror now clothed itself in the most unlikely forms?

But why pick on el-Gamal in particular? He was, according to the carabinieri and the public prosecutor, an ugly customer. True, he had a valid residence permit, just like his companions. True, he worked as fisherman. That was just a façade, however, concealing an evil existence. As the prosecution would note, el-Gamal had come under suspicion on October 4, 2001, exactly a year before his arrest. On that date, a "confidential source" had approached Lieutenant Alessandro Perrino with a tip about the Egyptian, advising him to search el-Gamal's house for weapons. At the time, the fisherman was living on Via Mantova. His house was dutifully searched. No trace of a weapon was found. The carabinieri did confiscate some religious videocassettes and a pro-Palestinian flyer from the so-called International Communist Organization. And the public prosecutor of Velletri charged him with a serious crime: "Hostile acts against a foreign state, which expose the Italian state to the risk of war." That is, a violation of Article 244 of the penal code, with a sentence ranging from six years to life, in the event that the perpetrator's "hostile act" leads to war.

Nothing came of the charge. But there was something else. Two years earlier, in 1999, the carabinieri had already been sniffing around the Egyptian. Three different informants, all of them anonymous, indicated that el-Gamal was plotting to usurp the imam of Ostia, who he considered too moderate. He was also supposedly preparing to take part in some unspecified meetings for the recruitment of martyrs to fight in Kosovo, which was then plunged in civil war.

The Egyptian's goose was cooked. The same thing could be said for his two companions. The prosecuting attorneys, Erminio Amelio and Franco Ionta, had no doubts about what had been going on at Number 4, Via Furio Anziate. They considered it entirely irrelevant that at the moment of his arrest, Shalabej could hardly stay on his feet due to a surgical procedure performed on his knee the week before. Nor did it trouble the judges that the three suspects remained in jail after two requests for bail. Yet there were still some questions to be answered. Perhaps we should start with some peculiarities.

First: the pistol. The ballistics report confirmed that the Beretta had been manufactured in 1942 and was part of a stockpile issued to the Fascist railway police in 1943. The weapon was certainly capable of being fired, but it was in terrible condition. It bore traces of rust that led one to believe that it had been buried for a prolonged period. The cartridges, on the other hand, dated from the 1970s, and were of the type then distributed to the police and security services. Why would an operational kamikaze cell bother with such an ancient armament?

Next, the explosives. The seven bricks of TNT were military issue, but they were not of the type used by NATO or the Italian army. On the contrary, their casing—"greaseproof paper with a black border"—suggested that they came from the stockpiles of a former Warsaw Pact nation. More to the point, they were strikingly similar to a supply of TNT bricks that had been seized by the carabinieri in the same region on May 12, 2001. Perhaps this coincidence deserved some closer examination. But nobody bothered to think about it.

To explode, of course, TNT requires a trigger. The two hands from the clock and the battery charger found in the apartment would not be sufficient. Explosives specialists dismissed those items as junk. The three men lacked not only a detonator, but even the most elementary components to assemble a functional device. As it was, then, the TNT was good for nothing. It was inert material, like Silly Putty. Could the three Egyptians really have imagined that they would make use of it?

Then we have the kamikaze belt. When Shalabej first offered his explanation of the offending item, it struck the prosecutors as pathetic. "The belt is mine," he said. "El-Gamal gave it to me. It's for making a pilgrimage to Mecca, and I don't understand how it ended up in the cupboard, since I always keep it in my car." *Pathetic* is always a relative term. Nobody in the public prosecutor's office dwelled for even an instant on a troubling fact: During the search on October 4, the cupboard had been opened and nothing had been found inside it. (The prosecuting attorneys never even attempted to find out what ultimately became of Shalabej's car.)

Finally, the so-called documents. The map showing the McDonald's locations in Rome was an advertising hand-out. So was the map of the airport. It was the kind of wastepaper that might be found in anybody's home.

EL-GAMAL, SHALABEJ, AND EL-ZAHED were ordered to stand trial for the crime of "association with the intent to carry out international terrorism." In the criminal charges, they were accused of belonging to "a politico-military organization dedicated to violent acts meant to subvert the democratic system. Their goal was to attack such targets as the military cemetery at Nettuno, the airport at Fiumicino, and the McDonald's franchises located in Rome, as well as facilitating the gradual entrance of their accomplices into Italy."

The prosecution asked for a sentence of twelve years. And the president himself, acting in his civil capacity, demanded a sum in punitive damages so high that the three fisherman couldn't have scraped it together in ten lifetimes.

The trial began in 2003 before the First Court of Assizes in Rome. The three Egyptians were on hand, all of them in cages.

It was supposed to be a routine affair, argued before a sparse crowd. But things went awry almost immediately.

On November 19, 2003, the court heard the testimony of Alessandro Perrino, the officer who had led the raid and promptly reaped some professional dividends. He had left the armed services for a new job, which he insisted that he was not at liberty to explain. It turned out that he was employed by ACEA, a municipal supplier of water and electricity to the city of Rome. Perrino faced the judges, the defense, and the accused with brash assurance. His account began with the (fruitless) search of the premises on Via Mantova on October 4, 2001. Then he jumped forward to June 2002, when the lieutenant "casually" spotted el-Gamal "in the vicinity of the port at Anzio." Perrino recalled: "I was alone and didn't want to give myself away. So I entrusted my men with task of identifying his home, which turned out to be on Via Furio Anziate."

There's already something slippery about the whole scenario. El-Gamal, an extremely dangerous man identified as early as October 2001 as a potential terrorist—and denounced as such by the public prosecutor of Velletri—had vanished. Lieutenant Perrino let him slip away like any old petty grifter. And then, as luck would have it, he stumbled over the culprit amid the cobbled streets of Anzio. As he then recounted: "In the meantime, my close collaborator Marshal Paolo Gioacchini and I had established relations with a new confidential source. This was a person deeply familiar with small-scale and large-scale criminality, both in Rome and along the coast."

In September 2002, this faceless, nameless gentleman mentioned the presence of some Arabs in the area around Anzio, who "might have a supply of weapons and drugs." Perrino, then, was on the lookout. On the evening of October 3, 2002, he and Gioacchini were in plain clothes, in an unmarked police car. With them was "our source, who indicated three possible objectives. One of these was the establishment at Number 4, Via Furio Anziate."

"I dropped off our source. I checked the first two addresses that he had pointed out, and decided they were small potatoes. In fact, when we drove by the house on Via Furio Anziate, I tried out a syllogism on my colleague Gioacchini: 'And what if el-Gamal turns out to be the very Arab immigrant we're looking for, the Muslim with the weapons and explosives?'"

The lieutenant didn't wait for an answer. He summoned all the men at his disposal to a public garden along the edge of the beach, from which it was possible to observe the entrance to Number 4. He told them to wait until el-Gamal emerged, as he did every night, for his shift as a fisherman down on the docks. At 2:00 AM, the Egyptian strolled out the door. At 2:05 AM, the house on Via Furio Anziate was turned upside down by the carabinieri. El-Gamal and Shalabej were arrested on the spot. El-Zahed was picked up a few hours later on the *Titanic*.

Simple. An ambitious lieutenant. A precious and anonymous source. A lucky break. A "surgical strike."

Paolo Gioacchini, too, had left the armed forces. In his testimony, he confirmed Perrino's story. He still had a vivid memory of the map of the Nettuno cemetery: It was an "A4 format" photocopy from a *Tuttocittà* map, which they found in el-Gamal's diary. He swore that they had spent hours searching the apartment, and that nothing had been overlooked.

None of the military officers were able to explain why they had failed to find the kamikaze belt during the initial search. Nobody had any idea of what happened to Shalabej's car or his car keys, nor why they hadn't been confiscated. Nor was anybody able to offer a logical answer to another series of questions. Why had the former lair of a dangerous Al Qaeda cell been left unattended and unsealed after the operation? Why was it promptly handed back over to the landlady? And above all: When Signora Pergola returned to the apartment on October 9, she reported that "the Arabs had changed the locks." Who, then, had opened the door for her?

The prosecutor kept his cool. If anything, he seemed irritated by the stubborn insistence of el-Gamal's attorney, Carlo Corbucci.

And who was Corbucci? He was a fiery Roman, one of those lawyers who left no investigative stone unturned. He had a small office in the Delle Vittorie neighborhood, on the first floor of a Fascist-era building; the brass plaque on the front door transliterated his first and last names in Arabic. He had been defending the Muslim community in Italy since the seventies. He also had a profound knowledge of Islam, to which he had converted thirty years ago. Given his clientele, he had suffered a lot of headaches in the wake of September 11. A few messages from the intelligence community, asking which side he was truly on. A few curious "visits," which had convinced him to protect his office with a heavy armored door. The trial of the three Egyptians had a powerful affect on him— especially after Lieutenant Perrino lodged a complaint with the Bar Association on the eve of the hearing, insisting that Corbucci behaved in an unseemly manner. As the lawyer saw it, this bordered on slander, and was also "a veiled attempt to stop me from defending the accused." In response, he simply redoubled his efforts.

Corbucci had already measured the space between the water heater and the ceiling of the apartment, and discovered that it was too small to contain the pistol and the explosives that had supposedly been found there. Quite reasonably, he demanded an on-site inspection by the Court. At that point, though, he found that the bathroom had been renovated while the trial was in progress—

without any prior authorization, of course—and that he could no longer demonstrate this inconsistency.

Elsewhere, Corbucci made some headway. He was able to document that in the days leading up to the arrest, one of the windowpanes overlooking the balcony had been removed, allowing easy access from the outside. He examined every bit of evidence: the kamikaze belt, the map of the cemetery, the Beretta and the explosives. Corbucci also slipped in one question that seemed a little eccentric, and which wiped the smile off Lieutenant Perrino's face. "Do you know," he asked the ex-officer, "a certain Doctor Fausto?"

Perrino stiffened. "Certainly not," he said.

"Think about it carefully. You're sure you don't know Doctor Fausto?"

"Absolutely not."

Ah, Doctor Fausto. When Corbucci first dropped his name during the trial, its seemed like a desperate diversionary tactic, with no apparent outcome.

On February 10, 2004, el-Gamal took the witness stand. He told his story, which the prosecutors had heard immediately after his arrest and dismissed as nonsense. The judges, however, were dumbfounded. The Egyptian began his account in October 2001, during the days following the search of his apartment on Via Mantova: "I was approached by Lieutenant Perrino, and by another guy who introduced himself as Doctor Fausto. He explained that he worked for the intelligence services. Then he offered me money and protection in exchange for collaborating with him. I was supposed to gather information about the activities of Islamic extremists."

This was anything but an affable request. Fausto and Perrino made that clear. If el-Gamal refused, he would be "abandoned to the Americans and the Israelis." The Egyptian was terrified. He agreed to some further meetings with Fausto, but he was a fisherman, after all, and had no idea how to function as an informer. What's more, he had no information worth gathering or passing on. He left Via Mantova and moved to Via Furio Anziate, but continued to be frightened. He confided his fears to two friends: Rashid Nemri, a Tunisian who ran a *tavola calda* in Rome, and Aldo Giovanni Doro, an elderly marble salesman. The court summoned both of them in a great hurry.

Rashid Nemri displayed a phenomenal memory. On October 11, 2001, he told the judges, he was at el-Gamal's house on Via Furio Anziate. Somebody called from the downstairs intercom. The Egyptian answered, then explained that it was Perrino, the carabinieri officer who had searched his previous apartment. He went down to the street, and Rashid recalled that he had observed his friend talking with two men standing next to a police car. When el-Gamal returned to the apartment, he was frazzled. Perrino and Fausto had made an appointment with him for the next day: They were to meet down at the docks. "They want the names of people who frequent the mosque," he told Rashid.

As he told it, Rashid notified Aldo Giovanni Doro. The two accompanied el-Gamal to his appointment the next day. Concealing themselves nearby, they watched for an hour as he spoke with two gentlemen in a bar, one of whom was "definitely" Fausto. Then the Egyptian vanished into the carabinieri barracks. He emerged soon after with a forbidding document bearing the words *Tribunale di Velletri*. The message was clear: Collaborate or you're fucked.

The elderly marble salesman confirmed the whole thing. "Yes, it's all true," said Aldo Giovanni Doro. He recalled the conversation between el-Gamal, Fausto, and a second, unknown man: "They were at a small table at the Mennella bar." Above all, he recalled a second encounter between the Egyptian and the intelligence service operative in November or December of 2001. This time, the pair met at Fiumicino. Aldo spied on the interview, and may have snapped a few photos. And afterward, el-Gamal was told that the spooks had upped the ante: "A salary and an automobile worth 40 million lire." By now it was clear that Doctor Fausto—or whatever his name might be—was no figment of anybody's imagination. Aldo Giovanni Doro described for the court his facial characteristics, his height, and the sort of clothes he wore.

On February 20, 2004, Fausto stopped being a mere shadow. The chambers fell absolutely silent as he entered, and he greeted el-Gamal with a cordial handshake.

"My name is Fausto Del Vecchio. I am an official employed on the president's behalf by the security services."

By SISDE, as it would turn out.

His story lined up more or less with el-Gamal's. The Egyptian hadn't been lying. As Del Vecchio explained, the agency had decided to approach him as a source who was "potentially in contact with elements of the Islamic jihad, but not himself an adherent. He might also come into contact with other persons who could supply useful information to the intelligence agencies.... We tailed him until we figured out that he lived in Anzio. Then we decided to work with the local carabinieri—with Lieutenant Perrino in particular, who we asked to set up a direct meeting with el-Gamal. There was an initial encounter, immediately on the heels of the raid in October 2001. That took place in the carabinieri barracks, with Perrino on hand. We continued to meet through May 2002. Perrino was always present, and I never realized that we were being 'tailed' by Signor Aldo Giovanni Doro. At the end of May 2002, we gave up on the Egyptian, because he seemed like a liar, and certainly incapable of supplying us with useful information. Since then, the carabinieri have been working on their own."

The court showed Fausto the documents seized on October 4, 2001. "They seem meaningless to me," he responded. "And even if I had read or examined the communist flyer at the time, it wouldn't have been of any interest." Here was an admission that the first "visit" to the Egyptian's house was simply a ruse to establish contact. And what of the horrendous crimes denounced by the public prosecutor of Velletri? That too was a ruse, designed to frighten the man and make him more receptive to the carabinieri and, ultimately, to SISDE. Of course, Fausto denied ever making "real threats" to el-Gamal, but he had another task to accomplish. He needed to disentangle himself from the mess on Via Furio Anziate. He insisted on this point: "Ever since the end of May 2002, the carabinieri have handled this on their own."

On March 19, 2004, Perrino appeared before the court again. He was no longer so brash, and he was accompanied by a lawyer. He was afraid. He knew that he was in for trouble. His deposition was a true ordeal: He admitted that he had lied about Fausto, "but only to protect an experienced source." He also admitted that the initial raid on el-Gamal's house on Via Mantova had not been prompted by the news of a potential weapons cache. The "confidential source" Perrino had mentioned in his earlier testimony was sheer fancy. The former lieutenant continued his stammering account of Fausto's visit to his office on October 4, 2001: "I don't know whether he called me or I called him, but I'm sure that we saw each other immediately after the raid [on the Via Mantova house]... That was something we had already agreed on. He had requested some sort of contact with el-Gamal."

Again: The Via Mantova raid was simply a pretext. Three weeks had passed since September 11, SISDE and SISMI were under pressure, and the agencies were emptying their drawers to scrape together some substantial (or even insubstantial) leads on "Islamic subjects of interest." El-Gamal had the bad luck to end up in some intelligence report on Egypt: precisely the sort of leftovers that SISDE was now reheating. So Lieutenant Perrino staged the raid, picked up whatever odds and ends he could in the fisherman's apartment, and served up the whole mess to the Velletri public prosecutor.

The game worked. Nobody so much as blinked at it. So why not give it a second shot a year later, once SISDE had lost all interest? Perrino swore that even if the Via Mantova raid was mere pretext, the Via Furio Anziate raid was the real thing. He also stood by his tale of having stumbled across el-Gamal a few days prior to his arrest, without any knowledge of where the Egyptian was living. By now, however, the former lieutenant looked a little desperate.

Once Doctor Fausto made his appearance, in fact, the entire edifice that had been constructed to justify the raid on Via Furio Anziate came tumbling down. Two carabinieri officers who participated in the operation recalled that Perrino had alerted them early in the evening on October 3—hours before the lieutenant had his "intuition" about el-Gamal's terror den. And there was another strange inconsistency. Until May 2002, Perrino had been in such close touch with el-Gamal that the Egyptian even had his cell-phone number. How, then, could he suddenly lose track of him? In Anzio, a small city, no less.

And what about the contacts that were supposed to place the three fisherman at the center of an Islamic fundamentalist network? This extra effort to transform the Egyptians into a "sleeper cell" was also in complete shambles.

All three probably frequented the mosque on Via Peano (near Viale Marconi in Rome), but nobody had ever seen them there. The famous pro-Palestinian pamphlet seized on October 4, 2001, had been distributed by the Via dei Volsci Collective, a dated, nostalgic branch of the local Autonomia Operaia, a voluntary labor association that spurned the traditional union hierarchy. True, el-Gamal and el-Zahed had undertaken a pilgrimage to Mecca with one Ibrahim el-Gayyeshi: an Italian citizen, auto body repairman, and occasional imam at the Latina mosque. But nothing about that trip really justified any connection between Via Furio Anziate and the Middle Eastern masters of terror.

And let's not even bring up Ahmed Ibrahim Salah, sometimes referred to as "Khumaini" in the agency's murkier bulletins and a "sensitive contact" of the three Egyptians. He was a Spanish citizen who had lived in Italy for twenty years, organizing trips to Mecca through his Naka Travel Agency. Until Easter of 2002, the carabinieri and the intelligence agencies had considered him extremely dangerous. He was "probably involved" in a planned attack that never seemed to get beyond the drawing board. In his testimony before the court, however, Lieutenant Colonel Paolo Scriccia did some quick backpedaling: "Salah, alias Khumaini, turned out to have no involvement in any subversive plot."

There was one card left to play: Osama bin Laden. Only a single piece of "evidence" regarding bin Laden was introduced during the trial. A witness. His name was Antonio Cortese, and he too lived in the building on Via Furio Anziate. He told the court that twenty days before the arrest, he had eavesdropped on one of the Egyptians talking on the telephone in Arabic—and that he "heard him pronounce the name *bin Laden*." This had worried him so deeply that he had reported the incident to his landlady, Signora Pergola.

That left the pistol, the explosives, and the belt. The analyses heard by the court had already demonstrated that the Beretta was a wartime antique, and that the TNT was "inert material" without a proper detonator.

As for the kamikaze belt, that too proved to be an innocuous item. On March 19, 2004, the court heard the testimony of the expert who had been charged with examining the belt and studying its possible uses. His conclusions cast a grotesque shadow over those who had conducted the original investigation—and over those who insisted on bringing the case to trial. For starters, he told the court, not a single particle of TNT had been found on the belt. He added: "We inserted the TNT bricks into the inner pockets of the belt, experimenting with two different methods. First, we tried to insert all seven bricks in a vertical position. Then we inserted six of them in a horizontal position. Only this second method, which involved 1.2 kilograms of explosive, allowed us to snap shut the pockets on the belt…. In both cases (horizontal and vertical loads), a suspect attempting to wear the belt would be unable to close the buckle, and would be forced to fasten it in some other manner."

In other words, once the "terrorist" loaded up the belt with TNT, he would be unable to wear it. The kamikaze device would slip down to his ankles, unless he lashed it onto his waist with twine.

What was left of the whole story?

There still remained the "documents," with the targets picked out by the three Egyptians: the McDonald's chain in Rome, the airport at Fiumicino, and the military cemetery in Nettuno. We've already noted that the maps of the first two locations were throwaway advertisements. What about the third one, photocopied from a *Tuttocittà* map of the area? That, too, was pure rubbish—el-Gamal denied that he had ever possessed the map. He insisted that the carabinieri had slipped it into his datebook during the search of the Via Furio Anziate apartment. An expert witness confirmed that it was an old photocopy, as demonstrated by "the traces of rust present in the paper." But more importantly, he could detect neither el-Gamal's fingerprints nor those of his two companions on the map. None of them had handled that sheet of paper. It had, however, passed through the hands of some other, unknown individual, who had left no less than "eleven prominent fingerprints."

On April 30, 2004, the First Court of Assizes absolved el-Gamal, Shalabej, and el-Zahed of the two crimes they had been charged with: international terrorism and possession of weapons and explosives with subversive intent. The court ruled that the Al Qaeda cell in Anzio had never existed ("the facts did not support it"), that the Egyptians had never played any part in it, and that they never intended to form such a group. The court also stated that the trio of fisherman "had not possessed" the Beretta pistol or the TNT—and that somebody, therefore, had snuck these items into the location where they had been found on the morning of October 4, 2002.

The 42-page decision, signed by the presiding judge of the court, Francesco Amato, and by his fellow judge Giancarlo De Cataldo, is a harsh document.

> The obvious contrast between the statements of "Doctor Fausto" and those of Lieutenant Perrino on specific aspects of the affair causes us great concern…. It's unthinkable that in a locality as modest in size as Anzio, Perrino didn't know where el-Gamal lived, especially since they had tried to enlist his help on behalf of the intelligence services…. This casts a shadow over the entire reconstruction of the affair…. It seems obvious to add that although "Doctor Fausto" denied any role in the events, the arguments set forth by the accused relegate his testimony to a mere expedient, desperate and false to boot, which is further corroborated by complete testimony of Lieutenant Perrino.

The decision goes on to condemn the modus operandi of Perrino and his colleagues:

> The raid on October 4, 2001, was essentially a stratagem to establish contact between an intelligence operative and El-Gamal. It was also meant to exert pressure on El-Gamal, as were the charges filed against him by the Velletri Public Prosecutor, which led to no penal action of any kind: they were simply a form of intimidation…. As for the raid on October 4, 2002, we can observe that the stated importance of the information supplied by the "confidential source" regarding the presence of dangerous

Arabs in Via Furio Anziate should have led to further
investigative activities: surveillance, interception, the
shadowing of suspects. Instead, it seems, a nonexistent
situation was viewed as an existent crisis, and the raid was
launched. Satisfied with the results, Lieutenant Perrino
made no effort to locate and seize the cars belonging to
Shalabej and El-Gamal. The experienced personnel that
conducted the search failed to find the belt. And upon
terminating the search, they failed to secure the premises, to
place official seals on it, and to keep it under surveillance.

The Court of Assizes had participated in a theatrical performance,
totally lacking in substance and verifiable truth. The trial also
inspired some grave doubts about the fact-gathering capacities of the
intelligence agencies, which had led directly to the three Egyptians
being paraded before the public as terrorists. The relevant "sources"
were condemned as "legally useless or devoid of evidentiary value."
In the end, there was only one possible conclusion:

> The prosecution failed to demonstrate the existence of a
> subversive group in Rome or in any other location, in which
> the accused had participated.... Nor did they demonstrate
> any acts suggesting that the accused had sought to assist the
> entry of their colleagues into Italy.... Nor did they prove that
> El Gamal, Shalabej, and El Zahed had formed a subversive
> organization or participated in the same. They couldn't
> even show sufficient evidence regarding the custody of the
> explosives or the gun. The suspects are hereby acquitted.

On April 30, 2004, the three Egyptians were released. Innocent
men, they had spent 19 months in a maximum-security prison.
Shalabej had lost more than 48 pounds while he was in jail.

During the first week of May, Carlo Corbucci and his colleague

Giovanni Destito met with the Velletri Public Prosecutor. In light of the acquittal granted by the Court of Assizes, they requested an update on the charges lodged against el-Gamal in 2001: "hostile acts against a foreign state, which expose the Italian state to the risk of war." This was, of course, the device Lieutenant Perrino had used to reel in the Egyptian on October 4 of that year. Yet the folder, mysteriously enough, had vanished. As Destito recalls:

> I was told that the investigation had been archived, and that it would take a few days to dig up the papers and have copies made. Fine. But when I came back, I couldn't believe my eyes. The complaint appeared to have been archived several months before. Inside the folder, however, somebody had forgotten to remove a document filed by the public prosecutor just a few days before the Court of Assizes handed down its verdict, requesting an extension on the time limit for the original investigation. In other words, it was clear that after the verdict was delivered, somebody had taken note of this gaffe, and tried to patch things up by backdating the folder.

Corbucci made another discovery. The acquittal demanded that all property seized from the Egyptians be returned to them. Many of their possessions had ended up in the "twenty black garbage bags" filled by Signora Pergola and her husband when they were "putting things in order." When Corbucci opened them, he gasped: "I realized that along with their clothing and personal effects, there were hundreds and hundreds of clock hands, and dozens of battery chargers. Incredible, I thought. The carabinieri had confiscated only a few of these items, in order to prove that they were 'rare' and 'specific' components needed to make an accurate detonator."

Meanwhile, nobody bothered to apologize to el-Gamal, Shalabej, and el-Zahed. Nobody launched an investigation of those who had imprisoned them in the full knowledge that they were innocent. The public prosecutor in Rome filed an appeal, which allowed him to put a slightly better face on the whole disaster: During the final months of 2004, the three Egyptians were again absolved of terrorism, but found guilty of the possession of TNT. On June 6, 2005, however, the Supreme Court quashed this verdict and absolved them of any crime whatsoever.

Today el-Gamal lives in Goro, in the Po River delta, where he works in the clamming business. El-Zahed returned to his labours on the *Titanic*. Shalabej lives in Rome. His damaged leg no longer allows him to work as a fisherman or an ambulance driver. All three have told their lawyers that they wish to be forgotten by the public— and by Doctor Fausto, who still says that he retains a "positive impression" of el-Gamal and his lawyers. In the meantime, SISDE has transferred him to a city in the north of Italy.

ANOTHER STORY. On the morning of February 20, 2002, Rome awoke to a nightmare. At dawn, the ANSA press agency began batting around a few lines borrowed from the front page of the *Messaggero*, which shrieked: "Via Veneto to be attacked with cyanide." The agency went on to note: "Four Moroccans, in possession of a considerable quantity of a cyanide-based compound and maps of Rome with the American Embassy clearly marked, have been arrested in Rome. The operation was conducted by the carabinieri at the behest of Public Prosecutor Franco Ionta. The four Moroccans, at least two of whom were in this country illegally, had been followed by investigators for several days. The arrests took place the moment that they confirmed the existence of the receptacle containing the cyanide compound. The operation was linked to the arrest of another three Moroccans by the DIGOS branch in Rome four days ago."

That afternoon, the American Embassy released an official note thanking the government and the police for their "excellent" work. In Washington, the State Department and Justice Department were both aquiver. The FBI immediately contacted the Italian antiterrorism branch. And an old intelligence report, which mentioned that Al Qaeda might use cyanide to launch an "imminent" attack, was promptly dusted.

The outcry was deafening. The city was in an uproar. Television crews crowded the utility tunnels beneath Via Veneto, filming the water mains leading to the American Embassy. All the news shows went crazy, even as the authorities did their best to calm the frightened populace: The "hydraulic network" was free of contamination, the water was fine.

One thing was clear. Four Maghrebis were in jail. They had been caught with cyanide and some maps of Rome's subterranean tunnels. The police and the carabinieri had pursued parallel investigations and were now combining them into a single scenario.

HERE'S WHAT HAPPENED. On February 19, the carabinieri knocked on a door at Via Buscemi 36/A. The person living there was Aziz Jamile, a 32-year-old Moroccan from Casablanca. The officers had no warrant—just a hint from a "confidential source," who urged them to search for weapons and counterfeit documents in that apartment. It was a legal search.

According to the records, the carabinieri seized six photocopied maps of the area around Via Veneto, three of them with the location of the U.S. Embassy marked in red. Two of these were street maps. The other four showed the network of water pipes running underneath Via Veneto. The investigators also found a handwritten letter from one Said Iqbal, a Mustafa Kamil; two passports; an identity card; a driver's license issued to Fatene Hasan; boxes full of fireworks; and a booklet published by the City of Rome, with 19 small maps showing the network of maintenance tunnels used by ENEL, ACEA, Telecom Italia, and the other utilities companies during the first half of 1998.

And that wasn't all. Outside the apartment and accessible by a pair of French doors in the kitchen, there was a small landing. There the carabinieri pried open the locked cover on a narrow niche, which housed the gas meter. And inside, they found a pouch containing 4.44 kilograms of a reddish, crystalline substance. They also extracted a cellophane envelope, which contained 111 blank forms from the Ministry of the Interior, normally used to grant residency permits to foreigners.

When the raid took place, there were three other Moroccans at Jamile's apartment: Redouane Rijaoui, 30, from Casablanca; Charifi Faycall, 23, from Agadir; and Yassine Zekre, 21, also from Agadir. They were arrested for the possession of "counterfeit passports and residence permit forms." The crystalline substance found in the meter box was sent to the Department of Chemistry at the University of Rome for analysis. Within a few hours, a specialist identified it as "potassium ferrocyanide."

On the same day, the carabinieri and a team of experts from the utilities checked the tunnels housing the water, electricity, and telephone conduits leading into the U.S. Embassy. The inspectors photographed one oddity. In a wall that had been constructed to block access to the tunnel immediately below the embassy compound, somebody had made two openings, just large enough to admit a person. And on February 21, beneath a manhole cover leading to another tunnel, inspectors found a fiberglass ladder and some abandoned garments. True, these items were discovered one and half kilometers from the embassy. But under the circumstances, the security forces certainly took note.

At first it seemed that the carabinieri were the only ones involved in, let's call it, Operation Cyanide. But that wasn't the case. On February 14, 2002, five days before Jamile and his friends were arrested, the police had also shown up at Via Buscemi 36/A. They too wished to search the premises, as part of an investigation that had been going on for at least a month. But the public prosecutor denied their request, so nothing happened. Here was a small, revealing detail, which will help to reveal what was going on in the minds of the four suspects.

Between January and February of 2002, an unusually detailed report by the Italian intelligence agencies sent shock waves through the police department. According to the report, an Islamic terrorist group had decided to gather information on the water pipes leading into the American and English embassies. They were planning to attack the diplomatic missions by poisoning the water supply. The report included the names of three suspects. They were Aziz Jamile, who lived at Via Buscemi 36/A, and two other Moroccans from Casablanca: Said Iqbal, 37, and Zinedine Tarik, 35. Apparently this trio had been delegated with finding the appropriate maps to plan the attack.

The police requested and obtained several search warrants from the public prosecutor. But their first two raids, on Via Crespi (where Tarik lived) and Via Torraccio di Torrenova (where he ran a phone store) were a bust.

Things went a little better when they showed up at Said Iqbal's house at 10 Via Sava. There they confiscated some rubber stamps, which were "presumably counterfeit." The rubber stamps were from the police departments of Cagliari and Tangiers, the tax collection office in Rome, and the Ministry of Transportation. In a datebook left on a table in the bedroom, they found a sheet of paper, upon which somebody had sketched a crude street map, noting the locations of Via Nomentana, Porta Pia, Via XX Settembre, and Via Cadorna. Along a certain stretch of Via Nomentana, somebody had written *Ambassade*—which is to say, embassy. The words *Ambassade Angl.* were scrawled near Porta Pia. Obviously this indicated the location of the British Embassy. Studying the handwritten map more closely, the police noticed an arrow pointing to Via Cadorna, and a small square with a dot inside it.

They also confiscated a business card they found in the datebook, from the Desert Tiger Tea Room and Disco Pub. Somebody, presumably Tarik, had scribbled a couple of cell numbers on it, along with the words *Mary—Via Cadorna 20*.

When the raid on Via Sava was launched, there were four people visiting Iqbal at his apartment: his brother Mohammed Iqbal, Mohammed Khajali (another Moroccan from Casablanca), and two women, Fatima Mohsini and Amal Manfaloti. The three men were arrested for possession of stolen goods and clandestine activities with subversive intent. On February 14, as we have already seen, the police tried to raid Jamile's domicile as well, but the public prosecutor refused to issue a warrant. That very morning, in fact, the GIP—the judge in charge of preliminary investigations—had ordered the release of the three Moroccans arrested the previous day.

Then came the raid on Jamile's house on February 19. Once the carabinieri discovered the cyanide and the maps of the water mains, the whole picture looked very different. On February 23, the GIP office dramatically changed gears. It now viewed the three Moroccans from Via Sava and the four from Via Buscemi as a single entity. Taking into account the tips gathered by the intelligence agencies, the mutual acquaintance of the two groups, and the items seized during the raids, the judge sent all seven suspects to prison. The charges: "international terrorism" and "possession of a chemical weapon."

Meanwhile, the GIP ordered the arrest of Zindine Tarik, even though the investigators had failed to find a single item of interest when they raided his home and his store. He also sent off the police to collar Fatene Hasan, a 30-year-old Moroccan whose driver's license had been found at Via Buscemi. (After the raid, in fact, Jamile had suggested that Hasan might have hidden the potassium ferrocyanide in the meter box.) Now there were nine suspects. Nine Moroccans, who had planned to strike the two embassies with the deadly chemical.

Let's take it from the top for a moment. An "anonymous" source whispered something to the carabinieri, who promptly snagged the ferrocyanide from the house on Via Buscemi. That house was connected to a second one, on Via Sava, which had also been a target of the police during the same period—thanks to another source whose reliability was impossible to verify. Yet a third anonymous source had tipped off the intelligence agencies about a possible chemical attack on the embassies. The result: nine Moroccans in jail, four and a half kilograms of ferrocyanide at the lab, a handwritten map of the area around the British Embassy, additional maps of the maintenance tunnels and water mains, and a stash of blank forms for residency permits.

As of February 19, 2002, it looked like all the loose threads had been tied up. But there were more. Less than a month later, on April 22, the GIP sent three more men to jail: a 30-year-old Algerian named Chiab Goumri, a 39-year-old Pakistani named Nasser Ahmad, and a 33-year-old Tunisian named Khalif ben-Mansour Abd el-Moname. Nobody knew who they were or where they had come from. Their involvement with the planned attacks on the two embassies was unclear, yet they had been charged with the same crimes: international terrorism and the possession of a chemical weapon. And the carabinieri had already assembled a voluminous file of damning information on the three men. There were hundreds of hours of intercepted phone conversations. There were photos, reports, copies of terrorist propaganda. Taken as a whole, they told a frightening tale, which went like this.

The al-Harmini mosque on Via Gioberti, frequented by all three of the suspects, was incubating an Al Qaeda terror cell. The aims of this cell were twofold: the recruitment of martyrs for the Afghani front, and a series of lethal attacks in Rome. That was why the suspects had been carted off in such a hurry. Nobody knew when, where, or how they would strike. And if they were working in concert with the Moroccans, the failure of the embassy attacks might well encourage them to speed up their own violent enterprises. Besides, the "evidence" the carabinieri had dumped on the GIP's desk seemed enough. In his arrest warrant, the judge noted that conversations recorded inside the mosque alluded to "military operations, fund-raising for the Afghan conflict, pistols, rifles, Kalashnikovs, and bombs. In some cases, it's possible to hear a metallic noise, which may indicate the loading of a weapon."

LET'S TAKE A STEP BACK, THOUGH. Let's actually drop by Via Palos, a stretch of road on the western outskirts of Rome, running from EUR to the Ostiense neighborhood. It's May 2001. The Twin Towers are still standing. Al Qaeda and Osama bin Laden are known only to a handful of experts. As for Via Palos itself, well, it's a regular petri dish of illegality. The bottom of the barrel. Twenty hovels, some made of brick, others of wood, the doors secured with padlocks or chains. The carabinieri know the street very well. It's a great place to get information when they need it—a great place to shake down a few snitches.

May 18, 2001, was one of those occasions. The carabinieri pulled into Via Palos, and among them was one Brigadiere Racca, who notes, "We had received a series of reports from the intelligence agencies pertaining to several fundamentalist Islamic groups operating in Rome and in the provinces.... The reports had dwelled on some 'high-risk subjects' that hung around the shantytown on Via Palos. We put some surveillance in place to identify the persons specified in the intelligence reports. Then we decided to raid the area."

The brigadiere was fudging a little bit. What had prompted the raid was the fact that the lengthy "surveillance"—deployed along the edge of a road overlooking the shantytown—had been a sterile exercise. There was no sign of the "high-risk subjects" who supposedly hung around that wasteland. There were no activities that could be regarded as even remotely suspicious. That left only one option: Kick down some doors.

The result? In one shack, occupied by a guy named Karim

Idri, they found a file of papers in Arabic. As Brigadiere Racca recalled: "It was a dossier on the theories of Salafi Islam. Once we had it translated, we realized that it had been compiled by critic of those religious theories—by somebody who considered them too welcoming to the Western world. It was, therefore, a pro-fundamentalist tract."

No big deal. But the investigators hit some real pay dirt in the next shack.

It was a wooden construction with only one room. Whoever lived there had melted away the moment he saw the carabinieri, but he left behind enough clues to identify him. He was named Chiab Goumri, an Algerian whom the intelligence agencies suspected of former ties to the Gruppo Islamic Armato (GIA)—and he was also one of the men picked up during the bust at the Via Gioberti mosque.

The poor wretch was a cripple: He had lost his right leg some years before in a railway accident. In his shanty the carabinieri found the prosthesis he used to walk, a receipt made out to him from an orthopedic clinic on Via Prenestina, the battery holder for his cell phone, and 27 VHS videocassettes. Of these, 24 were of no interest. The other three brought a smile to the face of the investigators. The first contained footage of various political demonstrations held by FIS, or the Fronte Islamico di Salvezza Algerino (Islamic Front for the Salvation of Algeria). As for the other two, let's listen to Brigadiere Racca: "What we found was amateur footage of some attacks on the regular Russian Army in Chechnya. It wasn't just the attacks: there were also images of the ambush being staged, of the preparation and placement of explosives. After that we saw the bombs go off, then an attack on the heavily armoured troops. The video camera lingered over the gore…. The images on the two videocassettes displayed no logo from a television channel, so they couldn't have been transmitted by a satellite broadcast. And given the amateur quality of the footage, it couldn't have been shot by a professional. The cameraman had clearly participated in the action, lingering over the corpses of the reviled Russian soldiers."

Still, not much came from those reports by the intelligence service. All they found on Via Palos was an anti-Salafi screed, three videocassettes, and the name of a maimed man. Nothing more. The carabinieri could have easily buried the whole business—if September 11 hadn't changed the picture. At that point, the slim pickings recovered from the shantytown in May suddenly became a valuable seedling, well worth cultivation.

Brigadiere Racca recalls: "After the attacks on America, there was *clearly* some investigative input from various sources. Among these, *clearly*, were some contacts inside the fundamentalist groups, both in Rome and in the provinces. We were told that a number of high-risk subjects had been seen once again on Via Palos—that there could be hidden stockpiles of weapons in the very area we had already searched. So we decided to raid it a second time.

In the intelligence marketplace, any shred of information classifiable under the rubric of Islamic radicalism was currently worth its weight in gold. And Via Palos was a kind of soup, which needed only to be reheated in order for Chiab Goumri to come bubbling to the surface.

The second sweep through the shantytown was as inconclusive as the first. Again the carabinieri kept their eyes peeled for the high-risk subjects, the hidden stashes of weapons, and again they came up empty-handed. At least they were able to confiscate an abundance of papers. Of course it was hard to tell who they belonged to, or who had written them. The shacks were empty, after all, and none of the tenants were likely to put their names on the front door. As Brigadiere Racca recalls, the papers consisted of "propagandistic material by subversive groups.... Excuse me, I don't mean subversive groups: I mean Islamic groups.... There were also datebooks, in which the same names kept recurring. We're talking about Chiab

Goumri, Samir Lanani, Mohammad Giardi, Mouloud Ferdjani, Moussa Khalifa (also known as 'Mohammad the Libyan'). Just about all of these names popped up as often as they did in the course of our investigations."

The more the carabinieri sifted through the papers, the more promising they seemed. Mouloud Ferdjani had already been tried and convicted in Naples for terrorism-related crimes. Lanani and Khalifa made obsessive appearances in every report issued by the intelligence agencies. It appeared that something serious was going on in Via Palos after all.

Flipping through one datebook, in fact, an excited investigator seemed to discover a link between the shantytown and the attacks on the Twin Towers. Between the bums in EUR and the suicide squad in Manhattan. The datebook included an address for Sofian Lemeches, an Arab whose brother Nebil lived in Italy. And that address was accompanied by a second address in the United States: "West Orange Good—Phoenix—Arizona." *Bingo!* thought the investigator. Two of the September 11 pilots had done their flight training in Arizona, so here was another name to add to that list. The connection might have deserved a sceptical smile: Instead it went straight to the FBI, and was then soldered into the chain of evidence. All the carabinieri needed to do now was work on the cripple Chiab Goumri.

His shanty had been empty back in May, the first time the carabinieri swept into Via Palos. Apparently, however, it wasn't difficult to track down this suspect and dangerous Al Qaeda militant. All they did was return to the shantytown and leave a notice under his door, inviting him to drop by the barracks and sign a police report regarding his artificial leg, videocassettes, and so forth. Then these items would be returned to him.

As Brigadiere Racca recalls: "When he was invited to collect these materials, Goumri showed us a card from the hotel Cressy, near the Stazione Termini on Via Volturno 27. He said that he sometimes stayed there." The carabinieri visited the hotel, under the banal pretext of checking the register. And what they found were more suspects, according to Racca: "We identified another Algerian citizen, a certain Kamel Defeiri, who worked there as a bellboy. His residency papers were in order, he had no previous criminal record, and he was extremely cooperative. He told us that he usually frequented the mosque near the Stazione Termini, and that he had the keys, since he was the janitor there."

It was the al-Harmini mosque on Via Gioberti. "Defeiri mentioned that the mosque was also frequented by another Algerian with a mutilated leg. Obviously we figured out that he was talking about Goumri," remembered Racca.

The supposedly electrifying connections between Via Palos and the pension on Via Volturno, between Goumri and Defeiri, never had much juice in them. Goumri himself had mentioned the hotel—why was it a surprise, then, that he was a familiar figure there? And what difference did it make if he frequented the Via Gioberti mosque? Was that a problem? The problem, in fact, was that the carabinieri believed him to be a scumbag and a liar. It made no difference that he had told them the truth, nor that he had obediently shown up at the barracks to retrieve his prosthetic leg. Here is Brigadiere Racca again: "We shifted our attention to the mosque at Via Gioberti 63. The premises were located inside a courtyard, and the investigation got off to a smooth start: from the signatures on the lease, we deduced that person in charge of running the mosque was Nasser Ahmad, a Pakistani citizen, with no previous criminal record and with his residency papers in perfect order."

The Via Palos shantytown, the hotel Cressy, the mosque on Via Gioberti. In six months—from May through December of 2001— the carabinieri had assembled a scenario that even a moderately sceptical eye could identify as a complete zero. Anonymous sources had shunted them onto a pointless track. All it led to was a pair of truculent videos shot in the Chechnyan slaughterhouse, some datebooks, a crippled Algerian who made no effort to dodge the police, and a Pakistani imam with a spotless criminal record and no apparent connection to the whole mess.

But that's not how the carabinieri saw it. They still insisted on connecting the dots: There was the reference to Arizona, there were Goumri's previous connections to the GIA, there were the datebooks found in the shantytown…. So they put a tail on Nasser Ahmad, the imam at Via Gioberti. They tapped all of his telephone lines. And to add yet another Big Brother touch, they installed hidden cameras to record all activities in the courtyard, and planted microphones sensitive enough to pick up every last sigh.

Nasser Ahmad earned his keep by booking tours to the Middle East. He ran a travel agency, Raval International, located at 95 Via Giovanni Amendola, in a residential neighborhood north of Rome. (The landlord for his business was the same one who leased him the location for the mosque.) The carabinieri promptly searched the premises, and emerged with only a single document: a pseudo-political poster in Arabic, hung in clear view of the public.

The poster stirred Kosovo, Arafat, Saddam Hussein, bin Laden, 9/11, and the assassination of John F. Kennedy into one rhetorical stew. It began: "Stop the wartime killing of humanity! The civilians of Kosovo are dead, but Milosevic is still alive. The Palestinians are dying, but Yasir Arafat is still alive. Civilians were killed in the attacks on Libya, but Khaddafi is still alive. The civilians in Iraq are dead, but Saddam is still alive." Ultimately the tone was antiwar rather than anti-West.

This they considered an important piece of evidence. It also confirmed the suspicions of their new source, Yonas Samuel. He was a guy who had worked at the travel agency for at least three years, and clearly had a great desire to stab his boss in the back. Samuel recounted that Ahmad had studied at the Koranic school in

Burewala, Pakistan, where he had earned the title of imam. Then he had supposedly gotten involved with Jamiya Islamiya, an Al Qaeda-affiliated terrorist group. Samuel added that he had personally heard his employer rejoicing about the attacks on September 11, and that Ahmad was also raising money for the jihad in Afghanistan.

The poster and Samuel's testimony were more than enough proof for the carabinieri. They would now concentrate on the mosque. Between the end of December 2001 and March 2002, a microphone hidden in an electrical outlet would record everything uttered by the imam and his companions. Two concealed cameras—one in front of the entrance, the other pointed at the window—would perform a similar function.

The resulting footage made for quite a show.

Along with Ahmad and Goumri, the investigators now identified a third suspect: Khalif ben-Mansour Abd el-Moname, usually referred to as "Naim." Lacking even a roof over his head, he slept in the loft at Via Gioberti. In exchange for this rudimentary shelter, he stood guard over the mosque, which was actually a converted apartment. The three saw each other often, and functioned as a kind of brotherhood, joining each other at the mosque for prayer and chatting up in the loft.

They spoke in Arabic, but also in Italian, with the blunt inflections of Roman dialect. The hidden microphone recorded several hundred hours of such conversations. And their tone, as documented by the transcripts, was none too meek.

A few highlights.

On December 12, 2001, Naim spoke with an unknown companion: "Listen, how long is it since you last fired a weapon?"

On December 23, two days before Christmas, he progressed to some veiled threats: "We're going to do exactly as the Koran says." And his companion, again unidentified, began discussing a few friends who were coming up from the Abruzzo region:

"They live in Aquila, there must be twenty of
them, and they're raising some money."
"I've heard they're piling up cash...."
"Right, they're piling up some cash to fight the war...
bin Laden and Afghanistan, you know what I mean?"
"Do you know what the guy's name is?"
"Abdel Nasser."
"The guy with the office behind those buildings."

On January 7, 2002, Naim spoke with a certain Saharg, and
excitedly alluded to a *croccaro*, which is what Italians call the Soviet-
made Kalashnikov rifle:

"The army is in Pakistan. You should go train there!"
"Who are you talking about?"
"Abdu... I'm not kidding, I'm going to Egypt with
him... with a submachine gun! No! With a *croccaro*!"
"No, no, I don't want a *croccaro*!"
"Nasser is joining the army!"
"He needs those documents!"
"The documents will be ready today."

A week went by. On January 14, 2002, Naim, Ahmad, and a third,
unidentified companion had the following exchange:

"That guy killed somebody.... He
doesn't have the rifle anymore."
"He doesn't have the machine gun either!"
"There's an armory.... I want to kill Bush!"
"There are people in Syria... There are new people."
"Today we'll strike the blow."
"We need a bomb and a pistol."

"The carabinieri have already arrived."

"Do you have cartridges? Load up the Kalashnikov."

"Kalashnikov."

"A rifle will do the trick. And a .38.

I'll get you some other pieces, too."

Like the exchanges that came before and after it, this resembles a dialogue among lunatics. There's no logical connection, no real context. But one thing was clear: The loft at Via Gioberti was a virtual armory, where the game of war had moved beyond mere rhetoric.

On February 13, 2002, Naim seemed to up the ante again. Conversing with two companions, he said:

"They're already up in the mountains, then?"

"Three M16s."

"You grab the smallest one."

"The bomb."

"The government will be forced to free the hostages."

"The bomb isn't ready."

Four days later, on February 17, Naim got even more serious: "Will you be launching the attack on the carabinieri? You'll have to." And finally, on March 28, the investigator listening to the tapes with a set of headphones made an alarming notation: "The loading of an automatic weapon is audible."

For the carabinieri—not to mention the public prosecutor and the GIP—that was enough. On April 22, as we have already seen, Chiab Goumri, Nasser Ahmad, and Khalif ben-Mansour Abd el-Moname were arrested. The mosque on Via Gioberti was raided and shut down. In the loft, that den of iniquity, not even a slingshot was found. Still, the intercepted conversations left little doubt as to the guilt of the suspects. And it wasn't only the conversations that led to their arrest. The surveillance cameras installed by the carabinieri had allowed them to record the comings and goings of the congregation. Among those caught on film were Mouloud Ferdjani and "Mohammad the Libyan." These were precisely the two figures mentioned in innumerable intelligence reports—*and* in the datebooks seized in the Via Palos shantytown.

Between February 19 and April 22 of 2002, the public prosecutor in Rome hauled in the nets, in which twelve defendants were ultimately entangled: an assortment of Moroccans, Algerians, Pakistanis, and Tunisians. That was the entire catch. One cripple, some young guys from Casablanca, a Pakistani who ran a travel agency, an idler who slept in a borrowed loft at the mosque. Three addresses—on Via Buscemi, Via Sava, and Via Giolitti—sketched out a Triangle of Terror, in which Al Qaeda sleeper cells were preparing to go about their bloody business. In one case, the plan was already clear: the chemical attack on the two embassies. Nobody knew exactly what was being hatched on Via Gioberti. But obviously something big was afoot, hence the stockpiling of money and weapons.

Both investigations had a single origin: confidential sources working for Italian intelligence agencies. Both had moved forward at top speed, to soothe the jangled nerves of the nation after September 11. And it was the carabinieri at center stage in both cases. They had busted the operation on Via Gioberti, of course. But they couldn't have rolled up the entire "Moroccan cell" without discovering the chemical weapon on Via Buscemi. Nor, without the cyanide and the maps, could DIGOS have made a convincing case for the planned assaults on the embassies.

In the spring of 2002, it was only the experts who paid attention to such details. And none of them saw fit to air any doubts, because they all knew what counted: results. In one stroke, Rome had rid itself of two dangerous terrorist cells. You couldn't ask for a more "concrete" or "imminent" threat. That left only one remaining question. How were the Moroccans rounded up on Via Buscemi and Via Sava actually connected to the mosque on Via Gioberti?

No matter how much time the investigators spent panning for this evidentiary gold, they found nothing. Absolutely nothing. But this fact did little to slow the juggernaut. Spurred on by the prosecution, the GIP office ruled that the 12 suspects would be tried together. This defied not only procedure but logic. It was, however, an early warning of a major muddle, whose true nature would be revealed before long.

In July 2003, the Second Court of Assizes began the proceedings in Rome. Nine of the twelve original suspects were in the courtroom— but not a single one remained in detention. That fact itself said a good deal about the investigative activities of the preceding year.

In any case, the court began simply by trying to impose some order on the facts so assiduously shuffled around by the prosecution. Which is to say: Before sprinting up and down the deductive paths that connected one part of the case to another, the court tried to establish who had done what. And when. And why. It was a healthy exercise, which allowed the listeners to peek behind the curtain and see the investigation for what it was: a fabrication.

Let's start with the most sinister segment of the case. We're talking about the attempt to poison the water pipes underneath the American and British embassies.

Aldo Laganà is a professor in the Chemistry Department at the University of Rome. He was the specialist who examined the 4.4 kilograms of crystalline powder that the carabinieri had found in the gas meter enclosure on Via Buscemi. It was he who identified the substance as potassium ferrocyanide. But that wasn't all he said. As the professor explained to the court, he had immediately sent the carabinieri a long analysis on February 19, 2002—and in that report, he had already ruled out the possibility that the chemical could be used as a terrorist weapon against human beings.

As Laganà noted: "Potassium ferrocyanide is a substance easily obtained through commercial means. It's used as a toning agent in some photographic paper, and also to dye textiles. The chemical is soluble in water, but once it's been dissolved, it's almost impossible to extract the toxic components. The water will have a yellowish appearance—the higher the concentration of ferrocyanide, the more pronounced the color will be. To separate out the toxic components, the solution would have to be broken down. This only happens at temperatures of at least 500 degrees centigrade. At that point, yes, vapors would be released from the solution, but they would have to be inhaled in very great concentrations—the victim would have to be sealed inside a small space. There's no doubt that ferrocyanide possesses an intrinsic toxicity. I should, however, stress that the average lethal dose is 2,970 milligrams per kilo of body weight. To kill a man weighing 70 kilos, you would need more than 200 kilos of the powder."

So the chemical found in Via Buscemi was innocuous. Even worse, this was old news to the carabinieri and the prosecuting attorney: Thanks to Laganà's report, they had been aware of it since February 19, 2002. They knew that the quantity was much too small to massacre anybody. They knew that for the toxic fumes to be released, the liquid needed to be heated to 500 degrees centigrade—and that adding it to the water mains was a ridiculous idea, since the concentration would instantly diminish to a harmless (and essentially undetectable) level. And thanks to the ACEA technicians, they knew that the pressure in the hydraulic systems leading to the two embassies was strong: four atmospheres.*

LET'S RECAP, then. If the terrorists managed to open a main, the jet of water would knock them off their feet. If they somehow remained on their feet, they would need to pour a tremendous quantity of the solution into the pipe for it to reach a poisonous concentration:

1,800 kilos of ferrocyanide per minute. And to do so, they would require pumps too large to fit into the maintenance tunnel. Their only alternative would have been to perform the operation at street level, right in front of the guards at each embassy.

Yet nobody backed down. Not the carabinieri, and not the public prosecutor. The prosecuting attorney made a vigorous objection: Surely you could be tried and punished for planning an impractical attack—even for planning an *impossible* attack. Therefore the raid on Via Busecemi had left the guardians of order with no other choice.

But here, too, things didn't quite add up.

When the court tried to establish exactly what had happened at that apartment during the raid—who had seized which piece of evidence, and in what order—the case promptly fell to pieces. The initial report by the carabinieri had been filed at 9:00 AM on February 19, 2002. The document recorded all 33 confiscated items in a neat list. For the first three items, the report noted: "6 photocopied street maps of Rome, 3 of them with the location of the U.S. Embassy marked in red; a pouch sealed with brown adhesive packing tape, containing 4.4 kilograms of a dirty reddish crystalline substance, which we are currently having analysed; a transparent cellophane envelope containing 111 blank forms from the Ministry of the Interior, currently used by foreigners to apply for residency in Italy."

According to the report, these three discoveries had been "hidden

---

* Testifying before the Court of Assizes, an ACEA official named Sandro Cecili explained: "To add a foreign substance such as ferrocyanide to the mains, it would first be necessary to interrupt the flow of water. The next step would be to cut into the principle main leading toward the water meter. Once that was accomplished, though, you would need an electrical or manual pump to exert additional pressure on the liquid in the pipe—otherwise the foreign substance might back up on you." The whole operation, he noted, called for bulky equipment that couldn't easily fit in an access tunnel, and would therefore "have to be set up at street level."

inside a locked gas meter enclosure" on the apartment's balcony.

But the paper trail didn't end there.

At 11:00 AM on February 19, the carabinieri filed a second report. This one noted that the raid had been prompted by a tip from a "confidential source," who "had learned that some non-EC immigrants were hiding weapons and false or counterfeit documents in the apartment of Via Buscemi." And at 2:30 PM, yet a third report was filed. It explained that another squad of carabinieri, under the command of Captain Piero Vinci, had searched the apartment a second time. On this occasion they found and confiscated "several maps showing utility tunnels and construction sites in Rome, a great quantity of gunpowder-like material, as well as videocassettes, notes, and various papers."

At 8:00 PM, the carabinieri drew up an arrest report for the Moroccans they had collared at Via Buscemi: Aziz Jamile, Redouane Rijaoui, Charifi Faycall, Yassine Zekre. As part of this document, they listed the confiscated items, which had been the actual justification for the arrests. The list was complete. However, some of the items had suddenly shifted around. The "dirty reddish crystalline substance" and the blank forms were still in the meter box. Yet the maps of Rome had now ended up inside the apartment, along with the "gunpowder-like material," the videocassettes, and the papers.

Three hours passed. And by 11:00 PM, the list had mutated again. In yet another report, there was no mention of the gunpowder-like material. And the videocassettes were now listed as part of the haul seized at 9:00 AM, during the first raid.

These successive reports do indeed tell a story—the story of a giant muddle (and that's a generous way of putting it). The fact is that between the nights of February 18 and February 19, there was a constant flow of carabinieri in and out of Via Buscemi. The fact is that the confiscated objects kept migrating from one area to another, and that some of the items seized at 2:30 PM were then inserted into the documentation from the 9:00 AM raid. The fact is that this evidence was collected in a bizarrely piecemeal manner. Why? In the course of a search for "weapons and counterfeit documents," how could the initial investigators have forgotten to look in a china cabinet in the living room? Coincidentally, the maps of the utility tunnels and construction sites showed up in that very cabinet during the *second* raid. And so did the street maps indicating the locations of the embassies—which were supposed to have been discovered in the gas meter box.

It's obvious that on the morning of February 19, the scene of the cyanide-related crime was staged in a certain manner, then redesigned for more dramatic effect. At first the maps showing the embassies were stuck in the gas meter box with the ferrocyanide. This would suggest that they functioned as a single, dastardly package. But when the additional maps of the utilities sites turned up, it made more sense to put all the "strategic planning" documents in one spot: the china cabinet. The deadly powder remained in the meter box, along with the blank residency forms.

The Court of Assizes was flabbergasted. It summoned the participants in the initial raid on Via Buscemi. Damiano Laneve, Massimiliano Roccoli, and Pierfranco Miele were all useless, their accounts contradictory. Then Captain Piero Vinci appeared on the scene.

The judges could hardly believe their ears.

"Around 8:00 AM on February 19," Vinci told them, "I learned the outcome of a nighttime raid conducted by the carabinieri of the central Compagnia Roma." The captain had picked up this bit of news in a haphazard manner, "from one of the soldiers" with whom he shared billeting. As he went on to explain:

> I heard that Aziz Jamile was among those arrested. Then I recalled reading that very same name in a confidential report, which included a tip about the apartment on Via Buscemi

and made the situation sound fairly serious. At that point
I decided to search the apartment again, just to make sure
everything had been confiscated. Around 12:30 PM I went to
Via Buscemi. There I discovered the maps of the utility sites,
the gunpowder-like material, and the videocassettes. Around
8:00 PM we decided to draw up a single confiscation report,
combining the objects seized in both raids. That list was
definitely compiled in the evening, not at 9:00 AM—although
it was erroneously labelled as such. While we were drawing
it up, we noticed that we were missing the maps of the utility
sites. For that reason, we were forced to omit them from the
report. But later, after everybody else had left the office, I
found the maps in a wastebasket. An officer had thrown them
away, assuming they were useless papers. At 11:00 PM I drew
up yet another confiscation report, dedicated solely to those
utility maps. And according to what I was told by colleagues
who participated in the first raid, the only things they found in
the gas meter box were the ferrocyanide and the blank forms.

It's likely the captain was fudging a few details. But even if we take
his account at face value, it makes for an amazing story. He admits
to two major bloopers. First: The report drawn up on the evening of
February 19 was "erroneously" backdated to 9:00 AM. Next: Thanks
to an careless subordinate, a key piece of evidence seized from
the Moroccans—the utilities maps showing the network of water
mains beneath the American and English embassies—ended up in
a garbage can at the barracks. No doubt it was extricated from an
assortment of pizza crusts, coffee cups, and cigarette butts.

Captain Vinci may have been doing his best to mop up the
mess on Via Buscemi. He succeeded only in making himself look
ridiculous. After all, he chalked up the second raid to a personal
intuition. He admitted that the carabinieri had shuffled around the

objects discovered during the two searches. And the image of him bending over the wastebasket in the empty office, raking through the trash for a key piece of evidence, bordered on the grotesque.

At this point we might have assumed that the captain was in for some serious trouble. Perhaps some outside investigation would get to the bottom of the whole mess, since the public prosecutor seemed incapable of handling it. Perhaps we would even find out whether the evidence found at Via Buscemi had been planted there. But that's not what happened next.

Instead, the prosecution stuck to its guns. Granted, the ferrocyanide was harmless. Granted, the two searches of the Via Buscemi apartment conducted by the carabinieri were so tainted as to be worthless. The prosecution now clung to the *other* group of Moroccans, the ones nabbed on Via Sava. They had been caught with a handwritten map of the area around the British Embassy. If the prosecution could demonstrate their guilt, they might be able to double back and convict the Via Buscemi bunch as well. Hadn't the two groups been working on the same plan?

SO BEGAN ANOTHER ORDEAL. In an increasing mood of irritation, the Court of Assizes decided to give the handwritten map a careful examination. Yes, there were two clearly marked locations: the British Embassy and a second, unspecified diplomatic mission. And there was a small box with a check mark in it, in the area around Via Cadorna. What did the map mean?

The answer was disconcerting. The "unspecified" diplomatic mission turned out to be the Moroccan Embassy on Via Lazzaro Spallanzani. And the box with the check mark indicated the Desert Tiger Tea Room and Disco Pub.

The investigators had found a business card from this very establishment during the raid. On the heels of his arrest, Said Iqbal tried to explain it to the officers. He told them that the little map had been drawn by a friend of his, Mohammad Reguemali, who worked at the Moroccan Embassy. It was supposed to show the way to the Desert Tiger, where Iqbal planned to celebrate his brother's birthday. At the time, nobody believed him. But the Court of Assizes quickly demonstrated that it was the truth. In testimony before the court, both Mohammad Reguemali and the proprietor of the Desert Tiger confirmed this account. In fact the proprietor dug out phone records indicating that the Iqbal brothers reserved a table shortly before the arrests.

There was one final bit of evidence: the letter from Iqbal to Mustafa Kamil found at Via Buscemi. Here, insisted the prosecution, was a link showing the "operative" connection between the two Moroccan cells. Wrong again, as Iqbal explained to the court: "It's true that I know Aziz Jamile, the man who lives in Via Buscemi. But that's because I'm engaged to a cousin of his. And her brother, Mustafa Kamil, lives in the same house. That's why you found a letter of mine there."

The entire scenario of the cyanide attacks was now demolished. Every element had collapsed under scrutiny. Italy had been the victim of a swindle. The United States and Great Britain had been taken for a similar ride: There was no massacre in the making. At the most, the Moroccans had been planning to fake some residency documents. What they intended to do with four kilograms of an innocuous powder was anybody's guess.

The trial could have ended there. Yet the prosecution had inexplicably linked the Moroccans to the evidence gathered on Via Palos and Via Gioberti. Therefore the public prosecutor had one last card to play: the fiery conversations recorded in the mosque. Perhaps these would allow him to prove that in the spring of 2002, Al Qaeda had been on the verge of attacking Rome.

The actual recordings, however, told a different story. Not a single one of the conversations transcribed by the carabinieri matched the words pronounced on the tapes. The court took note of this immediately. On September 24 and October 1, the carabinieri played what they considered the most significant portions of the tapes in the courtroom. In fact, it was impossible to understand almost anything on the tapes. They consisted of "buzzing sounds and confused noises," interrupted by "occasional, disconnected words, which could not be assembled into complete or coherent statements," according to court documents.

The carabinieri were quick to defend themselves. Marshall Fortunato Scoscina and Brigadiere Davide Racca, who had supervised the recordings, explained that those apparently meaningless noises could be deciphered only with the aid of "sophisticated equipment." It was a curious argument, since the officers who had transcribed the tapes had used no such equipment. But the court gave them the benefit of the doubt, and ordered an analysis. An acoustic engineer, Andrea Paoloni, was asked to examine 23 different conversations. The results were suitably frightening, although at this point they probably surprised nobody.

As Paoloni testified: "In the recordings, we hear a mixture of various voices, and it's impossible to determine with any certainty whether they're talking to each other, or to other persons who were present. Also clearly audible are some whispered or murmured comments. We can't establish where they fit into the conversation, or who pronounced them. In any case there are numerous breaks in continuity and logic."

That wasn't all. Most of the statements transcribed by the carabinieri had never been uttered, or meant something else entirely. Paoloni had much to say about the transcriptions we saw earlier. It's an educational comparison. His response to the individual transcripts was this:

CARABINIERI TRANSCRIPT, December 12, 2001: Naim is speaking with an unknown companion: "Listen, how long is it since you last fired a weapon?"

PAOLONI: "This sentence was never spoken."

CARABINIERI TRANSCRIPT, December 32, 2001: Naim makes threatening comments: "We're going to do exactly as the Koran says." And his companion, again unidentified, begins talking about a few friends who were coming up from Abruzzo: "They live in Aquila, there must be twenty of them, and they're raising some money." "I've heard they're piling up cash...." "Right, they're piling up some cash to fight the war... bin Laden and Afghanistan, you know what I mean?" "Do you know what the guy's name is?" "Abdel Nasser." "The guy with the office behind those buildings..."

PAOLONI: "There are six people speaking. The sentences about raising money are spoken by unidentified individuals. It's impossible to deduce whether the parts about raising money are actually related to the parts about Abdel Nasser."

CARABINIERI TRANSCRIPT, January 7, 2002: Naim is speaking with a certain Saharg: "The army is in Pakistan. You should go train there!" "Who are you talking about? "Abdu... I'm not kidding, I'm going to Egypt with him... with a submachine gun! No! With a *croccaro*!" "No, no, I don't want a *croccaro*!" "Nasser is joining the army!" "He needs those documents!" "The documents will be ready today."

PAOLONI: "There are at least three people speaking, and they're not talking about a submachine gun. The *croccaro* is not Al Qaeda jargon for a Kalashnikov. They're talking about a fast-food joint in the Via

Gioberti neighborhood, which sells *crocchette*—potato croquettes."

CARABINIERI TRANSCRIPT, January 14, 2002: Naim, Ahmad, and a third, unidentified companion have the following exchange: "That guy killed somebody.… He doesn't have the rifle anymore." "He doesn't have the machine gun either!" "There's an armory.… I want to kill Bush!" "There are people in Syria.… There are new people." "Today we'll strike the blow." "We need a bomb and a pistol." "The carabinieri have already arrived." "Do you have cartridges? Load up the Kalashnikov." "Kalashnikov." "A rifle will do the trick. And a .38. I'll get you some other pieces, too."

PAOLONI: "There are seven people speaking. The words *kill, rifle, bomb,* and *Kalashnikov* are heard, but in the context of an incoherent conversation. The sentences alluding to a rifle [*fucile*] might also be alluding to a cousin [*cugine*]."

CARABINIERI TRANSCRIPT, February 13, 2002: Naim is conversing with two companions: "They're already up in the mountains, then?" "Three M16s." "You grab the smallest one." "The bomb." "The government will be forced to free the hostages." "The bomb isn't ready."

PAOLONI: "The drift of the conversation is incomprehensible, and it's possible that they're not talking about a bomb at all."

CARABINIERI TRANSCRIPT, February 17, 2002: Naim is speaking: "Will you be launching the attack on the carabinieri? You'll have to."

PAOLONI: "Naim is not speaking. And that sentence is not audible."

CARABINIERI TRANSCRIPT, March 28, 2002: The loading of an automatic weapon is audible.

PAOLONI: "The sound could also be attributed to a metallic lock or latch. It's impossible to make a definitive identification."

So the notorious Via Gioberti recordings were also trash. All of them. And it wasn't only Paoloni who shot their credibility to pieces. The expert witness summoned by the prosecution, Captain Davide Zavattaro of the carabinieri, introduced an extra (and perhaps unintentional) note of ambiguity: "The transcription of such ambient recordings involves a high degree of subjectivity. It often happens that you'll hear certain things simply because you've divided up the sentences in a specific way. But if you listen again, with a different mindset, you may hear something more pertinent."

The key phrase here was "a different mindset." It wasn't just the transcriptions that fell victim to that different mindset—it was the entire investigation. When the reality of the facts clashed with that mental scenario, those in charge simply tampered with the facts to bring them into line. And the main culprits in this case were the carabinieri and the Public Prosecutor's office. Once that was understood—and documented by the Court of Assizes—it became obvious that every part of the story, from the Via Palos shantytown to the mosque on Via Gioberti, meant exactly the opposite of what had been suggested by the prosecution.

So: Goumri the cripple wasn't lying. He had never been lying. He had willingly disclosed his whereabouts to the carabinieri. The violent videocassettes found in his shanty had been purchased from a street vendor. The allusion to Arizona in the datebook, which supposedly linked him (or some other shantytown resident) to the Twin Towers, was dismissed by the FBI as meaningless.

True, Goumri had once met the "dangerous" Mouloud Ferdjani (convicted of terrorism in Naples), and he knew Mohammad the Libyan. But this didn't prove that he belonged to a terror organization, nor that he was planning a massacre. Nor did Ferdjani hang around the Via Gioberti mosque, as the carabinieri originally insisted. At first they claimed that on January 29, 2002, a hidden camera trained on one of the apartment's windows had caught the fugitive Ferdjani changing his clothes. Alas, that wasn't true. The camera in question was installed on December 7, 2001. And as Major Roberto Zuliani later conceded to the court, it was essentially out of commission within two weeks, when somebody stuck a sheet of cardboard in the window.

And what was there to say about Nasser Ahmad? The Pakistani imam and travel agent was supposed to have been nailed for sending false identity papers to Mohammad the Libyan after he fled to Canada. At the trial, this proved to be false: What he sent was a valid residency permit, which the elusive terrorist had left behind by accident. There were also the accusations made by his employee Yonas Samuel. Hadn't Ahmad raised funds for the jihad in Afghanistan? What about his connection to Jamiya Islamiya, and his evident joy at the devastation on September 11?

Samuel turned out to be a liar—a fraud, really. The carabinieri knew this as early as March 16, 2002, when they intercepted a wiretapped conversation between the disgruntled employee and a friend of his, Hussein an-Awar:

> **Samuel:** Nasser made everybody believe he was some kind
> of village elder, a wise man. But that shithead was in Jamiya.
> And now that he's been caught, they'll fuck him up good.
> **An-Awar:** So you'll take over the travel agency.
> **Samuel:** Right, and that's what I wanted to
> talk to you about.... Tell me something. Is there
> any chance Nasser will be cut loose?
> **An-Awar:** If they don't have enough

evidence, they'll let him go.

Samuel: I'd rather he stay in there for a while. For some serious charges.

An-Awar: Then I'll unload on him. I'll testify against him, and that way he'll never get out. It's not a problem, I'll go the whole nine yards if you like.

Samuel: Go ahead. Because Nasser is a piece of crap, he's given me nothing but headaches.

The two friends concluded with a good laugh. But neither the carabinieri nor the prosecuting attorney dumped this witness in March 2002. Nor did they call him on the carpet to explain that fabricating evidence against an innocent man was a crime. All they knew was that Nasser was "a piece of crap." That was more than enough.

That left only Khalif ben-Mansour Abd el-Moname, better known as Naim. All they had on this penniless man was the material taped in the loft at Via Gioberti: which is to say, absolutely nothing. It wasn't true that he spent his free time assembling bombs, rifles, and Kalashnikovs. It wasn't true that he incited his companions to open fire on the carabinieri.

The trial, then, was truly over. The public prosecutor of Rome made an attempt at damage control. He requested that the most serious charges against the Moroccans—terrorism and the possession of a chemical weapon—be dropped. He acknowledged that the planned attacks on the two embassies were pure humbug. Still, he wanted to convict the tenants at Via Buscemi for the possession of stolen goods. He was equally committed to putting away the three hotheads from the Via Gioberti mosque. And at first, he got at least partial satisfaction: eight years and four months for Nasser Ahmad, eight years for Naim, and eight years for Chiab Goumri.

On April 28, 2004, however, the Second Court of Assizes absolved all of the defendants. Only the one-legged Goumri retained a blot on his record: the license plate on his Scarabeo moped turned out to have been stolen.

Years have passed since this story began in the winter of 2002. More than four, in fact, if we go back to the initial raids on the Via Palos shantytown. And all that came out of the entire enterprise was a conviction for the possession of a stolen license plate.

Nobody has demanded an explanation from the public prosecutor of Rome or from the carabinieri. On the contrary. The attorney general appealed the sentences with noisy (if impenetrable) disdain. In his view, the defendants had been absolved "by a judge who ignored the fact that such crimes have a preparatory phase." Even worse: The judge had, according to the attorney general "demonstrated little interest in proceeding to judgments based on established evidentiary facts, nor did he make use of the fundamental principles of hermeneutic logic.... Lacking any proofs, and in the most apodictic manner possible, he drew conclusions that went beyond our wildest dreams."

Knowing the sort of indigestible hodgepodge that the prosecution had served up the first place, it took a formidable sense of disconnection for the attorney general to make these complaints. Even more reckless was the chatter about evidence, proof, and logic. It was a desperate effort by a man who may have been ashamed of what happened, but lacked the courage to do anything about it.

It was also a useless effort. On March 3, 2005, the Court of Appeals confirmed the earlier ruling. In full. All the defendants were absolved.

CHAPTER FOUR

THE MUDDLE IN MILAN

Our previous chapter may have suggested that the judicial shenanigans, in Italy, have been confined to Rome and points south. Nothing could be further from the truth. Lombardy, too, has stumbled more than once in the War on Terror. But before we tell this particular story in detail, we will begin with two questions. Who is Stefano Dambruoso? And what is Ansar al-Islam?

Let's start with the easier question. For much of the decade prior to September 11, Stefano Dambruoso was a hard-nosed investigator of the Mafia in Sicily. That role familiarized him with intimidation, death threats, and elusive suspects. In 1996, however, he was appointed public prosecutor in Milan. And in the wake of the attacks on New York and Washington, he became one of Italy's best-known warriors against domestic terrorism.

Next question. Ansar al-Islam is a small and fairly marginal Kurdish Islamic group. It came into being in early 2001, when three groups split from the Islamic Movement of Kurdistan (IMK) to form a separate organization. The unity of the three groups—Markas-i-Islam, Hamas al-Tauhid, and Mullah Krekar's militants—didn't last for long. The factions seldom agreed about anything. As independent entities, they sent their youngest members to train in bin Laden's Afghan camps. Yet they never developed an operational relationship with in bin Laden. After all, he wanted to unleash a global war. They merely wanted to fight it out in Kurdistan.

In December of 2001, the three groups did launch a joint operation: a wave of attacks against the Patriotic Union of Kurdistan (PUK) and other targets. "The ferocity of the attacks, with ritual massacres of the peshmerga and suicide assaults against government offices, is without precedent," noted one contemporary source. Still, their bloody activities remained within the confines of northern Iraq, and were directed at Kurdish secularists. And soon enough, the umbrella group would be driven out of the country.

Ansar al-Islam's base was protected by a series of valleys and ridges not far from Halabjah. On three sides they were surrounded by the PUK peshmerga—Kurdish fighters—with the Iranian frontier on the fourth. In late March of 2003, the Kurds, supported by American air power, swept up into the base. According to their own reports—which are impossible to verify—the PUK forces killed 300 of the 600-900 militants camped up in the hills. Jason Burke, who covered this phase of the war for the *Observer*, disagrees. He argues that "most of the guerillas" managed to "melt away" and escape into Iran. In either case, Ansar al-Islam still exists today, although the name of the group has been changed to Ansar al-Sunna. According to Burke, "A few of the group's leaders have been arrested. Others still seem to be operating out of Iran. For the most part they have struck in northern Iraq, launching a series of suicide attacks against various elements of the Kurdish administration, especially the police."

The reality of Ansar al-Islam didn't bother Stefano Dambruoso. Investigators like himself had learned "an unwritten rule: study the little things, the local reality, but think on a large scale, an international scale." Such thinking allowed him to imagine Ansar al-Islam within the global struggles of radical Islam, even if the group's leaders remained fixated on only Iraq. According to Dambruoso, the situation was this: "This Kurdish faction has moved beyond its initial dream—an Islamic state, in a land where religion and politics do not mix—to share in a global movement. A struggle waged under the banner of holy war. It's a simple yet effective message, which has buttressed Mullah Krekar's 600 troops with an influx of North African militants. And since it's risky for them to recruit in Tunis (as opposed to Cairo), they find these' new soldiers in the Italian provinces." Yes, Dambruoso seemed to think, Ansar al-Islam was recruiting in Italy.

The public prosecutor's exclusive focus on this splinter group was almost incomprehensible. It appeared as if Dambruoso were in the grips of a poetic fancy. Heedless of any contradiction, he placed this marginal organization at the very top of a terrorist pyramid. And the man in charge of Italian operations, it was determined, was one Abu Omar: "the true light of the fundamentalists," the "beacon of extremism" who ruled the militants of Milan with "an iron fist."

Who is Abu Omar? He is a big blabbermouth, a vainglorious man, perhaps a mythomaniac. With his colorfully checkered past, he aroused a certain curiosity from the moment he arrived in Milan. Omar was born in Alexandria, Egypt, on March 18, 1963, and left his country during the 1990s. Intelligence archives (American, Italian, Egyptian) labeled him "a combatant in Afghanistan and Bosnia." In 1996 he was in Albania, where he married Marsela Glina. They brought a son into the world. His interval of domesticity would be short-lived. He was soon accused of planning the assassination of Egypt's foreign minister during a state visit to Tirana. He left Albania in a hurry and, after a layover in Munich, resurfaced in Bari, Italy, on May 1, 1997.

In 1999, officials in Rome granted him the status of a political refugee. He obtained a residency permit. In the summer of 2000, Omar moved to Milan. There he was accommodated in an apartment at Via Conteverde 18—"our temporary housing," explained the

Islamic Institute on Viale Jenner, "for those who arrive in the city without a penny."

Now, Via Conteverde was not simply any old address. A handful of notable fugitives had lived there during the city's initial investigation of "Al Qaeda sleeper cells." For the DIGOS branch in Milan, then, that apartment was a kind of membership badge. Omar's telephone was promptly tapped, and his friends and movements were noted. This didn't seem like idle curiosity. The man behaved like a big shot. He gave fiery speeches, wrote fiery articles. The police considered him a "hothead." To his companions he seemed like an imposter, and something of a narcissist.

For the intelligence agencies, however, Omar was a potential asset. They dispatched an undercover operative, who soon contacted the Egyptian newcomer. Would he be interested in joining a new terror network in Europe? Abu Omar declared himself ready and willing.

So he was a dangerous man, at least in theory. Having demonstrated this, it was now a simple matter for the prosecutor to present Omar as a fundamentalist chieftain, and to exaggerate the territorial ambitions of the Islamic Kurds.

In this way, Ansar al-Islam became the real thing, as fearsome as Al Qaeda. "Al Qaeda is the ideological umbrella," we were told, "while Ansar al-Islam is the logistical framework." In fact, the Kurdish splinter group was supposedly functioning as a kind of general armory for terrorists in Iraq.

This heated atmosphere prompted an unusual blooper on the prosecutor's part. He seemed unaware that Ansar al-Islam had changed its name to Ansar al-Sunna—or if he did know, he simply didn't care. For he wrote: "Cassettes and CDs have arrived from Kurdistan, featuring the militants of Ansar and those of a newer group, Al Ansar Al-Sunna—a faction allied to Al-Zarqawi." Apparently it was all grist for the mill.

Now, despite this embarrassing squishiness on the factual front, it's obvious that at least some Islamic emigrants in Europe were eager to participate in the Iraqi "resistance." There's no doubt about it. But were their numbers sufficient to demonstrate a genuine, concrete, ongoing danger to Italy? Did they really justify dozens of investigations, in the course of which Italian security agencies ran down all sorts of clues that were transparently ridiculous?

For Dambruoso, anyway, these efforts were worthwhile. With a whiff of narcissism, he noted that "with every passing day, the micro turns into the macro." The Kurdish killers were taking their orders from the enigmatic Abu Musab Al-Zarqawi, argued the prosecutor, and so were the "mujahideen and kamikazes recruited in Italy."

Even if we gave credence to the idea that suicide bombers were pouring into Iraq from Italy, the picture seemed a little confused. It wasn't clear who was giving the orders, or if indeed anybody was. The mantle of command, according to Milan authorities, was worn first by Osama bin Laden, then by Al-Zarqawi, then by Mullah Krekar (even though he was a citizen of Norway). The Antiterrorism Division in Milan was happy to float all these scenarios at the same time, shuffling around the particulars as necessary. The result was devoid of logic, choking on its own contradictions. As is widely acknowledged today, Ansar al-Islam had no organizational relationship with Osama bin Laden or with Al-Zarqawi. The whole conception was a house of cards, constructed in Milan.

Why anybody would bother to construct this shaky edifice is another question. The public prosecutor's conclusions about the centrality of Ansar al-Islam and Abu Omar certainly couldn't be justified by the evidence gathered in the course of his investigations.[*]

---

[*] The dozens of police operations, arrests, judicial inquiries, and trials in Milan produced only two convictions for terrorism: Noureddine Drissi (a Moroccan) and Mouldi Ben Kamel Hamraoui (a Tunisian). See P. Morosini, "Jihad e giustizia penale," in *Questione Giustizia*, No. 5.

In the courtroom, before a judge, those investigations fell to pieces. Dambruoso's tangled version of the relationships between various fundamentalist Islamic groups and Al Qaeda made sense in only a single context: the American agenda—which was, during the summer of 2002, all about the important links between Saddam Hussein and Al Qaeda, with Ansar al-Islam as the main go-between.

During that same summer, the American administration was considering an attack against a chemical weapons installation in northern Iraq, most likely run by the radical group Ansar al-Islam. A report of a ricin laboratory, which Washington believed to be linked to Al Qaeda, was picked up by ABC and CNN. Yet it soon led to embarrassment for the Pentagon. The Kurdish leaders in control of the area immediately let it be known that there were indeed Islamic militants there, "but no more than 100-150 individuals, with no connection to Bin Laden." These leaders also denied that Ansar al-Islam had any relationship with the ruler in Bagdad.

No connection with Saddam Hussein. No connection with Osama bin Laden. Ansar al-Islam, it turned out, was essentially an isolated meteor in the radical Islamic firmament. But for the intelligence community on the eve of the Iraqi invasion—which was only seven months away—the group had another identity: It was the missing link between Al Qaeda and the bloody regime in Baghdad.

At last we're beginning to glimpse the most authentic rationale for the public prosecutor's behavior: the paradigm of "espionage law." Shielded by the demand for collective security, and distorted by the doctrine of preemptive war, the Italian judiciary was free to operate in a kind of parallel universe. The Bush Administration needed to demonstrate that Saddam and Al Qaeda were in cahoots; it needed to win the hearts and minds of the West in order to legitimize the Iraqi invasion. Ansar al-Islam and Abu Omar—the sinister apex of Italian terror—would do the trick nicely.

And what were the results of these distorted assumption? One of them, at least, was the illegal kidnapping of Abu Omar in Milan. The suspect was grabbed by a CIA unit in full daylight, transferred to a military base in Aviano, interrogated and beaten for seven hours, and then turned over to Egypt, where he was tortured in a special prison. This seemed like the ideal strategy for squeezing some solid intelligence out of the suspect without taking any responsibility for the way it was obtained. The "target" could now be "worked on" without the slightest involvement by Italians.

The date was February 17, 2003. It was a Monday, shortly after noon. Abu Omar stepped out from behind the green gate at Via Conteverde 18. "I'm going to the mosque," he told his wife Nabila Ghali. He was referring to the mosque on Viale Jenner, less than a kilometer away as the crow flies. Omar walked briskly along Via Conteverde, with the traffic flowing in the opposite direction, and noticed a white van that slowed down as it approached him.

He picked up the pace and stepped into Via Ciaia. In the meantime, the van had circled around the block and was waiting for him in Via Guerzoni—a two-way street hemmed in on both sides by public gardens. It must have seemed like the ideal spot for a snatch. The area could easily be isolated from traffic. All it took were two cars clumsily parked in the intersections at Via Ciaia and Viale Jenner. The men in the white van could take their time, since the rented cars essentially sealed off the two ends of the street. There were at least 12 men involved in this phase of the operation. They were Americans. They communicated with each other via cell phone, having spent at least a week preparing for this "collection."

Abu Omar immediately noticed the man waiting next to the van, which was parked alongside Via Guerzoni 23. The rear doors of the van were open. The man spoke Italian. He identified himself as a "police officer," and asked Omar for his papers. A moment later, Omar was overpowered. Despite his bulk, he was quickly sprayed in the face with some blinding substance and flung into the back of the van. There were no cars in Via Guerzoni. Nobody was supposed to see the snatch.

But somebody did. A young Egyptian woman, who was just emerging from the public gardens with her children, stepped out onto the street behind Abu Omar. She noticed the two men chatting. She moved past them, and seemed to hear the sounds of a scuffle behind her. Next came the loud slamming sound of the door closing. Then the vehicle pulled out at high speed. When she turned around, Abu Omar was gone. The woman recounted this incident to her husband, who frequented the mosque on Viale Jenner. Clearly something very strange was going on. (The woman, incidentally, refused to say a word to the police, and then vanished from Italy.)

Now it was March 3. Two weeks after the disappearance of Abu Omar, American intelligence volunteered some information. They notified the Italian government that "according to unverifiable reports, Abu Omar may be in the Balkans." This was a shrewd attempt to muss the trail. The story should have ended there. Who would ever know exactly how it had played out?

The answer, of course, was Abu Omar himself. On April 20, 2004, Nabila Ghali got an unexpected call from her husband. He was calling from Alexandria, Egypt—and needless to say, their conversation was intercepted and recorded. Omar reassured his wife, asked her to send him 200 euros, and insisted that she not say a word to the press. Only his brothers were to be notified of his whereabouts. Beyond that he said nothing.

Later that same day, the telephone rang in the home of Elbadri Mohammad Rida. A fellow Egyptian and personal friend of Omar's, he was the imam of the mosque on Via Quaranta. The two managed to touch base for the first time on May 1. Then they had a lengthier phone conversation on May 8, at which point Omar described exactly what had happened to him from the moment he was thrown in the white van on Via Guerzoni. Here is what he told Rida:

> The two men who kidnapped me seemed to be Italians, at least in their appearance, but I don't know if they actually were. They thought they had stunned me with the spray. But once the van was underway, I managed to get back on my feet. And although I had a gag in my mouth, my eyes weren't covered, and they had left my watch on. We drove for five or six hours. When the van stopped and they opened the rear door, it was around sunset: between five and six o'clock. I had the feeling I was on an American military base, because I was able to recognize some of the insignias on the airplanes. The two kidnappers took me to a room and left me there alone. After about an hour, four other men showed up. They interrogated me until three in the morning. At first they tried to speak Italian, but they spoke it very badly, so eventually they switched to English. They kept hammering away at the same point: "You're agitating against the invasion of Iraq, you're inciting hatred for the Americans. Right? And aren't you recruiting militants to fight in Iraq?" I told them no, it wasn't true, and they kept repeating the same questions. At a certain point they showed me a pamphlet I had written, in which I took Italy to task for its misdeeds in Libya and Somalia. Then they began punching me. They beat me until late at night. Then, at around three in the morning, they put me on a small plane, with very few seats. We flew for about four hours, and at dawn, we made a stopover at another American military base. I think it was a base on the Red Sea.

The plane had stopped for fuel and maintenance. Soon it took off again, and an hour later it landed in Cairo, at the regular airport.

> The moment I came down the ramp, I was taken into custody
> by Egyptian officials. They blindfolded me and took me first
> to Lazoughli, where the Secret Service held me in a locked
> cell, and then to a room in the Egyptian Ministry of the
> Interior. At this point things began to move quickly. They told
> me: "If you want to go back to Italy, you can be home in less
> than 24 hours. On one condition: You agree to work for us."

Abu Omar refused: a fateful decision. On that same day—February
18, 2003—he was transferred to Tora, a high-security prison and
epicenter of suffering. The place was a virtual city of cells, an
underworld in which "there was always a more hellish circle than
the one you inhabited."

Abu Omar recalled:

> The interrogators worked with a light hand, the torturers
> worked with a heavy one. I was stuck in a refrigerated room
> completely nude. It must have been at least [four degrees
> below zero Fahrenheit] in there, because I felt the very bones
> of my body crumbling away. When I was almost frozen,
> they tossed me into a room that was burning like fire: at
> least [122 degrees Fahrenheit]. Once they stretched me out
> on a wet floor and then threw live electrical cables into the
> water. It was after those shocks that I began to have trouble
> moving my legs, and I can no longer feel part of my back.

What did the Egyptians want from Abu Omar? As he later told his
friend, "the questions were pointless. Were you in Bosnia? Were you
in Afghanistan? All they did was to give some semblance of purpose
to the torture."

In reality, they wanted something else from him. He confided this to Elbadri Mohammad Rida, almost with pride: "They showed me a list of names. Yours was at the very top, Mohammad! Then came Abu Emad, the imam from Viale Jenner. Mine was third. They told me that if I wanted to be released, I had to rat them out."

Abu Omar remained in Tora for 14 months. Finally, they told him he was a free man. With one proviso: "If you want to leave this place on your own two feet, and not in a coffin, don't ever tell anybody what happened to you. You'll have to explain that you came Egypt of your own free will, with a ticket you bought in Italy."

Abu Omar signed the agreement. On April 19, 2004, he was free. But the telephone calls he made between April 20 and May 8, reported by the Italian newspapers, must have violated his agreement with his captors. On May 12, the Egyptian security services picked him up at his apartment in Alexandria. He was again released on February 12, 2007.

That mechanism has a name: extraordinary rendition. The practice consists, according to a Milan tribunal that later investigated Omar's abduction, of "bypassing the extradition process, especially when those methods are not feasible. Instead, the subject is directly and violently removed from the territory of a foreign State. This action is performed by agents (official or not) of the abducting State and without the consent of the host State." For the Americans, this didn't seem problematic. Indeed, Washington embraced the practice. The United States Congress was informed of this fact on October 17, 2002, when CIA director George Tenet testified before the 9/11 Commission.

"Since the attacks on the Towers," Tenet told the panel, "the CIA, with the cooperation of the FBI, has brought to justice seventy terrorists throughout the world." The methods used for these arrests paid little heed to the sovereignty of the states where the suspects were rounded up. After September 11, then, the practice of "extraordinary rendition" became routine for the Bush administration. It was authorized on numerous occasions.

No, it wasn't a problem for the United States. It was, however, a major problem for Italy, because "for the first time in the history of the Italian legal system, a suspect was removed under judicial authority and forcibly transported to a third State." The kidnapping of Abu Omar was not merely an illegal act. It was "a grave violation of Italian sovereignty." So concluded the inquiry by Deputy Prosecutor Armando Spataro, which also resulted in 22 arrest warrants for the various CIA personnel involved in the kidnapping. (By this time, Stefano Dambruoso had left his post in Milan to advise Italy's permanent mission to the United Nations.)

The joint squad of CIA and FBI operatives had bungled the job pretty badly, leaving traces everywhere. According to the prosecutor's office, the squad's cell phones could be placed in Via Guerzoni around noon. Shortly after, the same group of cell phone signals began "moving" toward Aviano. The outgoing signals indicated calls to the American Consulate in Milan and to a number in Virginia. One of the phones traveled all the way to Cairo the next day, cheek by jowl with Abu Omar.

Having identified the cell phones, which were Italian, the investigators figured out who had used the appropriate telephone calling cards on those very days—and from the cards, they got some names. The names led them in turn to the hotels where the group had stayed in Milan, and to the rental agency where they had leased the van and the cars for the operation. With all this in hand—the phone records, the hotel bills, the rental agreements—the investigation was over. The kidnapping was a fairly cut-and-dried affair. But how had such a shabby enterprise come to pass? And had the Italians collaborated with their allies? Had some institution (the government, SISMI, the police, the carabinieri, the judiciary) given a silent wink, or even an operational nudge, to Langley's forcible abduction? At least five facts and one noisy contradiction suggest that this may be the case.

First: incomprehensibly enough, Public Prosecutor Dambruoso never issued an arrest warrant for Abu Omar. As far back as April 4, 2001, the Egyptian was seemingly embedded in a dense tissue of reports, connections, contacts, conversations, and messages, all of which identified him as "a *qa'id*, a Supreme Commander." In theory he was the missing link to other suspected terrorist organizations (such as Ansar al-Islam and Jamiya Islamiya). Omar was also supposed to have played a strategic role in steering the Islamic fundamentalists of Hizb ut-Tahrir toward retaliatory violence. Still, the Public Prosecutor's office in Milan never asked for his arrest until April 5, 2005. Four years after his name popped out of every antiterror inquiry. Two years and two months after his kidnapping.

Next: Abu Omar was customarily tailed and wiretapped by the police and the carabinieri. Everything, down to the last whisper, was recorded and transcribed. But for seven days, from February 10 to February 17 of 2003, the dogs were called off. The suspect was left in a state of splendid solitude, which allowed the CIA to spring its comfy trap. The experts defended this lapse, insisting that "you can't tail somebody 24 hours a day if you want the strategy to work." Yet this argument was something of a bust, and simply led to another question. How was it possible, given all the hours devoted to shadowing Abu Omar, that nobody noticed a squad of 20 Americans breathing down his neck? Of course it's possible that Omar's Italian minders had other orders. But what were they? And who gave them?

Stefano Dambruoso traveled to the United States on two occasions during those years. What information did he exchange with the FBI on June 17, 2002 (before the kidnapping, that is) and with the CIA the following May?

According to his "diary," Dambruoso did discuss Abu Omar

during his meeting with the FBI in New York: "The urgency of our work brings us back to reality—and to the FBI office. New colleagues, new dossiers. We're concentrating on the Hamburg cell, we're reconstructing the operative relationships between the soldiers of Allah scattered throughout Europe.... A kind of Ariadne's thread appeared right under our eyes, spun out of men and nations. Abu Omar in Milan led us to Admed in Cremona."

When Dambruoso journeyed to Washington after the kidnapping, did he discuss Abu Omar's disappearance with his new colleagues? There is no record of him doing so. But that silence, too, is curious. Right from the beginning, the experts in Milan had characterized the kidnapping as the work of a Western intelligence agency. And in his book *Milano-Baghdad*, Dambruoso would later hold the CIA responsible for the snatch, imputing more than a tinge of paranoia to the agency.

In fact, the very events surrounding the kidnapping reveal a telling contradiction. When Nabila Ghali spoke to her husband on April 20, 2004, she told him that on the "very same day" of his disappearance, the police had shown up to search their apartment. Yet the police report for that search is dated February 27—which is to say, ten days later.

Could the CIA really have planned an operation on Italian soil without notifying its valued collaborator? And if SISMI really had been left in the dark, did the agency subsequently demand an explanation of the whole muddle? If so, what answer did they get?

After the kidnapping, only a single CIA participant remained in Italy. This was Robert Seldon Lady, the agency's station chief in Milan. Having retired, he moved to a country villa in Penango, near Asti, and kept a low profile—at least until June 23, 2005. On that date, officers from DIGOS showed up at the gate to arrest him. Since the former spy was not at home, the officers were greeted by his wife, Martha. They turned around and left, but not without carting off

Lady's personal computer. The drive had already been wiped. Still, the technicians were able to recover some very interesting files.

There were some photographs of Abu Omar taken a month before the snatch in Via Guerzoni. There was an airline reservation for a flight from Zurich to Cairo (Omar's ultimate destination after his kidnapping), and driving directions from Milan to the military base at Aviano (where Omar was interrogated before his flight to Egypt). Best of all, there was an email that Lady had received on December 24, 2004.

It had been sent by one Susan Czaka, probably the pseudonym of another CIA agent. The woman told the former CIA station chief that she had "received a warning" about the public prosecutor's investigation, and advised Lady to stay out of Italy. Offering any possible assistance, she added: "I was really worried that you were sitting in some Italian prison cell." This was simply an affectionate touch. As the correspondent explained, Sabrina De Sousa—one of the agents who had participated in the kidnapping—had already informed her through an intermediary that the "chief" was in Geneva. So Lady knew about the Milanese probe *before* that date. Somebody had tipped him off: somebody who didn't want a single one of the 22 culprits to end up in front of an Italian tribunal.

The unanswered questions go on and on. After the 22 arrest warrants were issued, Washington (with the full complicity of Italy's minister of justice, Roberto Castelli) refused to extradite the CIA agents.* Again, it's hard not to suspect that the Italian government gave at least a tacit blessing to the American operation. And this conviction only grows when we take a look at the memo that Robert

---

* In November 2005, the minister of justice, having just returned from a series of meetings in Washington, announced that he would not transmit the extradition requests issued by the Public Prosecutor of Milan for the 22 CIA agents. Castelli argued that the investigation in Milan was tainted by "political prejudice."

Seldon Lady wrote from his exile in Geneva, passing it along to Armando Spataro by means of his Milanese attorney, Daria Pesce.

His argument was relatively straightforward.

First: In February 2003, Lady's purpose in Milan was no secret to the local authorities. He worked out of the American Consulate, and the government, the local judiciary, and the police all knew what he was doing there. "Thanks to a number of previous reports," we read, "the DIGOS branch in Milan was perfectly aware of the job he was carrying out in Italy." Lady was functioning as Langley's eyes and ears in the city. He was also a linchpin in the ongoing investigations of Al Qaeda and the Islamic centers on Viale Jenner and Via Quaranta.

Second: Abu Omar was being investigated by the Public Prosecutor of Milan because he was suspected of belonging to an Al Qaeda cell.

Third: When it came to the kidnapping, "Lady did not act out of private conviction, but for reasons connected to his official, clandestine role" as CIA station chief. The conclusion? "In carrying out his mission, Signor Lady undoubtedly enjoyed the full support of the U.S. government, acting in concert with the Italian political authorities." The station chief had been given "an explicit or at least implicit authorization by the Italian government." Even the photos of Abu Omar found on his personal computer had not been taken by the CIA, argued Lady. It was the Italian security services that had photographed the suspect "in the course of their preventive activities."

It was a substantial argument, and a damning one. Yet it bounced right off the wall erected by the government, as did the indisputable facts documented by Armando Spataro's investigations. Meanwhile, the chatty atmosphere over at the Chigi Palace had evaporated. Berlusconi was in an embarrassing fix: He needed to say something, but whatever he said would be violently refuted in the blink of an eye. His only option was the usual, apodictic denial, repeated in communiqués that even the American press understood to be worthless.

"The Italian government was never aware of Abu Omar's kidnapping, neither before nor after it took place," insisted Berlusconi. He said nothing about the facts. Nor did anybody else. Gianni Letta, the politician who supervised intelligence oversight, was silent. So was the minister of foreign affairs. The ministers of defense and the interior also kept their own counsel. Only Berlusconi stuck to his guns, firing off the same noisy, reckless denial, which nobody in Washington believed for a second. Over and over he said: "The CIA did not conduct any operations on Italian soil."

CHAPTER FIVE

A STRANGE MEETING

In the autumn of 2001, Rome was crawling with spies, military insiders, scientific consultants, diplomats of every stripe, and foreign ministers. One day in October 2001, the Italian minister of defense, Antonio Martino, summoned SISMI director Nicolò Pollari. He informed him of the arrival of an "American friend," an old acquaintance of Italian intelligence from the eighties.

His name was Michael Arthur Ledeen, and he was in Rome to deal with some matters on behalf of the Pentagon. SISMI would need to help him. Set up meetings. Listen to what he needed. Support his mission and protect him, above all, from meddlers.

"It's better if you talk face to face. Ledeen will call you." That's how Martino wrapped up the brief conversation.

Pollari decided that this visitor from Washington represented a solid opportunity. Ledeen was an alternate channel, which could allow the SISMI director to sidestep his official "interface" with the CIA. True, the whole business had a whiff of eccentricity. Perhaps this sprang from questions about Ledeen's past. However, whatever doubts existed about this new relationship, there was also a flip side. Ledeen would open a conduit to the Americans. Through it,

Pollari's agency could pass along reports, strategies, discoveries, contacts, all of it earning brownie points with the Americans and perhaps thrusting Italian intelligence to the very center of the Great Game. Pollari was overjoyed. If you had just become the director of SISMI, the return of Michael Ledeen seemed like a very lucky event indeed.

MICHAEL LEDEEN has many faces. None of the many formulas that might define him can possibly capture his—let's call it—*verve*. He's been described as a professor, for example—but that seems like a narrow, rather minimalist term for a guy like Ledeen, who's been variously identified as a journalist, analyst, Italianist, political scientist, consultant, insider, and researcher. (He's also been called a "schemer," an "agent of influence," and a "wirepuller and maestro of disinformation.") In the end, every definition seems to fall by the wayside. Yet there is an air of conjecture about his life. It's impossible to overlook—a kind of magic. He's always in the right place at the right time.

Ledeen was born in 1941. He graduated from the University of Wisconsin with a degree in Modern European History and was later appointed a visiting professor at the University of Rome. In 1978, when the kidnapping of Aldo Moro—a five-time prime minister of Italy—plunged the Italian government into crisis, Ledeen was on the scene, as part of a wonkish unit convened by Francesco Cossiga, who was soon to become prime minister. Two or three years later, Ledeen was coaching SISMI officials on how to battle terrorist attacks (he called these sessions *crisis management games*).

During the same period, Ledeen was in Rome to assemble a dossier on the Libyan travels of Billy Carter, the brother of Democratic president Jimmy Carter. He accomplished the latter task with the help of Francesco Pazienza, an operative with connections to the highest levels of SISMI, and with technical support (recording, elimination of background noise, money for the acquisition of compromising photos) from the famed P2 wing of SISMI.* His scoop, which he published in *The New Republic*, was fairly damning: Qaddafi had sent the zany presidential sibling $50,000 to smooth U.S.-Libyan relations. Ledeen's story also made a dent in the support the Democrats customarily enjoyed from the Jewish community and the state of New York, thereby contributing to Ronald Reagan's defeat of Jimmy Carter.

In 1981, Ledeen was in Uruguay, on behalf of Alexander Haig's State Department, negotiating with the Montevideo government to recover photocopies of Licio Gelli's papers. In May of that same year, when Mehmet Ali Agca shot and wounded Pope John Paul II, Ledeen was at the Center for Strategic and International Studies in Washington. There he lost no time in asserting the "Bulgarian connection"—which claimed that Agca was an agent of the Bulgarian government, and, by extension, the KGB—to explain who had armed and indoctrinated the assassin. Two years later Ledeen was in Grenada: The White House had asked him to rummage through the archives of the deposed Marxist regime to find retroactive justifications for the invasion.

On October 11, 1985, when the *Achille Lauro* hijackers were forced to land at an Italian air force base in Sicily, Ledeen was on the phone at the White House, translating Italian Prime Minister Bettino Craxi's statements for Reagan.

Given his tendency to put in an elusive appearance wherever something is happening or about to happen, it's no surprise that legends and fables and intrigues have flourished around Michael

---

* Francesco Pazienza is probably the best known of the Italian wheeler-dealers, with close ties to the notorious P2 Lodge. He was also on amicable terms with General Giuseppe Santovito, former director of SISMI, for whom he worked during the era when Michael Ledeen first came on the scene. Pazienza is currently in prison.

Ledeen. One such legend calls him "an agent of the Mossad," even though his only official, verifiable relationship with the government in Tel Aviv has been a short stint coaching the Israeli bridge team.

Rather than pursuing Ledeen down these twisting paths, it makes sense to stick to the facts that have been confirmed by such qualified sources as Fulvio Martini, Federico Umberto d'Amato, Richard Gardner, and Noel Koch. Even better, many of these statements are part of the official record. For example, Admiral Martini, a former director of SISMI, recounted the following to a parliamentary hearing:

> I asked the American ambassador to keep Mike Ledeen
> out of Italy. He was a guy who worked on the fringes of
> the CIA. When Ledeen came to Italy, he went directly
> to the president [Francesco Cossiga], who he had known
> when [Cossiga] was Minister of the Interior. And I didn't
> like that. Because Ledeen had been paid $100,000 by
> one of my predecessors to put together a conference
> on terrorism. Those were absolutely wasted dollars.

Federico Umberto d'Amato, head of special intelligence branch called the Ufficio Affari Riservati, discussed Ledeen in his testimony before a parliamentary commission on the Italian P2 scandal:

> After the American election in '80, we observed a
> strange, mirror-like phenomenon. Somehow, the relations
> between Italian politicians and the new group in power in
> Washington were controlled by the Ledeen-Pazienza duo.
> The American embassy in Rome was inactive, and so was
> the CIA. There were trips back and forth organized by
> Pazienza and Ledeen, who was said to be (and I believe he
> was) an adviser to the Secretary of State, Alexander Haig.

Richard Gardner, American ambassador to Rome during the Carter years, recalls:

> D'Amato was right. Those two, Pazienza and Ledeen, were very active. They kept behaving as if *they* were the embassy, which created huge problems. We thought of them as freelancers with dubious credentials. I don't know to what degree their activities were self-promoting or authorized.

Finally, Noel Koch, a former Pentagon official. Writing in *The Nation* in 1988, he noted: "During those years, the CIA station chief in Rome said that he considered Ledeen an agent of influence."

In light of these statements, we can sketch out a profile of Michael Ledeen's activities. He is a man who is entrusted with "institutional missions," even if he operates in territory not officially sanctioned by those institutions. He opens alternative or subterranean channels of diplomacy between governments. He influences trends. He manipulates information. He tinkers with opinions. He maintains a network of relationships. He organizes a consensus around his initiatives, which are the initiatives of the group in power that he represents. He steers public opinion and allied governments in particular directions, which are dictated (even if not explicitly) by the American administration.

This could be the very definition of a spy, of an agent of influence, of an opinion maker or a spin doctor. At this point it hardly matters. It's the job that Michael Ledeen performed in Italy during the late 1970s and throughout the 1980s. And now he has returned—a figure warmly welcomed by the Italian government, endorsed by the Pentagon and accredited by the Italian minister of defense.

Ledeen is no lone wolf, by the way. However stubborn he may be, he bats for the neoconservative team—the biggest political innovation of George W. Bush's presidency, and a group with a messianic faith in its own actions. These gentlemen share a sense of mission that is, in some cases, greater than the actual desire for power. Protected by Vice President Cheney, the neoconservatives believe that the ends justify almost any means because they are doing the right thing.

"The United States represents an idea," wrote Ledeen in a 1996 *Weekly Standard* article. "Our national interest cannot be defined in purely geopolitical terms, because in reality, we pursue the affirmation of ideals, and therefore our foreign policy must be ideological, designed to advance the cause of liberty."

The bylines that appeared in *The Weekly Standard* during those years anticipated the roster of George W. Bush's first foreign policy team: Paul Wolfowitz, number two at the Pentagon; Zalmay Khalizad, who would be the nation's "special envoy" in Iraq and Afghanistan; Donald Rumsfeld, secretary of defense; Richard Armitage, deputy secretary of state; John Bolton, already undersecretary of state for arms control and international security, and subsequently ambassador to the United Nations; Douglas Feith, undersecretary of defense for policy; and Dov Zakheim, undersecretary for defense and comptroller. But it was in that neoconservative rumpus room called the American Enterprise Institute that Ledeen found the combative team of his dreams. It was a group of hardliners, rough-and-ready hawks, aggressive and blunt to the point of unpleasantness. A few names: Richard Perle, Reuel Marc Gerecht, Jeane Kirkpatrick, Michael Novak, David Frum, Laurie Mylroie, Lynne Cheney, Michael Rubin.

ANTONIO MARRAPESE says that if you want to know what's going on in Rome—or what's about to go on—all you need to do is wrap a soft towel around your hips and slip into the Turkish bath at the Hotel de Russie on Via del Babuino. This is a *must* for the heavy hitters, or for those with any ambitions to become one.

This Marrapese—a slightly puffy man in his forties, with a perennial smile and guarded eyes—is in the security business. "I protect people's privacy," he tell us. He hires bodyguards. He organizes security escorts. His company, the Defense Security Training Service Corporation (DSTS)—which has offices in Rome, Panama City, and Miami—also does business overseas, and this has spread the rumor that Marrapese recruits and "exports" mercenaries. When it comes up that Salvatore Stefio, kidnapped in Baghdad with three other Italian bodyguards, worked for Marrapese in Nigeria, his voice seems on the verge of exploding: "We have 400 workers and 30 trainers in Panama. We have a presence in Colombia, in the United States. We've worked in Liberia as well as Nigeria. Mercenaries? Don't even joke about it, boys! Defense Security is the world's fifth-largest company in the sector. And we deserve respect, not suspicion."

On, therefore, to the Hotel de Russie. Marrapese seems to be at home there. He wanders into the hotel bar and gazes at the spectacle.

He's silent for a bit, to heighten the anticipation of his listener. He chuckles to himself, as if he were watching a particularly good film. Then he speaks: "Mike Ledeen stops by whenever he's in Rome. He visits the Turkish bath, but never for too long, since he has low blood pressure. Ten minutes on the treadmill. A massage, energetic and relaxing. A very dry Martini at the bar. They know how to make them at *de Russie*. While he's kicking back, Mike talks—he lights his strong Cohiba and chats away."

As far as we can tell, Marrapese does outsourcing for intelligence agencies (or so he would have us believe). What the agencies have no wish to do, or simply *can't* do, he does for them. On a contract basis.

In the fall of 2001, however, it wasn't SISMI asking him for a "favor." No, insists Marrapese, it was Ledeen in person. There was supposed to be a meeting in Rome, very soon. The participants would require protection. No snoops behind the door. No microphones under the table. No Peeping Toms to photograph the arrivals. No intruders disguised as waiters. In short, the usual job—but it needed to be performed in an impeccable manner, because this was a vitally important meeting. Ledeen hired DSTS, says Marrapese, "on behalf of the American Enterprise Institute."

Marrapese continues: "For that business I was paid by a travel agency in Miami, but I knew that I was working for the AEI and the United States government. It was a three-day meeting: November 6, 7, and 8. The location was the Parco dei Principi in Rome. I assigned 15 men to take care of the meetings and sweep the room, which was big enough to accommodate 24 people."

The Hotel Parco dei Principi, where this private room was located, is on Via Gerolamo Frescobaldi, in the Parioli neighborhood. It was essential that the participants be able to reach the room without crossing through the hotel's main lobby. Otherwise, there would be too many indiscreet glances. Too great a chance that the very people they wished to avoid would, by an unlucky accident, be in the lobby. So the guests—20 people all told—entered the hotel from a side door on Via Mercadante, and proceeded from there directly to the basement, where, to the right of the elevators, they found the meeting room. (Recent renovations have now transformed it into a fitness center.)

Let's see who's sitting around the table.

There are Lawrence Franklin and Harold Rhode, officials from the Pentagon. Franklin is a former Defense Intelligence Agency agent. Rhode is an Office of Special Plans kingpin—an assistant to Doug Feith and, according to Paul Wolfowitz, an "adviser for Islamic affairs." Naturally there is Mike Ledeen. And there is Manucher Ghorbanifar. This ambiguous figure may be called the promoter of the meeting.

Iranian by birth, a resident (as far as anybody knows) of Paris and Geneva, Ghorbanifar has a less-than-spotless reputation. For some, he is an arms trafficker. For others, a counterfeiter. For the civilian arm of Italian intelligence, a secret agent on behalf of Tehran. For the Americans, a Mossad agent. For still others, all of these things at once.

Much of Ghorbanifar's life is truly a mystery. There is, however, one solid fact: He helped Michael Ledeen launch that tangled mess called the Iran-Contra Affair, which promised weapons to Tehran in exchange for money to finance the anti-Sandinista guerillas in Nicaragua. Luckily for Reagan, the fallout from the scandal stopped at the NSC, bringing down only Robert MacFarlane, Oliver North, and a few others.

The hell unleashed by the attacks on September 11 had put Ghorbanifar back on track. He called his friend Mike from Paris. He told Ledeen that he was willing to put together a meeting with some Iranian exiles who were eager to help overturn the regime of the ayatollahs. Ledeen reputedly asked him if he was out of his mind.* What was he talking about? Then, according to the "official" version, he agreed. What possible harm could it do for him to "take a peek"?

It was the autumn of 2001. Even the invasion of Afghanistan was still in the future. Nobody (except those in the most secluded chambers of the White House) was explicitly discussing a war with Iraq. And Iran was even further beneath the radar. Why, then, did two eggheads from the Pentagon's OSP leave Washington to meet with an infamous troublemaker like Ghorbanifar in Rome?

---

* This reconstruction of the meeting can be found in a SISMI document entitled "Confidential Meetings between the Pentagon and Iranian Dissidents to Obtain Information on the Alleged Links to Al Qaeda and On the Role Played by Various Middle Eastern Governments in Relation to International Terrorism." The document was shown to the authors by SISMI director Nicolò Pollari.

Speaking to *Il Foglio* in December 2003, Ledeen declared that "thanks to these conversations, we obtained information that saved many soldiers in Afghanistan."

This reconstruction of events must have at least a few holes in it, since Donald Rumsfeld, in Rome for a few days himself at the same time, commented that the meeting had not produced the results they had hoped for and that he and his staff had not attended it. Or so he informed Stephen Hadley, then deputy national security adviser, and the State Department.

A few important points worth noting.

The meetings had not produced the results they had hoped for. We're not talking, then, about saving lives. If this had been the outcome of the meeting in Rome, if it had saved some lives in Afghanistan, then the cynical but patriotic Rumsfeld would have been less dismissive.

A second detail. Neither Colin Powell nor George Tenet nor the national security adviser, Condoleezza Rice, had been told about the secret meeting—they were informed only afterwards, about specific actions that were taken. Clearly something was going on.

An intelligence operation was being developed in Rome, concealed from the CIA and the State Department, approved by the Pentagon's OSP, organized by the American Enterprise Institute, conducted with such entirely discredited figures as Manucher Ghorbanifar. And with who else?

It's hard to figure out whether this Marrapese is indulging in pure fantasy or whether there's an element of hard truth to his statements. What he says about the other participants at the Parco dei Principi meeting, however, is at least partially confirmed by Nicolò Pollari.

Marrapese recalls: "On the big table in the private room of the hotel, there were detailed maps of Iraq, Iran, Syria. And along with the Americans, there was also an Iranian (no, not Ghorbanifar, another Iranian) and an Israeli and two Italians: a balding man, 46 or maybe 48 years old, wearing a checked jacket and dark pants, and a younger guy, 38 or so, with braces on his teeth."

Says Pollari: "I wasn't born yesterday. When the minister asked me to set up that meeting, I got curious: That's my job, you understand? So I sent a couple of my men to the meeting, which wasn't held at the Parco dei Principi but in an apartment leased by the agency near the Spanish Steps. The Farsi interpreter was one of my guys, and so was his assistant. I wanted to know what they were cooking up there. What they were preparing…. Yes, there were maps of Iraq and Iran on the table."

Regarding Ghorbanifar's presence at the meeting in Rome, the accounts given by the protagonists are contradictory. According to Michael Ledeen, Ghorbanifar "was present." Pollari takes the opposite tack: "Ghorbanifar wasn't there. And I can say that the Iranians at the meeting had no idea who he was, to the point that we actually had to spell out his name."

Antonio Marrapese insists that "there were two other meetings." The authors are unable to confirm this assertion. It should also be noted that according to Marrapese, the original meeting took place in early November 2001, while American sources (including at least one of the participants, Michael Ledeen), state that it was in December of the same year.

One other thing: In early 2002, Nicolò Pollari informed George Tenet that Michael Ledeen, under the aegis of the Italian Ministry of Defense, had come to Rome with some Pentagon officials to meet with "strange Iranian exiles." The SISMI director, according to an on-the-record interview with the authors, added that the Iranians could "hardly have been genuine exiles, since they come and go from Tehran brandishing their passports and without any difficulty, almost as if they were transparent to the eyes of the Pasdaran." The Pasdaran is the Iranian national security agency.

Passing on this information to Langley and to the State Department enabled Pollari to keep playing a double game, at home and abroad. In Italy, he could play the Farnesina Palace against the Ministry of Defense. In Washington, he could play State Department

against the Pentagon, the CIA against the Office of Specials Plans.
It was best to remain on the fence, poised between two opposing
policies—between those who wished to peacefully pressure Saddam
into exile, and those who wished to remove him by force.

LET'S INTRODUCE a final name: Haras Habib Karim. A credible State
Department source suggests: "If you know about Haras Habib
Karim, you can figure out the whole thing. Karim is one of the
Pentagon's prime assets, and even Pollari was hoping to notch a few
points with his help."

Who on earth is this guy? He's certainly an unknown figure in
Italy. Yet he seems crucial to the cosy entente between the Italian
government, the Pentagon, the AEI, and the mysterious Iranians
who popped up for those meetings in Rome. To pull this thread
out of the tangle, we must listen to a CIA "insider" about Ahmed
Chalabi. The source, who asked to remain anonymous, says: "In
Italy you have always underestimated Ahmed Chalabi's level of
toxicity. You tend to omit this chapter from your story because you
think Ahmed was our business. But he was your business, too, more
than you have imagined. As everybody knows, Chalabi was selected
by the Pentagon hawks to convey information obtained from alleged
scientists who had deserted the Iraqi regime."

The source continues: "The person in charge of gathering
the information was Haras Habib Karim, the head of Chalabi's
intelligence. Karim was a key player. He coordinated the Intelligence
Collection Program. He processed and manipulated the 'product.'
Now, Karim is a Shiite Kurd, just under 40 years old. He lives in
Mosul, and he's very shrewd, very nasty, a wizard at duplicity and
faking documents. He has, however, one peculiarity: He has always
been an Iranian agent."

Finally, the source says: "The second key player was an American,
Francis Brooke. For some reason, the fake Italian dossier on the

uranium sale got into his hands.* Brooke has ties to Condoleezza
Rice, Paul Wolfowitz, the Pentagon. As Chalabi's right-hand man,
he was highly regarded in Tehran. All of these guys—Chalabi
and Karim and Brooke—worked elbow to elbow with the Iranian
Pasdaran. They were the front line, the Dirty Dozen."

Let's recall once again who we know attended the meetings in
Rome. There was Michael Ledeen of the AEI. There was Larry
Franklin and Harold Rhode of the OSP.** There were also the
Iranian guests, who are actually, Pollari tells us, representatives from
the Iraqi Shiites of the Supreme Council for Islamic Revolution in
Iraq (SCIRI), who appear in Rome, again according to Pollari, with
the knowledge of the Pasdaran—the so-called "Guardians of the
Revolution."

The SCIRI organization was founded in Tehran in 1982 by
the Ayatollah Mohammed Baqir al-Hakim. At first, its goal was to
topple Saddam Hussein and create an Islamic republic along the
lines of Iran. But al-Hakim eventually put his dream of Islamic

---

* Francis Brooke confirmed, in a conversation with the authors in November 2005,
that he heard of the Nigerien dossier in January 2003. He recounts: "We must
have learned about the existence and contents of those papers in January 2003.
From who? I can't recall precisely. You're asking too much! Anyway, soon other
people mentioned the dossier to me. During those weeks in Washington, it was a
kind of recurrent piece of gossip. Did the DIA talk to me about it? I don't know....
Frankly, I don't even remember if I saw the papers. Certainly I was told about
what they contained. And we concluded that the dossier was garbage. As you
know, I was convinced (and am still convinced today) that Saddam had weapons of
mass destruction. But this was the first that our intelligence agencies heard about
a yellowcake deal between Iraq and Niger. Who did we tell that the papers were
junk? Certainly I spoke about it with people at the National Security Council and
the State Department."

** On January 20, 2006, Air Force Reserve Colonel (and DIA analyst) Lawrence
Franklin was sentenced to 151 months in jail for passing for information about
U.S. policy toward Iran to Israel via the American Israeli Public Affairs Committee
(AIPAC).

revolution on hold and limited the organization's scope to regime change in Baghdad and the unification of all Iraqi Shiite parties in exile. At the beginning of the war in Iraq, the ayatollah pledged himself to "the creation of a civil society that accepts the existence of pluralist political structures, a quasi-independent press, and free elections." Yet the Supreme Council's essential goal never changed: After centuries of persecution, al-Hakim meant to win the Shiites the clout they deserved as the most populous sect in Iraq.

Our sources tell us that the Iranian situation, at the time of the Rome meeting, was this: The Iranians knew that it would be a simple matter for the ayatollahs to cause major chaos before, during, and after a U.S. invasion of Iraq. After all, 65 percent of all Iraqis were Shiites, and that gave the Iranians enormous leverage when it came to their neighbor. With the grudging approval of the Americans, Tehran ultimately opted for "a reasonable guarantee of Iranian strategic interests in the area," and for a political and institutional future in Iraq that would favor the Shiites. Of course, the ayatollahs already hated Saddam, whose decade-long territorial war had decimated an entire generation of young Iranians. But now they found an additional reason to hasten the dictator's exit. An Iraq liberated from Sunni domination would give more political clout to Tehran. Perhaps it would even put the exiled Iraqi Ayatollah Muhammad Baqir al-Sadr—who was supported and protected in Iran, along with his substantial military arm, the Badr Brigades—in the driver's seat. Regime change was looking better all the time.

It was no wonder, then, that Chalabi's team had been greeted in Tehran with the dignity reserved for a diplomatic mission. In a November 2005 conversation with us, Francis Brooke recalls:

> It's true, I was in Tehran in late January 2003. War was imminent, and I flew to Turkey. I met Chalabi, and at four o'clock in the morning we drove across the Iranian border at a

frontier village called, if I remember correctly, Hagamaram. It
wasn't easy. The Turkish border was sealed, and we had to ask
the Americans for help. They took us under their protection
and we drove for another couple of hours, until we reached
a small airport where a plane was waiting: It was owned
by Caspian Air, a company used by Iranian intelligence.
Upon arrival at the Tehran airport, we were met
by a procession of cars from the Ministry for Home
Affairs. We didn't go through any frontier formalities.
I was received as a "non-person." I was viewed as Dr.
Chalabi's right-hand man. Nobody asked for my passport.
Nobody gave me a visa. We were taken to an apartment
north of the city, in the diplomatic neighborhood. A
nice place, where we stayed for a couple of days.
Chalabi and I met all the people it was logical to meet. The
Iranian president, the prime minister, the national security
adviser. The trip was no big secret: It was covered in the
Iranian press, and I even gave an interview. What did we
talk about? The Iranians were afraid the Americans were
preparing a military invasion of Iran, too. We reassured
them. We explained the general feeling in Washington,
and pointed out that America couldn't sustain a three-
front war in any case. Was there anything else? Yes.
We compared their intelligence with ours (meaning
the INC's). We exchanged information on the combat
resources of the Iraqi armed forces: divisions, artillery,
tanks. We were flattered, because our intelligence and
theirs concurred. And as I said before, there was nothing
better on the eve of war than Iranian intelligence.

From this we can deduce how the whole carousel works: Haras
Habib Karim cobbles together the revelations of his Iraqi deserters.

The Iranians then offer the Pentagon a confirmation of these revelations, which has actually been concocted by Chalabi's group under the supervision of Tehran's secret service.

Thus, we can return one last time to the specifics of the meeting in Rome. What a lot of nonsense has been vented about this gathering: According to one source, its purpose was "to save human lives in Afghanistan." According to another, it was meant to identify "Iran's interests in Afghanistan." Last but not least, we've examined a SISMI document that gave an entirely different explanation, that the meeting was held to obtain information about alleged links between Al Qaeda and various Middle Eastern governments.

In each of these scenarios, the leading actor would seem to be Manucher Ghorbanifar. In reality, the Iranian is a minor character, a red herring. His sources tend to be dead ends. As our State Department friend tells us:

> Manucher Ghorbanifar offered a single source in London
> who could tell them where Saddam had hidden his
> stockpile of enriched uranium. Ledeen then embroidered
> the story. He reported that Iran, too, was trying to acquire
> this uranium, and that the radiation emitted by the stored
> material must certainly have contaminated some Iraqi
> technicians, whose identities were known. The question was
> batted back and forth between the CIA and the Pentagon,
> amid the usual doubts from Tenet. Then Ghorbanifar's
> London source was flown to Baghdad on the CIA's dime
> to lead us to the uranium. He spent a few days leading the
> Langley people on a wild goose chase. Then he suggested
> that $50,000 might refresh the memory of a few contacts
> in Baghdad. Naturally the CIA kicked him to the curb.

Let's forget about Manucher Ghorbanifar, then.

The true protagonists in Rome, we've learned, are actually the Iranian guests, who are not really deserters. The meeting at Parco dei Principi was actually convened to bring together SISMI, the Pentagon's OSP, and SCIRI. Together, the three groups attempt to make a sound assessment of Saddam's military arsenal and help to plan the impending invasion of Iraq. Francis Brooke, as well as he can, concurs: "We of the INC were not in Rome, but it is possible that SISMI organized that meeting to establish relations with the Iranians of SCIRI in anticipation of the war. One thing is certain. They talked about everything, except Afghanistan." Our American source provides a stronger confirmation of the usefulness of the meeting for all involved: "The Iranians are used to having bilateral intelligence relationships. So they don't tell others who they are working with. Nobody else knows. Having said this, I'll repeat that on the eve of war, the Iranians had the best military intelligence available about Saddam's Iraq. The role of SCIRI? If we're talking about military intelligence, SCIRI and the Teheran government are the same thing. The same eye and the same ear."

Thus, out of all of the confusion about the Rome meetings, a few important facts can be summarized. They show that representatives from the Iran's SCIRI consulted early with Pentagon hawks about the Iraq War. It is a fact made more important once it is understood that the Iranians—via the collaboration with Haras Habib Karim and Ahmed Chalabi—shared actual intelligence with the Americans.

Despite the fact that little more is certain, the Rome meetings remain important.

After all, the feasibility of the Pentagon's operational plans for military intervention in Iraq depended on the U.S. military being fed constant information from friendly intelligence services, Iran most especially. These updates were eventually collected by the unified Anglo-American command in real time, and processed and turned into orders for fighting units in Iraq.

Over the course of recent months, the facts set forth in these pages have been confirmed in significant ways.

In Rome, as in Washington, there has been a political changing of the guard. As a consequence, some of the key players in the events we have described (the "Nigergate" affair; the meetings in Rome between officials of the Pentagon's Office of Special Plans and Iranian envoys; the extraordinary rendition of the Egyptian imam Abu Omar) have lost their jobs. They were forced out by their very participation in these events, long denied or hidden behind an official smokescreen.

Nicolò Pollari, the director of SISMI, was fired on November 20, 2006. He is scheduled to appear before a tribunal in Milan on June 8, 2007. The charge is kidnapping: More specifically, Pollari will be tried for the extraordinary rendition of Abu Omar, along with 26 CIA agents and six high-ranking SISMI officials. He could serve a maximum sentence of 15 years in prison.

Larry Franklin, who spent two years working for the Pentagon's Office of Special Plans, was found guilty of passing classified information about Iran to the Israelis. For this crime a federal judge sentenced him to 151 months in prison and a $10,000 fine.

Ahmed Chalabi is struggling with a politically precarious climate in Baghdad, where he is a participant in Iraq's controversial Supreme National DeBaathification Commission. According to official sources, the FBI continues its investigation of his role as a suspected double agent working on behalf of Tehran.

And that's not all.

On March 6, 2007, Lewis "Scooter" Libby, former chief of staff for Vice President Dick Cheney, was found guilty of perjury and obstruction of justice. This verdict is already the subject of heated debate. But aside from its judicial outcome, the trial also documented in great detail the origins and political context of the "Nigergate" affair.

The Administration's secret documents, declassified and exhibited during the trial (three of them are reproduced here as an appendix), confirmed the central role of Cheney and of a certain "foreign intelligence agency" (SISMI) in propping up the yellowcake swindle. Why had the White House ordered the "character assassination" of Ambassador Joseph Wilson in the summer of 2003? As the testimony made clear, this was an obvious effort to dodge responsibility for the manipulation of prewar intelligence. Meanwhile, the procession of journalists summoned to testify about their encounters with key Administration officials—from Libby to Richard Armitage to Karl Rove—conveyed exactly how the relationship between information and power had been perverted during the War on Terror.

In Strasbourg, on February 14, 2006, the European Parliament approved (by a vote of 382 to 256, with 74 abstentions) the final report of an independent investigative commission, which had spent the last year documenting repeated violations of sovereignty by the United States in at least twelve EU nations. According to the report, between 2001 and 2005 the CIA had overseen 1,245 clandestine flights within European airspace. The agency had secretly transported at least 21 "prisoners" from Europe to Egypt, Guantánamo, and to detention centers in former Soviet bloc countries. The governments of Italy, Germany, Great Britain, Poland, Switzerland, Austria, Greece, Cyprus, Portugal, Spain, Denmark, and Romania were directly involved in these acts. And in the Parliament's view, they constituted an open violation of international law.

Bit by bit, we have discovered how the War on Terror has politicized intelligence and amplified a climate of absolute animosity. And yet: The disclosure of these acts does not in any way signify the defeat of the "project"—still driven by ideology and ambition—on whose behalf they were committed.

APPENDIX

What follows are three unclassified documents exhibited during the trial of Lewis Libby. All of them concern the "Nigergate" affair and give a first hand glimpse at what happened behind the walls of the Bush Administration.

I.

DX439: THE CIA'S MEMO ON "NIGERIEN DENIAL OF URANIUM YELLOWCAKE SALES, TO ROGUE STATES" MARCH 9, 2002.

II.

DX64: CIA FAX TO HANNAH AND LIBBY, JUNE 9, 2003.

III.

DX71: U.S. DEPARTMENT OF STATE MEMO BY CARL FORD TO MARC GROSSMAN, JUNE 10, 2003

DX439.1

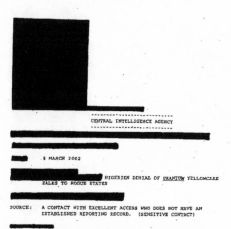

~~SECRET~~

CENTRAL INTELLIGENCE AGENCY

8 MARCH 2002

NIGERIEN DENIAL OF URANIUM YELLOWCAKE
SALES TO ROGUE STATES

SOURCE: A CONTACT WITH EXCELLENT ACCESS WHO DOES NOT HAVE AN
          ESTABLISHED REPORTING RECORD. (SENSITIVE CONTACT)

TEXT: 1. (HEADQUARTERS COMMENT: THE SUBSOURCES OF THE FOLLOWING
INFORMATION KNEW THEIR REMARKS COULD REACH THE U.S. GOVERNMENT AND
MAY HAVE INTENDED TO INFLUENCE AS WELL AS INFORM.) FORMER NIGERIEN
GOVERNMENT OFFICIALS CLAIMED THAT SINCE 1997 THERE HAD BEEN NO
CONTRACTS SIGNED BETWEEN NIGER AND ANY ROGUE STATES FOR THE SALE OF
URANIUM IN THE FORM OF YELLOWCAKE. THE FORMER OFFICIALS ALSO
ASSERTED THERE HAD BEEN NO TRANSFERS OF YELLOWCAKE TO ROGUE STATES.

          2. FORMER NIGERIEN PRIME MINISTER IBRAHIM ((MAYAKI)), WHO WAS
NIGER'S FOREIGN MINISTER FROM 1996-1997 AND NIGER'S PRIME MINISTER
FROM 1997-1999 AND WHO MAINTAINED CLOSE TIES TO THE CURRENT NIGERIEN
GOVERNMENT, STATED HE WAS UNAWARE OF ANY CONTRACTS BEING SIGNED
BETWEEN NIGER AND ROGUE STATES FOR THE SALE OF YELLOWCAKE DURING HIS
TENURE AS BOTH FOREIGN MINISTER AND PRIME MINISTER. MAYAKI, HOWEVER,
DID RELATE THAT IN JUNE 1999 BARKA ((TEFRIDJ)), A NIGERIEN/ALGERIAN
BUSINESSMAN, APPROACHED HIM AND INSISTED THAT MAYAKI MEET WITH AN
IRAQI DELEGATION TO DISCUSS "EXPANDING COMMERCIAL RELATIONS" BETWEEN
NIGER AND IRAQ. ALTHOUGH THE MEETING TOOK PLACE, MAYAKI LET THE
MATTER DROP DUE TO THE UNITED NATIONS (UN) SANCTIONS AGAINST IRAQ AND
THE FACT THAT HE OPPOSED DOING BUSINESS WITH IRAQ. MAYAKI SAID THAT
HE INTERPRETED THE PHRASE "EXPANDING COMMERCIAL RELATIONS" TO MEAN
THAT IRAQ WANTED TO DISCUSS URANIUM YELLOWCAKE SALES. MAYAKI SAID HE
UNDERSTOOD ROGUE STATES WOULD LIKE TO EXPLOIT NIGER'S RESOURCES,
SPECIFICALLY URANIUM, BUT HE BELIEVED THE NIGERIEN GOVERNMENT'S
REGARD FOR THE UNITED STATES (U.S.) AS A CLOSE ALLY WOULD PREVENT

001524

~~SECRET~~

DX439.2

~~SECRET~~

SALES TO THESE STATES FROM TAKING PLACE DESPITE *NIGER'S* ECONOMIC
WOES. MAYAKI CLAIMED THAT IF THERE HAD BEEN ANY CONTRACTS FOR
YELLOWCAKE BETWEEN *NIGER* AND ANY ROGUE STATE DURING HIS TENURE, HE
WOULD HAVE SEEN THE CONTRACT.

3. BOUCAR ((MAI MANGA)), *NIGER'S* FORMER MINISTER OF ENERGY AND
MINES UNTIL 9 APRIL 1999, A FORMER DIRECTOR OF THE NIGERIEN COMENAC
MINE AND CURRENTLY HONORARY PRESIDENT OF COMENAC, STATED THAT THERE
WERE NO SALES OUTSIDE OF INTERNATIONAL ATOMIC ENERGY AGENCY (IAEA)
CHANNELS SINCE THE MID-1990S. MAI MANGA SAID THAT HE KNEW OF NO
CONTRACTS SIGNED BETWEEN *NIGER* AND ANY ROGUE STATE FOR THE SALE OF
URANIUM. HE ADMITTED THAT YEARS AGO A PAKISTANI DELEGATION VISITED
NIGER AND OFFERED TO PURCHASE *URANIUM* BUT THAT NO SALES RESULTED FROM
THESE TALKS. MAI MANGA ALSO SAID THAT (FNU) ((BLASCHER)), THE FORMER
DIRECTOR GENERAL OF SOMAIR AND CURRENTLY A DIRECTOR AT COGEMA, CAME
TO HIM IN 1998 WITH AN IRANIAN DELEGATION TO DISCUSS BUYING 400 TONS
OF YELLOWCAKE FROM *NIGER*; HOWEVER, THE ONLY RESULT WAS A MEMORANDUM
OF CONVERSATION, WITH NO CONTRACT BEING SIGNED AND NO YELLOWCAKE
TRANSFERRED TO IRAN. MAI MANGA THEORIZED THAT *NIGER'S* MINES COULD
HAVE INCREASED PRODUCTION TO SUPPLY IRAN WITH THIS AMOUNT OF
YELLOWCAKE BUT THIS WOULD HAVE REQUIRED OPENING ADDITIONAL MINING
FACILITIES THAT HAVE BEEN MOTHBALLED FOR SEVERAL YEARS. MAI MANGA
THEREFORE CONCLUDED THAT A *SALE* TO A ROGUE STATE SUCH AS IRAN WOULD
HAVE BEEN DIFFICULT GIVEN THE NEED OPEN MORE FACILITIES. (SOURCE
COMMENT: MAI MANGA APPEARED TO REGRET THAT *NIGER* EVEN DISCUSSED
URANIUM SALES WITH IRAN IN LIGHT OF THE INTERNATIONAL PRESSURE THAT
RESULTED.)

4. MAI MANGA STATED THAT *URANIUM* FROM *NIGER'S* MINES IS VERY
TIGHTLY CONTROLLED AND ACCOUNTED FOR FROM THE TIME IT IS MINED UNTIL
THE TIME IS LOADED ONTO SHIPS AT THE PORT OF COTONOU, BENIN.
ACCORDING TO MAI MANGA, EVEN A KILOGRAM OF *URANIUM* WOULD BE NOTICED
MISSING AT THE MINES. ON-SITE STORAGE IS LIMITED AND HE SAID THAT
EACH SHIPMENT OF *URANIUM* IS UNDER ARMED MILITARY ESCORT FROM
THE TIME IT LEAVES ONE OF THE TWO NIGERIEN MINES UNTIL IT IS LOADED
ON TO A SHIP IN COTONOU. AIR TRANSPORT IS TOO EXPENSIVE TO SHIP
YELLOWCAKE AND TRUCKING BARRELS OF YELLOWCAKE NORTHWARD WOULD REQUIRE
AN EXPERIENCED GUIDE AND MANY ARMED GUARDS, DUE TO THE SHIFTING DUNES
AND BANDITS IN THAT REGION. MAI MANGA THEREFORE BELIEVED THAT IT
WOULD BE DIFFICULT, IF NOT IMPOSSIBLE, TO ARRANGE A SPECIAL SHIPMENT
OF *URANIUM* TO A PARIAH STATE GIVEN THESE STRICT CONTROLS AND THE
CLOSE MONITORING BY THE NIGERIEN GOVERNMENT AND THE TWO MINING
COMPANIES. MAI MANGA ALSO SAID THAT THE MINE AND YELLOWCAKE WORKERS
ARE TOLD THAT *URANIUM* IS DANGEROUS SO THEY DON'T KNOW HOW TO HANDLE
THE MATERIAL OUTSIDE OF THE STANDARD PROCEDURES.

5. MAI MANGA PROVIDED AN OVERVIEW OF THE TWO *URANIUM* MINES IN
NIGER, SOMAIR AND COMENAC. SOMAIR IS AN OPEN PIT MINE THAT PRODUCES
ROUGHLY 1000 TONS OF YELLOWCAKE PER YEAR. THIS HAS BEEN THE AMOUNT
PRODUCED FOR YEARS AT THIS MINE WHICH IS JOINTLY OWNED BY FRANCE AND
NIGER. COMENAC IS AN UNDERGROUND MINE THAT PRODUCES ROUGHLY 2000
TONS OF YELLOWCAKE PER YEAR. THIS MINE IS JOINTLY OWNED BY FRANCE,
JAPAN, SPAIN AND *NIGER*. IN THE EARLY 1980S THE COMBINED OUTPUT WAS
INCREASED FROM 3000 TONS TO NEARLY 4000 TONS OF YELLOWCAKE PER YEAR,
BUT PRODUCTION WAS CUT IN THE 1980S WHEN THE *URANIUM* PRICE FELL AND
SEVERAL YELLOWCAKE PRODUCTION LINES WERE MOTHBALLED AND HAVE YET TO
RESTART. *NIGER* DOES NOT TAKE ITS OWN PERCENTAGE OF THE PRODUCT; ALL
THE YELLOWCAKE IS SHIPPED TO FRANCE, JAPAN OR SPAIN. FRANCE'S COGEMA
OVERSEES THE PRODUCTION FROM BOTH MINES AND SETS THE PRODUCTION

001525

~~SECRET~~

DX439.3

SCHEDULE ALONG WITH THE MINE MANAGEMENT , FIRST FOR THE YEAR AND THEN
BREAKING THE PRODUCTION INTO MONTHLY TARGETS. PRODUCTION IS ADJUSTED
DEPENDING ON THE URANIUM YIELD FROM THE MINE ORE. ADDITIONALLY,
FRANCE CONTROLS THE FINANCIAL ASPECTS OF THE MINES BECAUSE URANIUM IS
PRICED IN U.S. DOLLARS ON THE WORLD MARKET, BUT NIGER'S CONTRACTS
WITH COGEMA ARE IN CFAS. WHEN THE CFA WAS DEVALUED, THIS EFFECTIVELY
CUT THE PRICE IN HALF--A CHRONIC SOURCE OF FRICTION BETWEEN FRANCE
AND NIGER.

DX64.1

FROM CIA OPS CENTER

SERRET
CLASSIFICATION

2003 JUN -9 FM 3:53

PROVISIONALLY
DECLASSIFIED

SITE 3
CIA
MESSAGE NUMBER
329

MONDAY
6-9-2003

TIME TRANSMITTED: 15:47   TIME RECEIVED:

FROM: Office/Desk: Phone:

SUBJECT: IRAQ - NIGER URANIUM (CONGRESSIONAL NOTIFICATION)

DELIVERY INSTRUCTIONS: Pages: 10
                                                       (Including Cover)

NOTE: FURNISH AFTER-DUTY-HOURS CONTACT TELEPHONE NUMBER FOR EACH
ADDRESSEE REQUIRING AFTER DUTY HOURS DELIVERY.

☒ IMMEDIATE / URGENT   * SIT ROOM *
☐ HOLD FOR NORMAL DUTY HOURS   CALL 6900
                                         FOR PICKUP
TRANSMITTED TO:

AGENCY	RECIPIENT	OFFICE / ROOM NUMBER	PHONE NUMBER / SECURE FAX
W.H. (VIA SIT ROOM)	JENNY MAYFIELD	V.P.s OFFICE Room 276	
	PLEASE PASS TO MR. HANNAH + MR. LIBBY		
	A.S.A.P.		

Remarks: 001472

WASHFAX COVER SHEET

SECRET
CLASSIFICATION

LL001-00499

LL001-00499

DX64.2

PROVISIONALLY
DECLASSIFIED

OCA 2003-1146
3 April 2003

Mr. Tim Sample
Staff Director
Permanent Select Committee
  on Intelligence
House of Representatives
Washington, D.C. 20515

Dear Tim:

SUBJECT: Notification

COUNTRY: Niger

ISSUE: ▮▮▮▮ Purported Iraqi Attempt to get Uranium from
       Niger

   (U) Enclosed is a background paper regarding the subject
mentioned above.

   (U) Should you have any questions regarding this matter,
please do not hesitate to call.

                    Sincerely,

                    Stanley M. Moskowitz
              Director of Congressional Affairs

Enclosure

001473

SECRET/

UNCLASSIFIED

DX64.3

CH 69

FROM CIA OPS. CENTER   (MON) 6. 9. 03 16:53:57.

SECRET

SUBJECT: Purported Iraqi attempt to get Uranium from
                    Niger

1.   Most agencies in the Intelligence Community
(IC) assess that multiple intelligence reports over the last few
years on Saddam's aggressive pursuit of aluminum tubes for
centrifuges, magnets, for centrifuge bearings, high-speed
balancing machines, and computer-controlled machine tools as well
as the reconsolidation of his cadre of nuclear technicians point
to ongoing reconstitution of his nuclear weapons program. In
addition to these reports, the IC received a number of reports
alleging that Iraq attempted to get uranium from several
countries. The reports on attempted uranium procurement were not
the essential elements underpinning our judgment that
reconstitution had begun. This point is underscored by the fact
that in more than a dozen briefings to Congress by senior
officials last fall, the uranium acquisition attempts were not
briefed. Because this issue has gained so much public attention,
especially after the IAEA's public announcement that the Niger
documents were forgeries, the chronology below lays out the key
events starting with the dissemination of the initial
report on the topic in October 2004.

2.   On 15 October 2001, the CIA's Directorate of
Operations issued a report
            that indicated as of early 2001; Niger planned to send
several tons of uranium to Iraq. The agreement for the sale of
uranium to Iraq reportedly was approved by the state court of
Niger in 2000.

3.   On 5 February 2002, the Directorate of
Operations issued a second report
            indicating Niger and Iraq had signed
an agreement regarding the sale of uranium in July 2000.

4.   In response to the Directorate of Operations'
report noted in paragraph three, CIA published a Senior Power
Executive Intelligence Brief (SPWR) on 14 February 2002 that
concluded, "Information on the alleged uranium contract between
Iraq and Niger comes exclusively from a foreign government
service report that lacks crucial details, and we are working to
clarify the information and to determine whether it can be
corroborated."

¹   The 14 February 2002 assessment erroneously stated the IAEA said Iraq already has some 150 tons of
yellowcake—200 tons of which were purchased in 1978 from Niger. The correct figures are 191.9 tonnes of

SECRET

001474

DX64.4

SECRET/

**PROVISIONALLY
DECLASSIFIED**

5.   ▮▮▮▮ In early March 2002, the Directorate of
Intelligence prepared an analytic update that reported on a
meeting between the U.S. Ambassador to Niger, the Deputy
Commander-in-Chief of the US European Command, and President
Tandja of Niger. The update noted that in this late February
2002 meeting, President Tandja indicated that Niger was making
all efforts to ensure that its uranium would be used only for
peaceful purposes. We also reported that President Tandja had
asked the US for unspecified assistance to ensure Niger's uranium
did not fall into the wrong hands. Our analytic update also
stated that we had requested additional information from the
▮▮▮▮▮▮ service that provided the original reporting on
this topic and that the service currently was unable to provide
new information.

6.   ▮▮▮ On 8 March 2002, the Directorate of Operations
disseminated information--obtained independently from a sensitive
source--that indicated a former Nigerien government official
claimed that since 1997, there had been no contracts signed
between Niger and any rogue states for the sale of uranium in the
form of yellowcake. While also asserting there had been no
transfers of yellowcake to rogue states, one subsource-a former
senior Nigerien official we are confident would have known of
uranium sales--also said that he believed Iraq was interested in
discussing yellowcake purchases when it sent a delegation to
Niamey in mid-1999. The Directorate of Operations collected this
information in an attempt to verify or refute ▮▮
▮▮ reporting on an alleged Iraq-Niger uranium deal. The
Directorate of Operations assesses their sensitive source to be
highly reliable ▮▮▮▮▮▮▮▮▮▮▮▮▮▮▮▮▮▮▮▮▮▮▮▮▮▮▮▮▮▮▮▮
▮▮▮▮▮▮▮▮▮▮▮▮▮▮▮▮▮▮▮▮▮▮▮▮▮▮▮▮▮▮▮▮▮▮. The
subsources, however, were described in the disseminated report as
knowing their remarks could reach the US Government and noted
these individuals may have intended their comments to influence
as well as inform.

---

uranium contained in 276.8 tonnes of uranium yellowcake, which were imported in the early 1980s. The precise
year of import of this material is in question as the IAEA indicates Iraq received 432 barrels of yellowcake (137,435
kgs total) from Niger in 1981. It also lists that in 1982, Iraq received another 426 barrels of the material (139,409
kgs total) from Niger, bringing the total to 276.8 tonnes. The Iraqi declaration from 7 December 2002, however,
indicates that two shipments of yellowcake occurred on 8 February 1981 and 18 March 1981. These are the same
dates noted by Iraq in one section of its 1998 "Full Final and Complete Declaration" on its nuclear program. These
discrepancies in dates have been flagged to the Department of State.

2

SECRET/

001475

DX64.5

SECRET

7. ▮▮▮▮ On 25 March 2002, the Directorate of Operations released the third and final report on the Iraq-Niger uranium issue ▮▮▮▮▮▮▮▮▮▮▮▮▮▮▮▮▮▮▮▮▮▮▮▮▮▮

8. ▮▮▮▮ On 24 September 2002, the British Government published a dossier titled "Iraq's Weapons of Mass Destruction," which stated that "there is intelligence that Iraq has sought the supply of significant quantities of uranium from Africa." CIA avoided making a similar reference in providing text for the U.S. White Paper entitled "Iraq's Weapons of Mass Destruction Programs" and expressed concerns about the credibility of the reporting to the British ▮▮▮▮▮▮▮▮▮ prior to publication of their assessment. ▮▮▮▮▮▮▮▮▮ prior to publication of the dossier, the British countered CIA concerns regarding credibility of the reporting by claiming they had corroborating evidence that Iraq sought uranium from Africa. This alleged corroborating information, however, was not shared with us. ▮▮▮▮▮▮▮▮▮▮▮▮▮▮▮▮

9. ▮▮▮▮▮▮▮▮▮▮▮▮▮▮▮▮▮▮▮▮▮▮▮▮▮▮ On 4 October 2002, while testifying before the Senate Select Committee on Intelligence, CIA officers were asked whether they agreed with the British dossier on Iraq's weapons programs. CIA's National Intelligence Officer for Strategic and Nuclear Programs referenced two points on which the US differed from the British: ▮▮▮▮▮▮▮▮▮▮▮▮

10. ▮▮▮▮ On 1 October 2002, the National Intelligence Estimate on Iraq's WMD program was published. It stated: "Iraq has about 550 metric tons of yellowcake and low-enriched uranium at Tuwaitha, which is inspected annually by the IAEA.. Iraq also began vigorously trying to procure uranium ore and yellowcake; acquiring either would shorten the time Baghdad needs to produce nuclear weapons. A foreign government service reported that as of early 2001, Niger planned to send several tons of 'pure uranium' (probably yellowcake) to Iraq. As of early 2001, Niger and Iraq reportedly were still working out arrangement for this deal, which could be for up to 500 tons of yellowcake. ▮▮▮▮ In an effort to include all information related to Iraq's nuclear-weapon program, reports of attempts to acquire uranium from abroad were included in the NIE, but not as one of the reasons that most agencies judged that

SECRET

001476

PROVISIONALLY
DECLASSIFIED

DX64.6

SECRET

Saddam was reconstituting his nuclear weapons program. In fact,
State/INR noted later in the document that "the claims of Iraqi
pursuit of natural uranium in Africa are, in INR's assessment,
highly dubious."

11. ███████ On 10 October 2002, Embassy Rome reported on a
meeting from the previous day with a journalist from the Italian
magazine *Panorama*. The journalist provided the Embassy with a
copy of documents alleging Iraq and Niger had reached an
agreement in July 2000 for the purchase of uranium. The
journalist identified her source as an Italian male who had
managed to obtain the documents in question and who was now
seeking 15,000 Euro in return for their publication. Embassy
Rome indicated that it had learned from CIA that the documents
provided by the journalist were the subject of the CIA report
issued on 5 February 2002, as described in paragraph three.
Embassy Rome shared copies of the documents ███████████████
███████████████ the Embassy forwarded the
documents through State Department channels to its Bureau of Non-
Proliferation (State/NP). The Directorate of Intelligence did
not request or place a high-priority on obtaining the actual
documents, at this time.

12. ███████ On 15 October 2002, an Intelligence Community
E-mail (ICE-mail) from the Bureau of Intelligence and Research at
the Department of State (State/INR) to CIA acknowledges receiving
the documents acquired by Embassy Rome and noted doubt about the
alleged uranium deal. State/INR also offered to provide copies
of the documents to CIA at a meeting of the interagency group
assigned to review nuclear export matters, occurring the next
day. The delivery did not occur, nor did CIA press State/INR for
the documents, for the same reasons articulated in paragraph
eleven.

13. ███████ On 13 November 2002, as part of a larger
briefing on the status of Iraq's nuclear weapons program, CIA
briefed ███████ "reporting on Iraqi attempts to procure
uranium from Africa are fragmentary, at best. We assess that
none of the deals have gone through, but it shows that Iraq is
probably trying to acquire uranium ore abroad." Two additional
points were provided which pointed to attempted uranium
procurement from the Democratic Republic of Congo (DROC).

14. ███████ On 22 November 2002, during a meeting at the
State Department (INR), French Ministry of Foreign Affairs
Director for Nonproliferation, Francois Richier, indicated France
had drawn no conclusion about Iraqi nuclear reconstitution; and
with one exception, the evidence available to France thus far was
"dual-use." However, there was one thing "nuclear," France had
information on an Iraqi attempt to buy uranium from Niger.
Richier said France had investigated and determined that no
uranium had been shipped. In response to a question from the

001477

SECRET

DX64.7

Exh. 64

(MON) 6. 9' 03 15:53 67

SECRET

Department of State as to whether France had confirmed that Iraq indeed had made this procurement attempt. Richier did not provide a direct response, but indicated that French officials believed this reporting to be true.

15. ██████ On 25 November 2002, the US Naval Criminal Investigation Service in Marseille, France reported information from two of its sources who claimed that a large quantity of uranium was currently stored in barrels at the Port of Cotonou, Benin and that Niger's President had sold this material to Iraq.

16. ██████ On 19 December 2002, the State Department, released a fact sheet illustrating omissions from the Iraqi declaration to the UN Security Council, prepared by State/NP. Under the nuclear weapons section it stated, "The declaration ignores efforts to procure uranium from Niger. Why is the Iraqi regime hiding their uranium procurement?" During coordination, CIA confirmed that of all the reported incidences of Iraqi efforts to acquire uranium from abroad since 1991, we had the most information concerning the alleged deal with Niger, yet still considered the overall reporting as fragmentary. That day, the Weapons center for Intelligence, Non-Proliferation, and Arms Control (WINPAC) in the Directorate of Intelligence recommended that Niger not be mentioned, but according to the State officer who drafted the fact sheet, our comments were not obtained in time to correct the listing on the State Department web site. The information was acted on in time, however, to remove it from Ambassador Negroponte's statement.

17. ██████ a 6 January 2003 ██████ IAEA's Iraq Nuclear Verification Office (INVO), INVO. Director Jacques Baute raised the issue of uranium procurement attempts from Niger and requested that the U.S. provide any additional details regarding this supposed transaction. Baute added that INVO had not been provided with any particular details and, as in the past, asked for whatever information we could provide, however limited. In response, ██████ began to review the reporting and analysis concerning the suspect Iraq-Niger Agreement ██████

18. ██████ State/INR sent CIA two ICE-mail messages—one on 12 January and another on 13 January 2003—that expressed concerns that the documents pertaining to the Iraq-Niger deal were forgeries. In response, the WINPAC officer conducting a review of this issue discovered that CIA did not have a copy of those documents. The officer took steps to obtain the original ██████ documents from State/INR, which occurred within days.

────────────

██████ CIA received this information from the US Navy through standard military/attaché channels, i.e., HR-series reporting.

001478

SECRET/ ██████

5

DX64.8

SECRET

19. ██████ A 17 January 2003 SPWR prepared in response to a request for additional evidence of Iraq's nuclear weapons program noted "Fragmentary.reporting on Iraqi attempts to procure uranium from various countries in Africa in the past several years is another sign of reconstitution. Iraq has no legitimate use for uranium." Although CIA was re-examining this issue, this "assessment reflected an extension of its previous analyses, because new data—such as a translation of the documents—had not yet arrived.

20. ██████ In a 20 January 2003 ██████ State/INR proposed adding points to the information ██████ to be shared ██████ on the Iraq-Niger uranium.issue. . The State/INR proposed talking points included details such as how the documents were acquired, but did not include any judgments concerning the authenticity of the documents. In the same message, State/INR also advocated that the actual documents obtained from Embassy Rome be passed to INVO. An exchange of ██████ messages over the next few days shows ██████ attempted to honor the State/INR requests. State/INR concurred in the final version of the talking points ██████ which are described in more detail in paragraph twenty-five.

21. ██████ January 2003, ██████ issued a report ██████ that noted that the presence of uranium is common in the port of Cotonou, Benin, as this is the terminus of the normal shipping route from Niger. ██████ claimed ██████ information related to discussions between Iraq and Niger dating from 1999 on a proposal to ship uranium.

22. ██████████████████████████████

23. ██████ On 29 January 2003, the President noted in the State of the Union address that, "…the British government has learned that Saddam Hussein recently sought significant quantities of uranium from Africa."

24. ██████ On 4 February 2003, a note from CIA/WINPAC.was sent to ██████ at the US Mission to the IAEA in Vienna and the United Nations Monitoring, Verification, and Inspection Commission (UNMOVIC) office in New York. The note contained copies of the original language documents obtained.by Embassy Rome. Instructions in that note indicated the

001479

SECRET 6

DX64.9

Exh 64

FROM CIA OPS CENTER   (MON): 5. 9' 05 15:153' 8

SECRET//

information could be passed to IAEA/INVO's Baute, which was
interpreted as permission to pass the original documents. As a
result, the original documents were passed to UNMOVIC who passed
them to INVO.

25. ▮▮▮▮ On 4-5 February 2003, the U.S. briefed INVO in
response to Baute's request from 6 January for information on the
alleged Iraq-Niger uranium agreement. Members of the US Mission
to the IAEA in Vienna presented the information and analyses as
compiled by CIA. This Intelligence Community-cleared briefing
indicated, "Two streams of reporting suggest Iraq has attempted
to acquire uranium from Niger. We cannot confirm these reports
and have questions regarding some specific claims. Nonetheless,
we are concerned that these reports may indicate Baghdad has
attempted to secure an unreported source of uranium yellowcake
for a nuclear weapons program." The two streams of reporting
referred to in this briefing came from the sensitive source
discussed in paragraph six of this notification.

26. ▮▮▮▮ During Secretary Powell's briefing to the UN
Security Council on 5 February 2003, he did not mention attempted
Iraqi procurement of uranium due to CIA concerns raised during
coordination regarding the veracity of the information on the
alleged Iraq-Niger Agreement.

27. ▮▮▮▮ CIA/WINPAC received the translated documents
from the State Department on 7 February 2003. A preliminary
examination of the document confirmed the identities of a key
Iraqi ▮▮▮▮▮▮▮▮▮▮ but did not
progress sufficiently to fully examine other claims in the
document. Key forensic clues—errors in format and grammar
contained in the original documents—were not conveyed in the
translation process.

28. ▮▮▮▮ On 10 February 2003, a US Defense Attaché
Officer reported that he had examined the warehouses, as
described by the reporting in paragraph fifteen, and found they
contained cotton rather than barrels of uranium bound for Iraq.

29. ▮▮▮▮ On 3 March 2003, IAEA/INVO ▮▮▮▮
▮▮▮▮ an analysis of the 17-page document that
the U.S. provided on this issue. INVO's review concluded that
these documents were forgeries and did not substantiate any
assessment that Iraq sought to buy uranium from Niger. The IAEA
noted their assessment was also based on interviews in Iraq and
discussions with officials from Niger. Copies of the IAEA's
assessment arrived at CIA Headquarters on 10 March 2003.

001480

7

SECRET/

DX64.10

Ex 64

FROM CIA OPS CENTER   (MON) 6. 9'03 15:53 '87.)

SECRET

30.   On 4 March 2003, the US Mission to the IAEA i-
Vienna reported that "Baute explained that the French based thei
initial assessment on the same documents that the US provided an
that after further review by the French, they appeared to be
"embarrassed" by their initial assessment."

31. (U) On 7 March 2003, IAEA Director General El Baradei
stated in his report to the UN Security Council that day that
documents provided by member states indicating that Iraq sought
to buy uranium from Niger in recent years are "not authentic."
The IAEA concluded that these specific allegations were unfounded
and promised to follow up if additional evidence were provided by
member states.

32.   An 11 March 2003 SPWR and memo concluded that
"We do not dispute the IAEA Director General's conclusion—last
Friday before the UN Security Council—that documents on Iraq's
agreement to buy uranium from Niger are not authentic."

001481

SECRET

DX71.1

United States Department of State

Washington, D.C. 20520

PROVISIONALLY
DECLASSIFIED

June 10, 2003

INFORMATION MEMORANDUM

TOP ~~SECRET~~/

TO: P - Under Secretary Grossman

FROM: INR - Carl W. Ford, Jr.

SUBJECT: Niger/Iraq Uranium Story and Joe Wilson (

          This memo summarizes what we have been able to
discover about the role that Ambassador Joe Wilson played in the
Niger/Iraq uranium story, especially the allegations that INR
played a role in his early 2002 trip to Niger and the (non)
dissemination of reporting on what he learned. What follows is
based on our paper and electronic files; we are confident that
these records and the recollections of persons involved at the
margin are basically accurate but the two INR staff members who
were most involved are not here (one has been reassigned to
Pakistan, the other is on leave) to guide us through the files
and emails. What is clear, however, is that INR was not
Ambassador Wilson's point of contact in either the Department or
the Intelligence Community. INR did not meet with Wilson after
his trip and did not receive any information on his trip and
what he learned except what appears to be his reporting cable
(his name is not mentioned) disseminated throughout the
intelligence and policy communities by CIA. The reporting we
have from his trip makes no mention of documents, fraudulent or
otherwise.

          From what we can find in our records, Joe Wilson
played only a walk-on part in the Niger/Iraq uranium story. In
a February 19, 2002, meeting convened by Valerie Wilson, a CIA
WMD manager and the wife of Joe Wilson, he previewed his plans
and rationale for going to Niger but said he would only go if
the Department thought his trip made sense (Tab 1). Both the
memo of this meeting prepared by INR's West Africa analyst (now

~~TOP SECRET~~

DOS-00547

PROVISIONALLY
DECLASSIFIED

LL001-00511A

TOP SECRET

-2-

in Pakistan) and other material indicate that the CIA believed
the Ambassador and the Embassy were unlikely to ferret out the
truth from their Nigerien contacts. INR strongly demurred from
this view at the February 19 meeting. We have no record of any
other INR written or personal contact with Wilson regarding
Nigerien uranium.

The impetus for the Ambassador's demarches
in this period (Tabs 2 and 3), and the investigative trip by Joe
Wilson (Tab 4 is the CIA account of his trip findings) was a
"report of questionable credibility from a foreign service."
This was INR's conclusion in an assessment of March 1, 2002,
entitled "Niger: Sale of Uranium to Iraq is Unlikely" (Tab 5).
In a May 8, 2002 INR assessment of Iraq's WMD and missile
programs, we noted "There have been provocative allegations of
Iraqi nuclear activities, such as an alleged contract for the
provision of uranium from Niger, but we regard such information
as questionable."

The Niger allegations were
included but did not figure prominently in the 90-page October
2002 NIE on "Iraq's Continuing Programs for Weapons of Mass
Destruction." The major point of contention in differing
judgments about the likelihood of Iraqi nuclear weapons program
reconstitution efforts centered on the CIA's assessment that
Iraq was bent on acquiring aluminum tubes to produce parts for a
gas centrifuge uranium enrichment plant. In a lengthy dissent
entitled "INR's Alternative View: Iraq's Attempts to Acquire
Aluminum Tubes," INR noted "... the claims of Iraqi pursuit of
natural uranium in Africa are, in INR's assessment, highly
dubious." The main text of the NIE related a foreign
intelligence service report "that, as of early 2001, Niger
planned to send several tons of "pure uranium" (probably
yellowcake) to Iraq." The NIE later noted laconically that "We
cannot confirm whether Iraq succeeded in acquiring uranium ore
and/or yellowcake" from Niger and other alleged African sources.

In October 2002, an Italian journalist passed
purported copies of a Niger-Iraq agreement of July 2000 for the
purchase of uranium to Embassy Rome. These documents, which
were sent to Washington via both CIA and Department channels,
were not adequately analyzed until much later and were judged to
be fraudulent. However, they appear to have added new life to
the Niger/Iraq uranium story. These documents appear to be
related to, if not the actual basis of, the February 2002
foreign liaison service report that sparked original concerns
about a Niger/Iraq deal.   DOS-00548

TOP SECRET

DX71.3

-3-   PROVISIONALLY
        DECLASSIFIED

(█████   In November 2002, WINPAC briefed the █████
████ that fragmentary reports indicated Iraq was trying to
acquire uranium ore in Africa; however, WINPAC pointed to other
potential African sources, not Niger. In mid-December 2002, the
Department (NP) released a fact sheet that pointed "to efforts
to procure uranium ore from Niger," this despite the alleged
objections of WINPAC. The WINPAC caution was reportedly "not
obtained in time to correct the listing on the State Department
web site," but "was acted on in time, however, to remove it from
Ambassador Negroponte's statement. On January 12, 2003, INR
"expressed concerns to the CIA that the documents pertaining to
the Iraq-Niger deal were forgeries." The conclusion may,
however, have been reached and communicated for the first time
somewhat earlier; the record is not clear on this point. After
considerable back and forth between the CIA, the Department, the
IAEA, and the British, Secretary Powell's briefing to the UN
Security Council did not mention attempted Iraqi procurement of
uranium "due to CIA concerns raised during the coordination
regarding the veracity of the information on the alleged Iraq-
Niger agreement." (Citations here from Tab 6, an April 7, 2003,
CIA retrospective on "Purported Iraqi Attempt to Get Uranium
from Niger").

(█████   Our records contain an extensive paper and
electronic trail on the Niger/Iraq allegations, including other
retrospective accounts differing somewhat from the CIA
retrospective mentioned above. There is no indication, however,
that anyone in INR met with Ambassador Wilson except at the
February 19, 2002 meeting hosted by CIA, or discussed his trip
and what he learned with anyone in the Department or at CIA.

ATTACHMENTS:
        Tab 1: Notes - Niger/Iraq uranium Meeting CIA, 2/19/02
        Tab 2: Cable from Embassy Niamey "Niger: Taking Another
Hard Look at GON Uranium Sales"
        Tab 3: Cable from Embassy Niamey: "Niger: President Tandja
Tells DCINC Niger's Uranium is Secure; Slams Terrorism"
        Tab 4: CIA Account of Ambassador Wilson's Trip Findings:
"WP/Nuclear Weapons: Nigerian Denial of Uranium Yellowcake Sales
to Rogue States"
        Tab 5: INR Assessment: "Niger--Sale of Uranium to Iraq is
Unlikely"
        Tab 6: CIA retrospective on "Purported Iraqi Attempt to Get
Uranium from Niger"

DOS-00549

TOP SECRET █████████████

PROVISIONALLY
DECLASSIFIED

DX71.4

TAB   1

DX71.5

PROVISIONALLY
DELASSIFIED   ~~SECRET~~

~~SECRET~~

Notes - Niger/Iraq uranium Meeting CIA, 2/19/02

Meeting apparently convened by Valerie Wilson, a CIA WMD managerial type and the
wife of Amb. Joe Wilson, with the idea that the agency and the larger USG could
dispatch Joe to Niger to use his contacts there to sort out the Niger/Iraq uranium sale
question. Joe went to Niger in late 1999 in regard to Niger's uranium program,
apparently with CIA support.

Two CIA WMD analysts seem to be leading the charge on the issue, ███████████
the other guy's name not available. They appear to believe that the Embassy will be
unable to ferret out the truth on the Niger/Iraq matter. INR made it a point to, gently, tell
them that the Embassy has very good contacts and the Ambassador is a Tandja
confidante. Later when the WMD guys failed to get the hint they were informed, a little
less gently, that the Embassy was a reliable interlocutor and could be trusted to protect
US interests.

If Wilson goes ██
████████████████████████████████████
stressing again that the Embassy, however, does have a wide range of high-level contacts.

The alleged contract between Niger and Iraq says that Niger will sell Iraq 500 tons of
Uranium in two tranches per year. INR explained that would mean somewhere between
one sixth and one eighth of the total output of the two mines and that twice a year 25
semi tractor trailers loads of yellow cake would have to be driven down roads where one
seldom sees even a bush taxi. In other words, it would be very hard to hide such a
shipment.

When the idea of moving the stuff across the desert to Sudan (???) was broached INR
responded that while it is not difficult to drive across much of the hard packed, flat desert
terrain, there are many problems including heat up to 130 degrees F, wear and tear on the
vehicles, water, fuel and drifting sand that would make such a trip difficult in the
extreme.

INR also explained that the French appear to have complete control of the entire mining,
milling and transportation process, and would seem to have little interest in selling
uranium to the Iraqis. INR suggested that perhaps the most cost-effective way of
handling the problem would be talking to the French. They have a much thicker presence
on the ground in Niger, and even if they for some unknown reason were conspiring with
a rogue state to on WMD sales, our contacting them would let them know that we know
and probably thereby disrupt the operation.

Amb. Wilson mentioned two guys he would talk to in Niamey, former Prime Minister
Myaki and somebody named Mai Manga. The only Mai Manga known to the Embassy

PROVISIONALLY   DOS-00552
DECLASSIFIED

DX71.6

during the 1999 - 2001 period was a colonel in the Army. The Amb. said that it was not
the same, Mai Manga. Wilson believed that the Nigeriens, understanding that he had
worked at the NSC, would believe that he represented "national command authority" and
that word of his presence would stir things up to such an extent that information would
tumble out and/or the Nigeriens, if they were indeed planning on selling uranium to Iraq,
would get scared and discontinue the sales project.

Wilson, not wanting to get too far ahead of State or the Embassy, backed INR up in
regard to Ambassador Owens-Kirkpatrick's prerogatives and said he would only go if we
thought that it made sense.

███

DOS-00553

DX71.7

TAB 4

DOS-00560

DX71.9

NIGER AND IRAQ. ALTHOUGH ▮▮▮▮▮▮▮▮ ▮▮▮▮ PLACE. MAYAKI LET THE
MATTER DROP DUE TO THE UNITED NATIONS (UN) SANCTIONS AGAINST IRAQ AND
THE FACT THAT HE OPPOSED DOING BUSINESS WITH IRAQ. MAYAKI SAID THAT
HE INTERPRETED THE PHRASE 'EXPANDING COMMERCIAL RELATIONS' TO MEAN
THAT IRAQ WANTED TO DISCUSS URANIUM YELLOWCAKE SALES. MAYAKI SAID HE
UNDERSTOOD ROGUE STATES WOULD LIKE TO EXPLOIT NIGER'S RESOURCES,
SPECIFICALLY URANIUM, BUT HE BELIEVED THE NIGERIEN GOVERNMENT'S
REGARD FOR THE UNITED STATES (U.S.) AS A CLOSE ALLY WOULD PREVENT
SALES TO THESE STATES FROM TAKING PLACE DESPITE NIGER'S ECONOMIC
WOES. MAYAKI CLAIMED THAT IF THERE HAD BEEN ANY CONTRACTS FOR

YELLOWCAKE BETWEEN NIGER AND ANY ROGUE STATE DURING HIS TENURE, HE
WOULD HAVE SEEN THE CONTRACT.

3. BOUCAR ((MAI MANGA)), NIGER'S FORMER MINISTER OF ENERGY AND
MINES UNTIL 9 APRIL 1999, A FORMER DIRECTOR OF THE NIGERIEN COMINAC
MINE AND CURRENTLY HONORARY PRESIDENT OF COMINAC, STATED THAT THERE
WERE NO SALES OUTSIDE OF INTERNATIONAL ATOMIC ENERGY AGENCY (IAEA)
CHANNELS SINCE THE MID-1980S. MAI MANGA SAID THAT HE KNEW OF NO
CONTRACTS SIGNED BETWEEN NIGER AND ANY ROGUE STATE FOR THE SALE OF
URANIUM. HE ADMITTED THAT YEARS AGO A PAKISTANI DELEGATION VISITED
NIGER AND OFFERED TO PURCHASE URANIUM BUT THAT NO SALES RESULTED FROM
THESE TALKS. MAI MANGA ALSO SAID THAT (FNU) ((BLASCHER)), THE FORMER
DIRECTOR GENERAL OF SOMAIR AND CURRENTLY A DIRECTOR AT COGEMA, CAME

TO HIM IN 1998 WITH AN IRANIAN DELEGATION TO DISCUSS BUYING 400 TONS
OF YELLOWCAKE FROM NIGER; HOWEVER, THE ONLY RESULT WAS A MEMORANDUM
OF CONVERSATION, WITH NO CONTRACT BEING SIGNED AND NO YELLOWCAKE
TRANSFERRED TO IRAN. MAI MANGA THEORIZED THAT NIGER'S MINES COULD
HAVE INCREASED PRODUCTION TO SUPPLY IRAN WITH THIS AMOUNT OF
YELLOWCAKE BUT THIS WOULD HAVE REQUIRED OPENING ADDITIONAL MINING
FACILITIES THAT HAVE BEEN MOTHBALLED FOR SEVERAL YEARS. MAI MANGA

THEREFORE CONCLUDED THAT A SALE TO A ROGUE STATE SUCH AS IRAN WOULD
HAVE BEEN DIFFICULT GIVEN THE NEED OPEN MORE FACILITIES. (SOURCE
COMMENT: MAI MANGA APPEARED TO REGRET THAT NIGER EVEN DISCUSSED
URANIUM SALES WITH IRAN IN LIGHT OF THE INTERNATIONAL PRESSURE THAT
RESULTED.)

4. MAI MANGA STATED THAT URANIUM FROM NIGER'S MINES IS VERY
TIGHTLY CONTROLLED AND ACCOUNTED FOR FROM THE TIME IT IS MINED UNTIL
THE TIME IS LOADED ONTO SHIPS AT THE PORT OF COTONOU, BENIN.
ACCORDING TO MAI MANGA, EVEN A KILOGRAM OF URANIUM WOULD BE NOTICED
MISSING AT THE MINES. ON-SITE STORAGE IS LIMITED AND HE SAID THAT
EACH SHIPMENT OF URANIUM IS UNDER NIGERIEN ARMED MILITARY ESCORT FROM
THE TIME IT LEAVES ONE OF THE TWO NIGERIEN MINES UNTIL IT IS LOADED
ON TO A SHIP IN COTONOU. AIR TRANSPORT IS TOO EXPENSIVE TO SHIP
YELLOWCAKE AND TRUCKING BARRELS OF YELLOWCAKE NORTHWARD WOULD REQUIRE
AN EXPERIENCED GUIDE AND MANY ARMED GUARDS, DUE TO THE SHIFTING DUNES
AND BANDITS IN THAT REGION. MAI MANGA THEREFORE BELIEVED THAT IT
WOULD BE DIFFICULT, IF NOT IMPOSSIBLE, TO ARRANGE A SPECIAL SHIPMENT
OF URANIUM TO A PARIAH STATE GIVEN THESE STRICT CONTROLS AND THE
CLOSE MONITORING BY THE NIGERIEN GOVERNMENT AND THE TWO MINING companies.

DOS-00562

LL001-00526A

CHAPTER ONE

THE YELLOWCAKE FOLLIES

Quotes from Hans Blix are from a phone conversation with the authors in Milan, December 2005. Blix has dedicated a good part of his professional life to the issues of disarmament and nuclear proliferation. He is the author of *Disarming Iraq* (New York: Pantheon, 2004) and served as general director of the International Atomic Energy Agency (IAEA) from 1981 to 1997.

The Iraq Nuclear Verification Office (INVO) at the IAEA first caught wind of the alleged uranium traffic between Niger and Iraq on September 24, 2002, when Tony Blair submitted *Iraq's Weapons of Mass Destruction: The Assessment of the British Government* to the House of Commons. The relevant text appears on page 25, paragraph 20. IVNO director Jacques Bauté invited the British to Vienna to discuss the matter. The answers to his questions, however, remained vague. The only information conceded by the British representatives was that they were relying upon "second-hand information" supplied to them by a "foreign intelligence agency."

Rocco Martino was the object of intense scrutiny, beginning in August 2004, by a number of international news organizations. In conversation with the authors, or with other representatives of the media, Martino never hesitated to repeat various accusations. Much of the biographical information here, however, resides in the SISMI and SISDE archives.

For more on Adamou Chékou and Zakaria Yaou Maiga, see F. Kpatindè, "New revelations about a state-sponsored lie," in *Jeune Afrique/L'intelligent*, No. 2221, August 3-9, 2003.

The authors had three long conversations with Nicolò Pollari in Rome between July and August of 2004: In the bar at the St. Regis Grand Hotel; in a private room at the Hotel Rex; and in his office at the Baracchini Palace (which is to say, the Ministry of Defense). All of the SISMI director's statements are drawn from these conversations, unless otherwise specified.

We assert that Martino was selling information about the French to the Italians, because, on November 5, 2005, Rocco Martino confessed to the *Giornale*: "It's true, I worked for the French. But I also worked for SISMI. Was I playing a double game? Sure: double, triple, quadruple." Martino had been even more explicit when he spoke to Joshua Marshall, then working for *60 Minutes*, in the spring of 2004. In November 2005, Marshall spoke to the authors in New York, and recalled: "Rocco Martino told me that the Italian agencies knew every time he lifted a finger for the French. Before and after every contact, Martino reported directly to Antonio Nucera—and Nucera, I was told, then passed the information to his superiors at SISMI."

The quote "This is my profession… I sell information" is from N. Ruffors and N. Fielding, "Tracker Down: The Man Who Fooled the World and Was Duped Himself," *The Sunday Times*, August 1, 2004.

Although both Pollari and Nucera describe our source "Signora Laura" as "unproductive," their accounts show some major discrepancies. According to Nucera, it wasn't Rocco who asked for his help. It was Signora Laura who requested some help from her contact at the agency, and Rocco Martino who agreed to involve this SISMI "source" in his schemes. See Nucera's interview in the *Giornale*, November 6, 2005.

The quote from Rabiou Hasan Yari is from V. Thorin in *Jeune Afrique/L'intelligent*, No. 2219, July 19-25, 2003.

Eventually Maiga left Italy: "Zakaria Yaou Maiga was recalled to his homeland at the end of July 2003, even though his assignment in

Italy was supposed to run through 2004.... At present he may be the subject of an administrative inquiry. Is he guilty? Is he a scapegoat? We contacted him on July 30, 2003, while he was still in Rome. 'I have no statement to make, but you might direct your questions to the authorities in Niamey. Many thanks,' he replied, he voice shaking with emotion." From F. Kpatindè, "New revelations about a state-sponsored lie," *op cit.*

Martino's line that he "didn't even know where Niger was" is taken from an Interview in *Giornale*, November 5, 2005.

The *Libero* and a *Panorama* reports referred to here are by Farina, in *Libero* and titled "Ecco le prove di un intrigo di spie francese per screditare Italia e Usa sull'Iraq," August 2004, and Buongiorno, in *Panorama* and titled *"Rocco lo spione,"* August 19, 2004.

The quotation from Franco Ionta is from a conversation with the authors, Rome, October 2005.

We spoke with Alain Chouet near Nîmes in November 2005. The quotations in this chapter are from our conversation.

We know that Gianfranco Battelli sent a cable to Langley because Nicolò Pollari confirmed this fact to both *Il Messaggero* in November 2005 and to the Parliamentary Commission on Intelligence Oversight.

Wolbert Smidt's statements come from an interview on ZDF, the German public television station, which was aired on December 11, 2003, as part of an investigative documentary called *Die große Lüge. Bush, Blair und Saddams Bombe* ("The Big Lie: Bush, Blair, and Saddam's Bomb"). The entire program can be accessed at www.zdj.de/ZDFe/inhalt/17/0,1872,2088145,00.html.

The U.S. official who anonymously confirms Alain Chouet's version of events is quoted in Tom Hamburger, Peter Wallsten, and Bob Drogin, "French Told CIA of Bogus Intelligence," *Los Angeles Times*, December 11, 2005. Also, in Washington as well as Paris, "two additional sources close to DGSE" confirm Alain Chouet's story, and accuse SISMI of having manipulated Rocco Martino." See J. Guisnel, "Il Servizio italiano è all'origine dell'intossicazione," Embrouilles franco-italiennes, in Le Point, December 8, 2005.

As for British examination of events surrounding prewar espionage, there are only a few nebulous passages in the discredited Butler Report, thrown together to blur Tony Blair's culpability. As many know, Robin Butler, formerly a senior official in the British government, was asked by Tony Blair to conduct an "independent" investigation of MI6's counterespionage activities and of Downing Street's role in assembling prewar intelligence about Iraq. On July 14, 2004, Lord Butler released his commission's findings to the public. The 195-page report revealed a lengthy series of "defects, imprecisions, weaknesses, omissions, and serious mistakes" in the intelligence gathered prior to the war. For a cross-section of skeptical reactions from the press, see Norman Dombey, "Butler Wrong On Iraq Uranium Link," *Independent on Sunday*, July 25, 2004; B. Spinelli, "The Mandarins' Mandarin Does It In Style," *The Times* (London), July 15, 2004; and "I disastri della buona fede," *La Stampa*, July 28, 2004.

Despite several requests for interviews in the spring of 2004, Antonio Martino declined to meet with the authors. The quote we use from Admiral Martini is recorded in the record of the Parliamentary Commission on Security and Information Services and State Secrets, June 1, 2000.

The quote from Federico Umberto d'Amato is recorded in the record of the P2 Commission, October 20, 1982. See also S. Acciari and P. Calderoni, "C'ero io, c'era Pazienza, c'era," *L'Espresso*, November 11, 1984 and A. Carlucci, "Per Reagan a con Pazienza," *Panorama*, August 25, 1985.

The quote we use from Richard Gardner is from *The Wall Street Journal*, August 9, 1985. See also *The New York Times*, March 15, 1985 and R. Gardner, *Mission Italy: On the Front Lines of the Cold War* (Lanham, MD: Rowman & Littlefield Publishers, 2005).

Our quotations from Frum and Perle are from *An End to Evil: How to Win the War on Terror* (New York: Ballantine Books, 2004), p. 5 and p. 171. Other quotes used to explain the neocons are also from this text.

For more on the operations of the Pentagon's Office of Special Plans, see Seymour Hersh, "The Stovepipe," *The New Yorker*, October 27, 2003.

Robert Baer was a CIA agent from 1976 to 1997. He served in Iraq, Rabat, Beirut, Khartoum, New Delhi, and many other locations. In 1997 he received the Career Intelligence Medal "for having repeatedly run personal risks [and] for choosing the most difficult objectives in the service of his country." He is the author of *Sleeping with the Devil: How Washington Sold Our Souls for Saudi Crude* (New York: Three Rivers, 2004) and *See No Evil: The True Story of a Ground Soldier in the CIA's War on Terror* (New York: Three Rivers, 2003). We spoke Baer in May 2004; and February and July 2005.

Born in 1945, Sir Richard Dearlove was the director of MI6 from 1999 to May 6, 2004. He was only the second director in the history of the agency whose name was disclosed to the public. When Dearlove stepped down, he was succeeded by John Scarlett, who was already head of the Joint Intelligence Committee and a figure of some controversy, having worked with Tony Blair's former spin doctor, Alastair Campbell, on WMD-related intelligence. For more about MI6's gathering of Iraq intelligence, see Stephen Dorril, *MI6: Fifty Years of Special Operations* (London: Fourth Estate, 2000) as well as Seymour Hersh, "Who Lied to Whom?", *The New Yorker*, March 31, 2003.

We spoke to Rocco Martino in Rome, June and July 2003. The quotation that begins "I got a call from a former colleague at SISMI" was taken from N. Ruffors and N. Fielding, "Tracker Down," *op cit.*

For the complete text of the SISMI note read by Under Secretary of Defense Filippo Berselli on the evening of July 17, 2003, see *Iraq. Uranio: Berselli, raccolta di notizie di gennaio 2001. L'Italia non ha dato alcun dossier a nessuno*, Agenzia Nazionale Stampa Associata (ANSA), July 17, 2003.

Born in Gravina (Bari) in 1941, Giovanni Castellaneta began his diplomatic career in 1967, with successive postings in Mogadishu, Chambery, and Lisbon. He served as ambassador to Iran (1992-95), ambassador to Australia and various Pacific Island nations (1998-2001), and as foreign policy advisor to the Italian prime minister. Between 2002 and 2005, he was also vice chairman of the Finmeccanica Group, Italy's largest defense congomerate. He was appointed ambassador to the United States in October 2005.

For more on SISMI's two claims to the CIA in 2001, see *Report on the U.S. Intelligence Community's Prewar Intelligence Assessments on Iraq*, p. 36. For

the entire text of the report, see: www.globalsecurity.org/intell/library/
congress/2004_rpt/iraq-wmd-intell_toc.htm.   For   more   on   Pollari's
October 18, 2001 letter to the CIA, see M. Martinelli, "L'Italia non forní
prove false. Pollari pronto a spiegare in Parlamento le ragioni del SISMI,"
Il Messaggero, November 1, 2005.

The October 18 report we refer to here is "Senior Intelligence Executive
Brief, Iraq, Nuclear-Related Procurement Efforts." See footnote 74.

The authors spoke with Greg Thielmann in Washington, May 2004.

The quote we use from Tony Blair, that Iraq had "sought
significant quantities of uranium from Africa, despite having no
active civil nuclear power programme that could require it" is
from page 6 of *Iraq's Weapons of Mass Destruction: The Assessment of
the British Government*, issued on September 24.

CHAPTER TWO
A FINE ITALIAN TUBE

For more on American intelligence on the Aluminum Tubes, see D. Barstow,
W. J. Broad, and J. Gerth, "The Nuclear Card: The Aluminium Tube Story.
A Special Report: How the White House Embraced Suspect Iraq Arms
Intelligence," *The New York Times*, October 3, 2004.

For more on the cascade process, see L. Rothstein, "Phony Stories,"
Bulletin of the Atomic Scientists, September/October 2002.

The full text of Colin Powell's UN Security Council speech is online at
www.whitehouse.gov/news/releases/2003/02/20030205-1.html.

For more on the Silberman-Robb Commission, see *Report of the
Commission on the Intelligence Capabilities of the United States Regarding Weapons of
Mass Destruction*, pp. 67 and 207 (note 138). To see the report online: www.
gpoaccess.gov/wmd/index.html.

The September 8, 2002, *New York Times* report we discuss is M. Gordon
and J. Miller, "U.S. Says Hussein Intensifies Quest for A-Bomb."

The report we cite by Roberto Reale is *Ultime notizie. Indagine sulla crisi
dell'informazione in Occidente. I rischi per la democrazia* (Rome: Nutrimenti, 2005),

p. 160. A frequent guest on radio and television, Roberto Reale runs the "Media e Democrazia" project at Informazione senza frontiere.

In 2004, Representative Henry A. Waxman, ranking member of the committee on government reform, commissioned *Iraq on the Record: The Bush Administration's Public Statements on Iraq*. According to this report, the administration's top five policymakers consistently misled the public on four fronts: the imminence of the Iraqi threat; Iraq's nuclear program; its supply of chemical and biological weapons; and its links to Al Qaeda. For the text of the report, see: www.democrats.reform.house.gov/story.asp?ID=448&Iss ue=Iraq+Reconstruction. We spoke with Congressman Henry Waxman in Washington, November 2005.

The Times mea culpa we discuss here is "The Times and Iraq," *The New York Times*, May 26, 2004.

In 1991, George H. W. Bush signed a presidential order authorizing a "covert campaign" to destabilize Saddam Hussein, and John Rendon obtained the sum of $150 million from CIA sources to build an Iraqi opposition around Chalabi. According to investigative journalists Seymour Hersh and Jeff Stein, the bulk of this cash was expended on pricey PR consultants, elegant London real estate, tickets on the Concorde, and so forth. See J. Steinberg, *Executive Intelligence Review*, February 21, 2003.

Our characterization of the Rendon Group's activities is based on I. Urbina, "This War to You by Rendon Group," *Asia Times Online*, November 12, 2002. See www.gvnews.net/html/Shadow/alert3553.html.

The quote "Chalabi's group wouldn't even be on the map" is taken from M. Chossudovsky, "War Propaganda and the Capture of Saddam Hussein," December 2003, at globalresearch.ca/articles/CHO312D.html.

Behind his genteel façade, "behind his boyish features and blond hair and informal manner of dress," Francis Brooke displays a steely temperament. Born in Charlottesville, Virginia, married with children, he currently lives in Washington, although since 2003 he has divided his time between there and Baghdad. "Fifty percent here, fifty percent there," he told us. "My wife keeps careful track." His first assignment for John Rendon's PR firm in 1991, "working for the London office of the INC," convinced him that he was in the right business. During that same period, he also struck up his first connections with the CIA and the DIA, with whom he would deal extensively on behalf of the INC during the crucial months preceding the invasion of Iraq. Today he directs the Washington office of the INC. The authors spoke with Brooke in Washington, November 2005.

In May 2004, the Iraqi police, assisted by American officials, raided the offices of Ahmed Chalabi in Baghdad, accusing him of embezzlement. At the same time, the FBI in Washington began investigating Chalabi on charges of espionage: There was some speculation that he had passed sensitive information to Tehran. The FBI probe appeared to put the final kibosh on the ex-banker's reputation. But it was not to be so. In mid-November of 2005, Chalabi was in fact welcomed with all honors in Washington. He was received by Secretary of State Condoleezza Rice, and chaired a crowded conference on the future of Iraq at (you guessed it) the American Enterprise Institute. He flitted around the city accompanied by a sturdy fleet of armored vehicles, disturbed only by a few dozen protesters carrying placards that read: *Liar!*

On September 17, 2001, only six days after the attack on the Twin Towers and the Pentagon, former CIA director James Woolsey had a long conversation with the authors, in which he anticipated the rough outlines of the War on Terror that the White House was about to launch. "We can't fight malaria by squashing one mosquito after another," he said. "Bin Laden might be the most deadly mosquito. But he can't survive without the swamp. And Afghanistan and Iraq are his swamp. There will be a military reaction, of course. But it has to be substantial, because there's no time left for symbolic blows." See C. Bonini and G. D'Avanzo, "La CIA annienterà i terroristi, rovesceremeo chi li auita," *La Repubblica*, September 18, 2001.

For more of our conversation with Nabil Musawi (which occurred in October 2001 in London), see C. Bonini and D. D'Avanzo, "La pista del terrore porta a casa di Saddam Hussein," La Repubblica, October 20, 2001.

For more on attempts to connect Saddam Hussein to the War on Terror, see also our "Atta era un agente di Saddam," *La Repubblica*, November 3, 2001.

We spoke to Scott Ritter in Washington, November 2005.

The book by Miller and Mylroie that we discuss here is *Saddam Hussein and the Crisis in the Gulf* (New York: Three Rivers Press, 1990). Laurie Mylroie's other book is *Saddam Hussein and the World Trade Center Attacks*, first published by the American Enterprise Institute and reissued by ReganBooks in 2001.

The quote from Chalabi—"I'm just waiting for the moment to move."— was first used in C. Bonini, "Tra sei mesi a Baghdad con l'aiuto degli USA," *La Repubblica*, January 31, 2002.

The Buongiorno article we quote from is "La guerra è cominciata?", *Panorama*, September 12-19, 2002. An earlier reference to the same claims can be found in *The Washington Times*, July 26, 2002.

Elisabetta Burba's story about Rocco Martino was published in *Panorama*, July 31, 2003.

The testimony of George Tenet that is mentioned here is from July 17, 2003.

CHAPTER THREE
ROMAN BLUNDERS

We summarize Luigi Ferrajoli by drawing on *Diritto e Ragione* (Rome-Bari: Laterza, 1989).

Regarding Fattah el-Gamal: In a classic manner, the Egyptian fisherman's name popped up in the wrong place at the wrong time. El-Gamal had some contact with a young woman named Bombina Morrone, who in turn knew the fundamentalist imam of the mosque in Latina, who in turn was associated with one Ahmed Ibrahim Salah (known as "Khumaini"). It was a deductive daisy chain. Yet el-Gamal knew Bombina Morrone for one reason only: Her husband was a lawyer, who had assisted the fisherman after the raid in October 2001.

According to a report by Luca Franceschini, a consultant to the Defence Ministry, the TNT bricks we discuss here were of a type used by the Russian and Albanian armies. During the trial of the three Egyptians, it was ascertained that the TNT seized by the carabinieri in May 2001 was stored in a military warehouse on Via Appia Pignatelli in Rome. It was not destroyed until April 2004.

Regarding the clock supposedly intended for detonating the TNT: According to the report, "the clock hands could not be employed for an explosive device without the presence of an ignition switch." The battery holders might theoretically be used for such a device, but not "without the presence of an ignition switch, instrumentation, and flammable materials." None of which happened to be on hand.

For Alessandro Perrino's statements, and for those of the other carabinieri quoted in the text, see the sentencing document of the First Court of Assizes of Rome, April 30, 2004. The relevant material begins on page 6.

Carlo Corbucci is the author of an important text, which was recently published in a third edition: *Il terrorismo islamico in Italia. Realtà e finzione* (Roma: Gruppo Editoriale Agorà, 2003). We spoke with Carlo Corbucci in Rome, June 2005.

Fausto Del Vecchio gave his deposition during a hearing on February 20, 2004. The excerpts we reproduce in the text are drawn from the sentencing document of the First Court of Assizes of Rome, April 30, 2004. The relevant material begins on page 14.

The quote from the TNT expert comes from the deposition by a Professor Romolo, given at a hearing on March 19, 2004. See the Court of Assizes sentencing document, p. 32.

Giovanni Destito spoke with the authors in Rome, June 2005.

Brigadiere Racca's account comes from his testimony before the Second Courts of Assizes in Rome. (A *brigadiere* is a non-commissioned officer in the Carabinieri or the Guardia di Finanza.)

The transcript that begins "Listen, how long is it since you last fired a weapon?" is numbered 884 in the trial proceedings. The numbered conversations below and in the text are drawn from the same documentation.

The transcript that begins "We're going to do exactly as the Koran says..." is number 4202.

The transcript that begins "The army is in Pakistan. You should go train there!" is number 9535

The transcript that begins "That guy killed somebody…" is number 1370.

The transcript that begins "They're already up in the mountains, then?" is number 6787.

The transcript that begins "Will you be launching the attack on the carabinieri?" is number 8394.

The transcript for conversation 15292 is the one that notes: "The loading of an automatic weapon is audible."

The Vinci quote that begins "Around 8:00 AM on February 19…" is from the deposition of Captain Vinci before the Court of Assizes.

The quote from Davide Zavattaro is from the sentencing document of the Second Court of Assizes, April 28, 2004, p. 12.

The quote from the conversation between Hussein an-Awar and Samuel is drawn from the sentencing document of the First Court of Criminal Appeals, March 3, 2005. The relevant material begins on page 37.

CHAPTER FOUR
THE MUDDLE IN MILAN

In his book *Milano-Baghdad: Diario di un magistrato in prima linea nella lotta al terrorism islamico* (Milan: Mondadori, 2004), Dambruoso provides the following capsule bio: "Currently a judicial adviser to Italy's permanent mission to the United Nations in Vienna, he spent eight years as a public prosecutor in Milan. There he was also a member of the Antiterrorism Division and supervised some of its most important domestic and international investigations. *Time* has called him a 'European hero.'"

Our quotations from Jason Burke are from his book *Al-Qaeda: The True Story of Radical Islam* (London and New York: I B Tauris, 2003).

On June 15, 2002, Abu Omar dropped by the offices of the Islamic center and mosque at Via Quaranta 54. He spoke with a stranger who had just arrived from Germany. A hidden microphone recorded their conversation, which was then included in the remandment order issued by the Milanese GIP Guido Salvini. What follows is a significant excerpt, in which Omar seems less than ecstatic about his potential role in the revamped terror network. *Unknown speaker*: "To eliminate the enemies of God, a lot of things will have to change. There was a meeting of the sheiks in Poland on May 16. They decided to completely revamp Hizb ut-Tahrir and replace it with a new organization. We're going to need skilled people at every level.... There are brothers returning from Chechnya, and Abu Serrah is planning to create a battalion with 25 or 26 units to carry on the Jihad." *Omar*: "Just keep the Devil out of it." *Unknown speaker*: "It all goes back to Saudi Arabia. The man in charge there is Abu Salman, who's from the same family as Emir Abdullah. We need new structures, we're trying to obtain seven to nine buildings, because the mosques are too visible. We've already bought a four-story building." *Omar*: "How are things going in Germany?" *Unknown speaker*: "There's ten of us now, and we're investigating possibilities in Belgium, Spain, Holland, Turkey, Egypt, France, and Italy. The entire formation will be called the Force 9 Islamic Army, with its headquarters in London." *Omar*: "And how would I be involved?" *Unknown speaker*: "Selling, buying, printing, keeping records. Just wait, and somebody will get in touch with you."

According to Said Mahmoud Abdelaziz Haraz, a 36-year-old Iraqi who planned and carried out the massacre of Italians in Nasiriyah, there was only one *shahid* (Arabic for "witness") who came from Italy— a former hockey player. This Italian participated in the suicide attack on the United Nations office in Baghdad. The conversation between Abu Omar and Nabila Ghali is now filed with the remandment order for the 22 CIA agents. The long citation from Abu Omar is from his conversation with Elbadri Mohammad Rida, who relayed the conversation to us.

The Milan GIP Guido Salvini has observed that the term *extraordinary rendition* seems to have been coined by the CIA, then taken up by the press. It is, however, a non-technical term with "an intrinsically self-justifying flavor."

Since the 1800s, international law has labeled such activities as *abduction*. The definition of extraordinary rendition we cite here comes from Tribunale di Milano, Judiciary Section for Preliminary Investigations, No. 19838/05 R.G.N.R./No. 1966/05 R.G. GIP.

The quotations from the memo written by Robert Seldon Lady come from a 57-page memo handed over to the attorney Daria Pesce in November 2005. It was Robert Seldon Lady's hope that this document would help to revoke the warrant issued for his arrest.

On December 18, 2005, former Secretary of State Colin Powell discussed extraordinary rendition in a BBC interview. He expressed some annoyance at the very public breast-beating of America's European allies: "There's a little bit of the movie *Casablanca* in this, where, you know, the inspector says 'I'm shocked, shocked that this kind of thing takes place.' Well, most of our European friends cannot be shocked that this kind of thing takes place... The fact that we have, over the years, had procedures in place that would deal with people who are responsible for terrorist activities, or suspected of terrorist activities, and so the thing that is called rendition is not something that is new or unknown to my European friends." See news.bbc.co.uk/2/hi/americas/4538788.stm.

CHAPTER FIVE
A STRANGE MEETING

We spoke with Antonio Marrapese in Rome, June 2004. For more information on Antonio Marrapese and the Defense Security Training Corporation, see the company's website at www.defensesecurity.com, which includes this note on the proprietor: "Although he is increasingly called upon by celebrities, he insists that he is 'allergic' to VIPs. 'They show off their bodyguards like *status symbols*. I don't want to be anybody's *status symbol*.'"

Paul Wolfowitz's quote about Harold Rhode is taken from J. Lobe, Il nuovo consigliere di Cheney punta gli occhi sulla Siria, available at www.ipsnews.net and www.decoder.it.

Ledeen's quotation from *Il Foglio* is from the December 15, 2003, edition.

We spoke to the State Department source we quote here in Washington, May 2004.

For more on the Supreme Council for the Islamic Revolution in Iraq (SCIRI), see G.M. Del Re, "Gli uomini che vorrebbero farsi rais," *Limes*, 1/2003.

The authors spoke with Muhammad Baqir al-Hakim in Tehran, March 2003. See also C. Bonini and G. D'Avanzo, "No all'occupazione Americana. L'Iraq deve restare agli iracheni," *La Repubblica*, March 18, 2003. Mohammed Baqir al-Hakim was killed in Najaf on August 29, 2003.

INDEX